Lingerie Design

A Complete Course

Lingerie Design

A Complete Course

Pamela Powell

LAURENCE KING PUBLISHING

Published in 2016 by
Laurence King Publishing Ltd
361–363 City Road, London,
EC1V 1LR, United Kingdom
T +44 (0)20 7841 6900
F + 44 (0)20 7841 6910
enquiries@laurenceking.com
www.laurenceking.com

Reprinted 2019

A catalogue record for this book is available from the British Library

ISBN: 978-1-78067-791-0

Design by The Urban Ant Ltd

Printed in China

Frontispiece: Burlesque dancer Dita Von Teese wearing a corset by
Jean Paul Gaultier (Spring/Summer 2014). Victor Virgile/Getty Images.

Front cover: Modern version of the Tango corset or tight diminisher from
1914. Made from silk duchesse satin, spiral and plastic boning, a latticed
ribbon front panel, and appliqué lace. Garment made by the author and
photographed by Simon Pask.

Back cover: (top left) boned bra; (top right) waspie; (second and third rows)
stages in the construction of a triangle cup bra; (fourth row) pattern pieces

Contents

Lingerie and Foundations
A brief history from 1850

Throughout the centuries undergarments have served two functions: to provide a layer of modesty, comfort, and warmth, and latterly as foundations for outerwear, often shaping and supporting the body to fashion it into the current ideal silhouette. Undergarments have continually evolved and changed to work with current fashions, and they have also developed as new materials and haberdashery have become available. Despite being largely hidden from view, underwear has had no less attention paid to it than outerwear, often being the subject of highly skilled needlework, embroidery, and embellishment.

It was not until the nineteenth century, however, that underwear openly became the subject of fashionable discourse. In the late 1850s storefronts began to display underwear and, with the advent of photography and the spread of advertising, visual images of lingerie became more prevalent. Up until this time the mention of underwear was considered scandalous. Underwear now moved from the realm of modesty to become the height of glamour, and the allure of sensuous materials and styles became an acknowledged and vital part of the industry.

A Parisian lady at her toilette, early 20th century.

Antoine Doucet and his wife Adèle Girard opened a lingerie and haberdashery shop on the rue de la Paix, Paris in 1816. Their prosperous store was passed on to their son Edouard Doucet, who in turn passed it on to his son Jacques before his twentieth birthday. In 1874 Jacques Doucet opened his own couture salon next to the shop opened by his grandparents. Madeleine Vionnet joined Doucet in 1907 and her first collection consisted of lingerie-inspired dresses (*déshabillés*), which were uncorseted dresses designed to be worn in public. Her inspiration was taken from the paintings of the seventeenth and eighteenth centuries. These uncorseted dresses in delicate pastel-colored mousseline, satin, and iridescent silk fabrics were adorned with embroidery, lace, pin tucks, ruffles, and ribbons. Corsets, however, were still de rigueur with most fashions.

Lady Duff Gordon opened Maison Lucile in London in the 1890s. Famed for her lingerie, tea gowns, and eveningwear, some of her dresses were designed around the personality of the wearer. Reflecting her belief in dressing clients from the "inside out," she freed women from restrictive corsets and petticoats, making her designs both revolutionary and scandalous. The nightgowns and lingerie from the Maison Lucile used chiffon and layers of lace in nude tones embellished with ribbons and flowers, said to reflect female intimacy and allow a glimpse into a woman's soul. Lady Duff Gordon's creations were a must-have, considered chic by British society ladies and worn by the most alluring women of the Belle Époque, from London and Paris to New York and Chicago. Today, Lucile has been revived by Lady Duff Gordon's great-great-granddaughter, Camilla Blois, as a British luxury lingerie brand with a unique heritage.

Lindsay "Layneau" Boudreaux, a French immigrant regarded as the first professional underwear designer, opened the first pantie company in the US in 1912. Sadly the company closed within the year, but not before it had set a precedent in the manufacture of lingerie. Boudreaux not only created and revolutionized the underwear industry but also established the basis for today's upmarket lingerie stores.

Hollywood glamour characterized the lingerie of the 1930s, while in the 1940s it was the pin-up-girl style of a bullet bra worn beneath a figure-hugging sweater that defined lingerie fashions.

In the 1960s and 1970s Janet Reger became the most sought-after designer of fashionable lingerie, producing handcrafted garments that were decorated with lace and appliqués. Daring and risqué, her designs were nevertheless comfortable and functional. She started a lingerie catalogue business called the Bottom Drawer and had a celebrity following.

Luxurious designer silk lingerie was still being worn under the power suits of the 1980s, while in 1983 Jean Paul Gaultier launched his "underwear as outerwear" Spring/Summer collection. The trend was followed in the 1990s by Versace, who designed lingerie-style outerwear. The line between what is lingerie and what is outerwear is blurred still further today, but lingerie is still an important market in its own right.

The corset and its evolution into the girdle

The corset evolved in the first half of the sixteenth century in Spain and/or Italy, when the felted, laced bodice of previous decades began to be stiffened with rigid materials such as whalebone, horn, and buckram. The "stay" or busk – often a piece of whalebone – was first placed down the front of the bodice to create a flat front beneath a gown, and later, additional pieces of whalebone were introduced around the sides to further stiffen the shape. These garments became known as whalebone bodies, a term that distinguished them as garments designed to shape the flesh of the body.

Changing in shape as fashion required the body to be contorted into different silhouettes, and updated with the latest materials – such as steel boning, introduced from 1810 – corsets continued to be worn by most women in one form or another up until the early years of the twentieth century. They were worn by some older women or those anxious to contain an increasing avoirdupois up until the 1960s, and still have their fans today.

The containment of the body for the general public was not, however, completely over. By the early twentieth century the fashionable silhouette had slimmed down, with less emphasis placed on the upper half of the body. As a result a style of corset emerged that reached from the waist to the top of the thighs, containing the hips and buttocks. This corset would be the precursor of the girdle, a rigid, figure-controlling garment that became

Opposite / Lingerie-style *déshabillés* being worn in Calvados, France, 1910.

Above / Lady Duff Gordon of Maison Lucile.

the principal item of foundation wear from the 1920s through to the 1980s, worn by every respectable woman.

Girdles, like some other corsets in the 1920s and 1930s, were initially made from rubber, some even being advertised as "reducing corsets," designed to encourage weight loss – the wearer sweating, especially in the spring and summer months, inside garments made from a nonbreathable fabric. Perforated rubber corsets, like those created by Charnaux in the late 1920s and early 1930s, were introduced to mitigate the problem and remain popular in the fetish community.

The girdle evolved and changed as new elasticized fabrics – such as Lastex, introduced by the US Rubber Company in 1931 – were developed. Roll-ons were made from a tube of Lastex and "rolled on" over the hips with no additional fastenings. Step-ins were partially closed with hooks and eyes or zippers, and wrap-arounds had a long closure down one side. Some also had lacing to further alter the body's contours. Girdles extended from the waist down to the upper thigh, but some incorporated the bra.

With today's interest in retro fashion and burlesque, the girdle has once again become a popular garment. The panty girdle has evolved into much more comfortable shapewear, made from fabrics with a high percentage of spandex (elastane) and now featuring woven panels.

In addition to the girdle, other foundation garments have come and gone, depending on the silhouette required by the fashions of the day. One such is the waspie. The waspie briefly emerged before World War II in response to a fashion for small waists and curved hips, but was ultimately adopted after the conflict, when clothing restrictions were lifted and fashion was once again able to flourish, culminating in Dior's New Look of 1947 with its famous nipped-in waist.

What to wear under and over the corset

Designed at first to be worn under or over the corset to protect and provide a layer of modesty, the chemise, camisole, slip, and drawers would all evolve as the fashions of the early twentieth century were shaped and reshaped.

The shift, or chemise as it was known from the late eighteenth century, had been the primary undergarment for women and was worn next to the skin. Usually knee- or calf-length and made initially from linen and later from cotton, it began to rise above the knee in the 1920s as dress lengths shortened. Finally it became a vest worn mainly by the older generation or during the winter months. During the course of its demise it had become interchangeable with the slip, a more shapely garment combining a bodice and skirt. The camisole, usually fastened with buttons at the front, was a waist-length garment initially worn over the corset to protect the outer garments from any friction caused by the boning. It, too, fell out of fashion in the 1920s as the corset moved downward, and instead became combined from 1916 with wide-legged knickers to create a single garment known as the teddy (cami-knickers). The teddy could either be stepped into or could fasten with buttons between the legs and was the most popular undergarment of the 1930s, when it became more streamlined with narrow straps on the shoulders. Today the camisole has once again become a single garment – a lingerie item usually combined in a set with French knickers or tap pants, as designers work to make them prettier, sexier, shorter, and tighter to the body. It is also worn as outerwear.

Drawers made from flannel, muslin (calico), or cotton were introduced for women in the first half of the nineteenth century. Initially they consisted of two leg-shaped tubes sewn onto a waistband and were worn open at the crotch, probably for reasons of sanitation. By the 1870s, closed styles were created, partly as the vogue for cycling and sport grew among women; these were known as knickerbockers, or knickerbocker drawers, or occasionally bloomers (a reference to the original bloomer of the mid-nineteenth century, also developed for women who cycled). By the end of the century a new garment had emerged which combined knickerbockers with the chemise: combinations. Knickerbockers, meanwhile, would continue to become shorter, in line with the rise of the hemline – the name itself was even shortened to knickers – and by the 1930s they would be known as panties or pants.

The brassiere evolves into the bra

Brassieres were initially worn for modesty as the corset became shorter in the early years of the twentieth century, moving downward away from the bust toward the waist and hips. Often insubstantial, brassieres were made of cotton, linen, and lace and were based on the design of the camisole. It was not until the 1930s that the brassiere was made to separate the breasts. It became known as the bra, and its manufacture grew into a major industry, evolving with every new improvement in textile technology. The use of elastic, adjustable straps, and sized and padded cups – with the addition of Hollywood glamour and advertising – pushed the bra toward the specialized garment we see today.

In the 1990s, Versace designed what was termed "lingerie style" outerwear, following in the footsteps of Jean Paul Gaultier's "underwear as outerwear" Spring/Summer collection of 1983, and the bras worn over garments in Vivienne Westwood's Buffalo Girls (Nostalgia of Mud) Fall/Winter collection of 1982/3.

Opposite top / Girdles in an illustration from Alden's Spring and Summer catalog, Illinois 1955.

Opposite bottom / The Calypso Girdle Dress by Atelier Bordelle, 2015.

Above / A 1930s silk bra and tap pants set.

Creating the fashionable skirt silhouette

Over time the silhouette of the skirt has increased and decreased in width as different parts of the hips and buttocks have been emphasized in turn. To help support all this volume, a wide assortment of supports has been created, including bum rolls, bustles and crinolines, and layers of petticoats.

At various times throughout dress history a petticoat, whether layered or not, has been sufficient support for the skirt, but that changed in the mid-nineteenth century, when the increasing girth of a skirt requiring layer upon heavy layer of petticoats meant a frame, known as a crinoline, was needed for support. Crin, or horsehair, had originally been threaded horizontally through petticoats but eventually this was replaced with hoops of cane or whalebone and, finally, flexible steel. The existence of the frame made the adoption of drawers a necessity.

When the skirt eventually collapsed, with the removal of the crinoline in the 1870s, a bustle was required to support the volume of a skirt that was now drawn to the back. Throughout, the underskirt was worn immediately beneath the outer garment while the petticoat beneath – often made of flannel and even quilted – provided volume and warmth. In the early years of the twentieth century, underskirts were made from silks in bright colors, while in the 1920s the princess petticoat, a skirt and bodice combined, evolved into the princess slip, and then into the slip. Layered petticoats would once again be required to support the volume of the skirt in the late 1940s and 1950s.

Above / An advertisement from 1951 for the Perma-Lift brassiere.

Opposite top / A 1943 negligee by Charles James.

Opposite bottom / Poster for the 2009 film *Coco Before Chanel*, showing Audrey Tautou as Chanel, in her famous pajamas.

The evolution of sleepwear

For centuries the nightgown was a shapeless long shirt made from linen with only the quality of the linen indicating the economic status of the wearer. By the middle of the nineteenth century, ready-made nightwear became available, with the nightgown becoming very elaborately embellished by the end of the century. By the 1930s the nightgown resembled an evening gown, clinging to the body as it fell to the floor.

The peignoir and the negligee emerged as loose wrapped gowns in the eighteenth century. The peignoir was originally worn in the morning while brushing the hair and was sold with matching gloves and stockings; it was the original robe or dressing gown. The first negligee was long and heavy, designed in France in the 1700s for purely utilitarian purposes. It remained a dressing gown or robe to be worn in the bedroom until after World War II, when it was transformed into a sensual, even erotic form of lingerie. Today a peignoir is usually made from satin and lace and is often sold with a matching nightgown. A negligee is made from sheer, semitranslucent fabrics trimmed with lace, ribbons, and even feathers.

Pajamas entered fashion in the 1880s. South Asian in origin (the name comes from the Hindi word pājāma, meaning "leg covering") they were exported back to England from India. Men wore pajamas almost exclusively in cotton flannelette and cotton twills with a stripe, a style that is still popular today.

Women also wore pajamas as nightwear, but in the 1920s they migrated to the beach, where they were worn as cover-ups. They were also worn informally around the home; Coco Chanel created her lounge pajamas in the 1920s. In the 1930s the pajama leg was cut wide to look like a skirt and worn as loungewear in the evening for entertaining at home. Loungewear pajamas were not, however, to be confused with those worn for nightwear, which could be decorated with lace and made from satin.

Pajamas eventually became the stylish alternative to the nightdress. Between the wars pajamas grew in popularity, becoming more tailored for women, with tunic tops and a narrower leg. Palazzo pajamas, designed by Princess Irene Galitzine in 1960, once again took PJs out of the bedroom. The trend is happening again today, with pajamas now being worn in public by celebrities.

Tools, Supplies, and Fabrics

Before you begin to design your lingerie or foundation, it is important to have an understanding of some of the tools and supplies you will need. You may have the basic sewing tools, but if you are just starting out there are some other necessities. Using the correct needle and thread to sew your fabric is as important as the choice of boning.

Pattern-drafting tools

- Paper – this can be dot, poster, or craft paper. The most important consideration is transparency, to make it easier to trace off the pattern pieces.
- Paper scissors – to cut out the pattern pieces and to be used only for paper products; once you have cut paper with them you will blunt them, making them unsuitable for cutting fabric.
- Rulers and curves – used for drafting the pattern.
- Pencil – drafting with a pencil means that you can make corrections. It is important to keep a very sharp point on the pencil for accuracy.

Sewing tools

- Fabric scissors or shears – keep for cutting fabric only.
- Tape measure – for taking accurate measurements.
- Pins – fine silk pins for lightweight fabrics, and stronger pins for heavier fabrics. Throw away bent or broken pins. Beware of colored plastic beads on pin ends; if you iron over them they can melt, spoiling the base of your iron and marking the fabric.
- Magnet – to collect dropped or spilled pins.
- Needles for hand sewing – betweens are a good starting needle to hand-hem a garment or to embellish. Embroidery needles or large-eyed needles are needed for embroidery or ribbon work, and a beading needle to attach beads to your garment.
- Sewing machine, either industrial or domestic – look for a machine with a three-step zigzag stitch for attaching all the elastics found in both bra making and lingerie.
- Serger (overlocker) – great for sewing knit fabrics and finishing seam allowances.
- Iron and ironing board – a must for all sewing projects.

Boning

Polyester boning or rigilene requires no casing and is stitched down both sides directly onto the foundation. It is very lightweight. A negative aspect of rigilene is that it bends in all directions, so it is very easy to bend a garment out of shape. Think of using rigilene in a bustier or as the foundation behind an overlay on a gown bodice, where a rigid shape is not so important. A positive is that this boning can also be sewn with one piece on top of another, making it easier to sew a piece vertically with another crossed over it horizontally. Rigilene can also be used with other types of boning because it is easy to cut and shape. The cut ends must be tipped with caps or fabric bound so that the boning does not break apart; this can also be done by holding the ends over a flame until they melt slightly.

Plastic boning is usually sold inside a casing, but you can also buy it cut into lengths or on a roll. It is semi-transparent. It is not very strong and does not have the strength required for tight lacing as it will bend and distort, often in very unflattering ways. Plastic boning cannot be sewn into curved casings. You will find it used in strapless ready-to-wear gowns and lingerie because it is inexpensive.

Flat steel boning and baleen (whalebone) were the dominant materials for boning at the beginning of the nineteenth century, and were occasionally used together. Today this type of boning is made from spring steel flat wire and has a white nylon coating. It is very durable and the coating prevents rusting. While it is flexible, it only bends in one direction and is rigid lengthwise, so it cannot be sewn into curved casings. It does, however, have the strength required for tight lacing, making it a favorite of corset makers and costumiers. Flat steel boning can be both laundered and dry cleaned safely.

Spiral steel boning is a flexible galvanized spring steel wire that is sold in precut lengths or rolls that are either ¼in (6mm) or ½in (1.3cm) wide. It is a strong, flexible boning that can be sewn into curved casings because it bends easily in two directions. It is rigid lengthwise and the ends have to be finished with metal tips. It can be dry cleaned.

1.1

1.2

1.3

1.4

Busks

Busks are the clasps placed down the center front of a corset. A busk consists of two long pieces of steel, one with raised domes and the other with eyes or loops that fit over the domes to close the busk. Once only available in the natural color of the steel, today they are plastic coated in a variety of different colors. Busks are sold by the length in different weights and shapes; heavier busks are less flexible but give more support, while the curved shape of a spoon busk fits over the shape of the stomach.

1.1 / Polyester boning or rigilene.

1.2 / Plastic boning.

1.3 / Flat steel boning.

1.4 / Spiral steel boning.

1.5 / Busk.

1.6 / Spoon busk.
(1.2–1.6 all MacCulloch & Wallis Ltd)

1.5

1.6

Fabrics and lace

Choosing the correct fabric for the garment style and type is important. In most cases it will be next to the skin so must feel soft and not irritate in any way. Also consider how fabric and garment must be cared for and laundered.

Silk remains a popular choice for luxurious lingerie as it is soft and cool to the touch but warms quickly with body heat. It is very durable, long lasting, and comes in many different weights and a wide choice of colors.

Synthetic satin is also popular because it has a similar feel to natural silk, is inexpensive, and easy to launder. Satin is a type of weave and not a fiber, so a synthetic satin is a fabric woven from synthetic fibers. Spandex (elastane) and Lycra® can be blended into the fabric for elasticity.

Cotton and fabrics derived from cellulose such as rayon and modal are also good choices; they have a soft feel and natural sheen. They can be blended for added softness, with latex or spandex added for elasticity. Cellulose-derived fibers are also used in lace making.

Microfibers are very thin fibers of polyester and nylon combined into a single thread 100 times thinner than a human hair, or less than 1 denier. Microfiber fabrics have excellent wicking or moisture-removal properties, are soft to the touch, hold their shape, and are easy to launder and care for. They are found in every type of lingerie garment.

Powernet is an elasticized fabric in different weights and strengths. Made from a mix of nylon and spandex filament fibers, it has a two-way stretch and does not fray. Powernet is also sold as powerknit, girdle fabric, and power mesh. It is used in the construction of both bras and form-fitting garments.

Tulle is a lightweight, very fine netting made from nylon, cotton, rayon, or even silk. The fibers are tightly spun, producing a fabric that is used to add fullness or act as a support fabric. Tulle is also the background for most lace.

Lace is an intricate, delicate fabric with no grainline, sometimes with spandex for extra stretch. There are many types, from fine bobbin lace to heavier crochet, knotted lace, and knitted lace. Most laces have a net background and edges are often scalloped; ribbon or tape can be sewn on for extra texture. Lace comes in various widths, from narrow trimming and insertion lace to all-over patterned fabric, and is used in every type of lingerie from bras to sleepwear. Lace motifs can also be used as appliqués.

Stretch fabrics

Today more and more woven and knit fabrics are blended with spandex or Lycra®. The difference between the two is that spandex fibers contain no natural latex or rubber and Lycra® fibers may contain either. Spandex fibers can be woven into a fabric in its purest form or wrapped around a non-elastic yarn. Adding spandex to a garment increases comfort, gives stability, and helps it hold its shape. Adding spandex to a knit fabric not only increases stretch but also helps the stretched garment recover its original shape. Stretch fabrics are the best choice for form-fitting garments.

To find the amount of stretch in a fabric both vertically and horizontally, first cut an 8in (20cm) square. Secure a tape measure along the edge of a table, then tape card or even a ruler down both sides of the fabric. Hold one side of the reinforced fabric at one end of the fixed tape measure on the table. Stretch out the fabric horizontally along the tape measure to its greatest stretch before it starts to distort. The amount the fabric has stretched past its original length is the amount of horizontal stretch.

High stretch: more than 2in (5cm)
Medium to high stretch: 1–2in (2.5–5cm)
Medium stretch: ½–1in (1.3–2.5cm)
Low stretch: less than ½in (1.3cm)

Vertical (bi-fabric) stretch is measured in the same way. The recovery should also be measured to make sure the fabric returns to its original length and width.

The percentage of stretch in the fabric must be subtracted from the pattern. Divide the amount of stretch by the original width/length of the fabric and then multiply by 100.

$$\frac{\text{Amount of stretch}}{\text{Original fabric size}} \times 100 = \% \text{ of stretch in fabric}$$

$$\text{Example:} \quad \frac{\text{1in (2.5cm)}}{\text{8in (20cm)}} \times 100 = 12.5\%$$

Elastic trim

Elastic trim is used in bra making and in lingerie, where you will find elastic at the waistline of petticoats and around the legs and waistline of briefs.

Elastic can have a scalloped edge along one side, known as a picot edge, and may also have an added ruffled edge that looks really pretty on the neckline of a bra. Both ruffled and picot-edged elastic trim come in a multitude of color choices. The most common width is ¼in (6mm) but there are other widths available.

Clear elastic is used behind lace and sheer fabrics. It is also used behind stretch lace as reinforcement and to keep the lace stable.

Band elastic is used on both the top and bottom edges of a bra band and around the legs of a brief. It may also have a small picot or scalloped edge, and a slight shine on the front with a brushed finish on the back. These elastics are made from either spandex or latex.

Gripper elastic is used on the bottom of a longline bra or at the top edge of a strapless bra. It can also be used for waistbands. In its widest form, gripper elastic can replace the back of a foundation behind a backless gown. Some gripper elastic has tiny silicone beads or small stripes of rubber running down its center that grip the skin.

Fold-over elastic has a seam down the middle along which it can be folded, usually over the raw edge of a strap or neckline, around the leg of a brief or maybe even across the back of a camisole or nightgown. Fold-over elastic can also be finished with a scalloped or picot edge.

It is important to measure the stretch of any elastic trim. To find the stretch hold one end of the elastic at the end of a ruler, measure down the ruler 4in (5cm) and place a pin in the elastic to mark. Holding the elastic at the beginning of the ruler, stretch the elastic to its fullest stretch capacity at the pin, and note the amount of stretch. Take the measurement of the waistline or leg on your pattern before adding the seam allowance and apply this to the elastic trim. Now reduce the amount of extra stretch from the elastic trim to find the correct length. Finally add seam allowance to the elastic trim.

Waistline - Amount of stretch in elastic = Length of elastic

Example: 28in (71cm) - 2in (5cm) = 26in (66cm)

Rings and sliders

Rings and sliders are sold together, usually in a set of two. You will find them on bra and camisole straps, and any other straps that need adjusting. They can be made from nylon-covered metal or plastic.

Slide locks

The slide lock can be snapped closed, stopping the strap from sliding down, helping to eliminate a problem commonly faced by heavy-busted women. The slide lock is threaded onto the strap with the small hinged part open, then – when the strap has been adjusted to the required length, using a slider and ring – it is snapped shut and the row of small blunt teeth securely grip the fabric of the strap, preventing the slider from moving further.

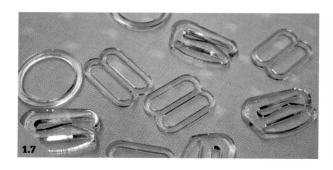

1.7 / Rings and sliders. (MacCulloch & Wallis Ltd)
1.8 / Slide locks.

Hooks and eyes

Hooks and eyes can be bought and sewn on individually, or they can be bought already attached to nylon or cotton tape. The tape can be purchased in a long strip with a single row of hooks on one side and one of eyes on the other, suitable for a corset or girdle. Shorter lengths arranged with a column of two, three, or four hooks on one side and multiple columns or rows of eyes on the other for adjustability can also be purchased – these are suitable for the back of a bra. This tape is ordered by the spacing of the hooks and eyes, or the number of columns. Most bras sold today have three columns of eyes.

Garter clips

These are also known as suspender clips. They are used with garter belts (suspenders), girdles, and corsets to hold up stockings. They come in either plastic or metal.

1.9

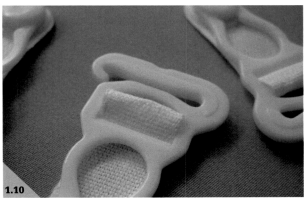

1.10

Needles

It is important to have the correct needle and needle size for your choice of fabric. Needles come in many different sizes, lengths, and shapes, designed for different functions. Some are round and others have a straight back and a round front.

Needle sizing

The two most commonly used sizing systems today are American and European (also called number metric, or NM). When you buy needles they will often be labeled, say, 70/10 or 90/14, indicating both American and European sizing. The smaller the diameter of the needle, the lower the number.

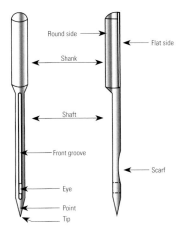

AMERICAN	EUROPEAN (NM)
8	60
9	65
10	70
11	75
12	80
14	90
16	100
18	110

1.9 / Hooks and eyes.
1.10 / Garter (suspender) clips.
(both MacCulloch & Wallis Ltd)

Sewing machine needles

Universal		A general-purpose needle.	Sizes 60/8 to 110/18	Single, twin and triple	For both woven and knit fabrics.
Jersey or Ball point		The rounded point slips between the fibers rather than cutting them.	Sizes 70/10 to 110/18	Twin	For knit fabrics.
Stretch		A slightly more rounded point and a tiny hump between eye and scarf that allows the thread to make a large loop on one side of the needle. This loop makes it easy to complete a stitch.	Sizes 75/11 or 90/14	Twin	For both knit and woven fabrics such as satin.
Microtex (Sharp)		A thin shaft, and a slim, sharp point.	Sizes 60/8 to 100/16		For lightweight fabrics, delicate wovens, and any heirloom sewing.
Embroidery		A large eye and a special scarf that protects fragile threads.	Sizes 75/11 to 90/14	Twin	Use with embroidery thread.
Metallic		The elongated eye prevents shredding and breaking of metallic threads.	Sizes 80/12 and 90/14	Twin	Use with metallic and other specialty threads.
Leather		A special cutting point.			For leather, artificial leather, heavy non-woven synthetics. Do not use on knit or woven fabrics.
Wing or Hemstitch		A wing on each side of the needle.	Size 100/16	The twin needles are a universal needle and a wing needle separated by ⅛in (2.5mm) gap.	For light- or medium-weight loosely woven fabrics. Popular for heirloom sewing and creating decorative cutwork.

Hand sewing needles

Crewel		A sharp point with a long, narrow eye.	Sizes 1 to 10	Used with embroidery floss and silk ribbon. For heavier fabrics.
Betweens		Short, fine needles with a large eye.	Sizes 3 to 12	Most often associated with quilting, but also used for fine hand sewing.
Sharps		Fine, medium-length needles.	Sizes 5 to 12	Used for hand sewing and also in fine hand embroidery.
Milliners or Beading		Long, narrow needles with a small, round eye.	Sizes 3 to 9	Used for sewing beads and French knots.
Tapestry		Stout needles with a long eye and a blunt point.	Sizes 13 to 28	Used for pulled and drawn work, and silk ribbon embroidery.

Thread

It is important to choose the correct thread for the type of sewing you are going to be doing. If the thread is too weak, then your garment is not going to hold together. If the thread is too heavy, it can tear or split the fabric. In manufacturing, thread performance is evaluated by seam length, Tex number (see opposite), raw material, abrasion resistance, elasticity, type of finish, chemical resistance, flammability, and colorfastness.

1.11

MONOFILAMENT THREAD	REGENERATED THREADS
This is a single synthetic filament. It is available in a number of sizes, .004 and .005 being the most popular for the home sewer when an invisible thread is required.	■ Cellulose – rayon, acetate For smooth, strong stitches with a sheen for machine embroidery. These are long, continuous filament threads.
NATURAL FIBERS	MAN-MADE
■ Animal – silk ■ Plant – cotton Silk thread is rarely used today in production because of its high cost. It is used with silk fabrics and for attaching lace in couture lingerie. Cotton and mercerized cotton thread is the most commonly used in both machine and hand sewing. Mercerized cotton is a cotton thread with a slight sheen. It is strong and smooth. Use for stitching cottons.	■ Synthetic – polyester, nylon, acrylic, elastic, polypropylene ■ Mineral – metallic The most common synthetics are polyester and nylon. They are stronger than cotton threads of the same size. Use with synthetic fabrics. Core-spun thread is cotton-wrapped polyester or polyester-wrapped polyester. It is suitable for most fabrics. Metallic thread has a strong polyester filament core with a metallized polyester foil wrap that gives a reflective sheen.
SERGER THREAD	EMBROIDERY THREADS
A light spun polyester thread usually purchased on a cone. It can give off lint and have thick and thin spots along its length. Only recommended for sergers. Textured threads are also used for serged rolled hems – the best known is Woolly Nylon.	Made from rayon, silk, both cotton and mercerized cotton, metallics, nylon, and polyester for hand embroidery. Embroidery threads can also be textured for different effects.

1.11 / Threads.
(MacCulloch & Wallis Ltd)

Thread sizing

While the Tex system of sizing thread is used in industry, there is no set standard for the home sewing market. The Tex system involves calculating the weight in grams of 1,000 meters of thread:

1 Tex = 1 gram per 1,000 meters

Thread can also be produced in different thicknesses that depend on the relationship between the length and weight – better known as the linear density, yarn count, or size. Both thread sizing and the tex system are metric sytems and used worldwide. Thread size is given as a number: the finer the thread, the lower the number assigned; the coarser the thread, the higher the number.

Lightweight threads: Tex 10 – Tex 24
Sulky rayon
R&A rayon
Mettler Poly Sheen
Woolly Nylon
Mettler cotton
Madeira cotton
YLI Heirloom
YLI Silk

Medium-weight threads: Tex 27 – Tex 35
Mettler all purpose polyester
Gütermann all purpose polyester
Coats Dual Duty
YLI Silk
YLI Select, cotton
Finishing Touch
Elite
Maxi-Lock

Heavyweight threads: Tex 40 – Tex 90
LI Jeans Stitch
YLI Silk
YLI Colours
YLI Quilting
Mettler Quilting
Gütermann Quilting
Signature cotton
Quilting
Sulky #30 rayon

Sizes Conversion Chart		
US	UK	EUROPEAN
6–8	8–10	36–38
10–14	12–16	40–44
16–20	18–22	46–52
22–24	24–26	54–56

2 Designing and Pattern Drafting
Slips, panties, and petticoats

The term "lingerie" traditionally covers all ladies' undergarments and those garments not designed to be seen in public. Hidden though they may have been, however, these garments have often been elaborately made and embellished. Just as fashionable dress evolved, the garments that are worn beneath them have evolved in both style and function. Today, lingerie includes camisoles and slips, panties or briefs, French knickers, teddies (cami-knickers), bodyshapers, petticoats, nightwear, and, finally, foundation garments and bras. The design of foundation garments and bras, which require a specialist cut, is discussed in later chapters. In this and the next chapter, the design of garments not designed to sculpt the body will be explored.

A rare Doucet *déshabillé*, circa 1905–10, made of pale lavender chiffon edged with needle-run lace, ruched ribbons, and large satin rosettes, finishing with a trained hem.

The lingerie sloper (block)

A sloper is a basic pattern that has no added seam allowances; by manipulating it, many different designs can be created. The sloper for underwear garments fits closely to the contours of the body and has less ease added than you would normally add for outerwear garments. The choice of fabric is an important factor in drafting your sloper. Underwear can be made from both woven and knitted fabrics, with the choice often dictated by the type and function of the garment.

Woven fabrics do not have as much stretch as knitted fabrics. Any stretch will usually come from the fiber or the weave structure and will usually be horizontal stretch. Woven fabrics can be cut close to the body using a close fitting sloper and can also be cut on the bias to give a more closely fitted finish with the added feature of a soft drape.

Mixed fibers can add a stretch component to the fabric, especially with the addition of spandex (elastane), giving a closer fit. The amount of stretch in such fabrics needs to be calculated and removed from the body measurements before cutting the sloper.

Knitted fabrics can have the unique combination of both drape and stretch, and the stretch can be both horizontal and vertical. Spandex can also be added to a knitted fabric to give it some stability and stretch recovery. The amount of stretch in the fabric has to be calculated before you can start drafting your sloper. A close fitting garment sloper can be developed with measurements that are smaller than those of the body if the fabric has high stretch.

A sloper can be built from personal body measurements or by using a standard body measurement chart. These charts vary from company to company and school to school. The measurements listed below are those you will need to draft your slopers, or you can work off your company's or school's measurement chart.

2.1 / Where to take body measurements.

2.1

1	Bust	
2	Waist	
3	Hip	
4	Chest	
5	Nape to waist	
6	Armhole (armscye) depth	
7	Back width	
8	Neck size	
9	Shoulder	
10	Bicep	
11	Wrist	
12	Sleeve length	
13	Body rise / Crotch depth	
14	Ankle	
15	Waist to floor	

The close-fitting sloper

Use your standard measurement charts or work from personal measurements to draft this sloper.

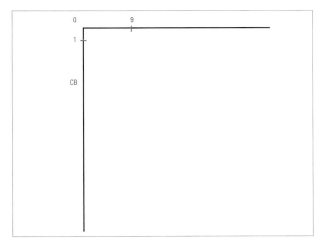
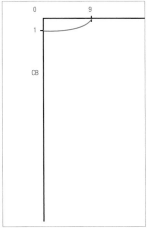
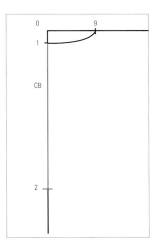

Step 1

Start with the back sloper.

- Draw a line down the left-hand side of a piece of paper the length of the measurement from nape to waist plus the measurement from waist to floor. Label it as the center back (CB).
- Label the top of the line as 0.
- Square a line across to the right-hand side of the paper from 0.
- Measure down ⅝in (1.5cm) from 0; mark this point as 1. Measure across one fifth of the neck measurement less ⅛in (3mm) from 0; mark this point as 9. Draw in the back neck curve from 1 to 9.

Step 2

- Measure down from 1 the armhole depth and mark this point as 2.

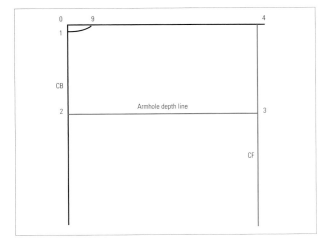

Step 3

- Square across from 2 half the bust measurement plus 2in (5cm); mark this point as 3.
- Square a line up from 3 to the top line; mark as 4. This line is the armhole depth line.
- Draw a line down from 4 the same length as the center back. Label this line as the center front (CF).

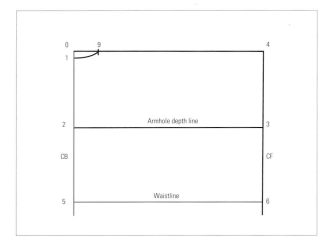

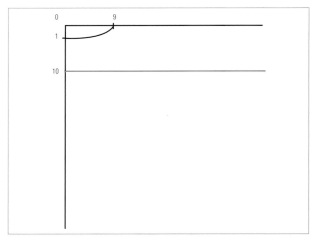

Step 4

- Measure the nape to waist measurement down from 1; mark this point as 5.
- Square across to the center front line; mark this point as 6. Label this as the waistline.

Step 5

- To begin to plot the detail of the back shoulder area, first measure down from 1 one fifth of the armhole depth measurement less ¼in (6mm); mark this point as 10.
- Square a line halfway across the paper.

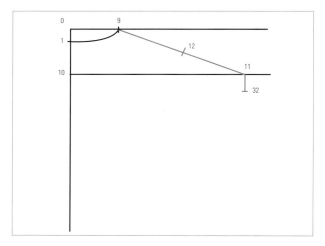

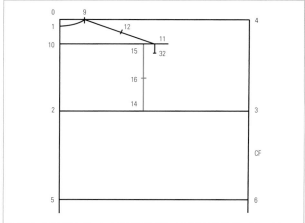

Step 6

- To shape the back shoulder, draw a line from 9 the length of the shoulder plus ⅜in (1cm) and angle it down to touch the line you drew from 10; mark this point as 11.
- Divide the line from 9 to 11 in half and mark as 12.
- Square down ⅝in (1.5cm) from 11 and mark as 32.

Step 7

- Next, continue shaping the back sloper down to the waist. From 2 measure across half the back measurement plus ¼in (6mm) and mark as 14.
- Square up from 14 to the line you drew from 10 and mark as 15.
- Divide the line from 14 to 15 in half and mark as 16.

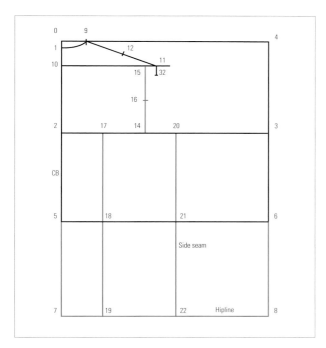

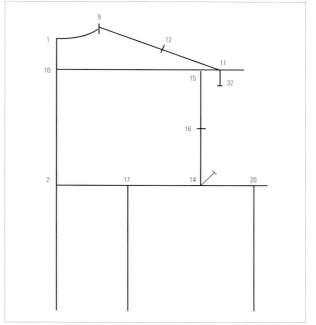

Step 8

- Square a line down from 5 the waist to hip measurement; mark as 7.
- Square a line across from 7 to the center front and mark as 8. Label this line as the hipline.
- Divide the line from 2 to 3 in half and mark as 20.
- Square a line down from 20 to the waistline and mark as 21. Continue down to the hipline and mark as 22. Label this line as the side seam.
- Divide the line from 2 to 14 in half and mark as 17.
- Square a line down from 17 to the waistline and mark as 18. Continue down to the hipline and mark as 19.

Step 9

- Draw a line out from 14 at a 45° angle; mark. The length of the line will depend on the size of the sloper you are making:

    sizes 6–8   ⅞in (2.2cm)
    sizes 10–14 1in (2.5cm)
    sizes 16–20 1⅛in (3cm)
    sizes 22–24 1¼in (3.3cm)

See the conversion chart on page 23 for UK and European sizes.

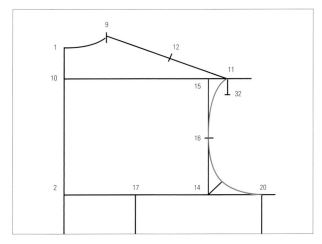

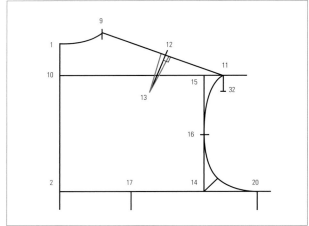

Step 10

- Draw in the back armhole curve, starting at 11, touching the mark at 16 and the mark you made from 14, and around to 20.

Step 11

- Draw the back shoulder dart; square a 2in (5cm) line down from 12. Draw in two dart legs the same length on either side of this line to make a dart that is ⅜in (1cm) wide. Mark the end of the dart as 13.

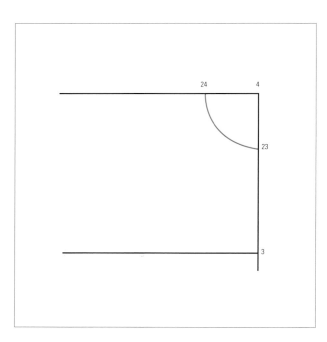

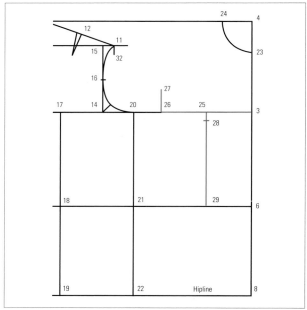

Step 12

Now draw the front sloper.

- From the center front at 4 measure across one fifth of the neck measurement less ¼in (6mm); mark as 24.
- Measure one fifth of the neck measurement less ¾in (2cm) down the center front line from 4; mark as 23.
- Draw in the front neck curve from 24 to 23.

Step 13

- From 3 measure across half the chest measurement plus half the dart measurement and mark as 26.
- Square a line up from 26 one third the measurement from 3 to 23 and mark as 27.
- Divide the measurement from 3 to 26 in half; mark as 25. Square down from 25 to the waistline; mark as 29.
- Locate the bust point (BP) 1in (2.5cm) down from 25 and mark as 28.

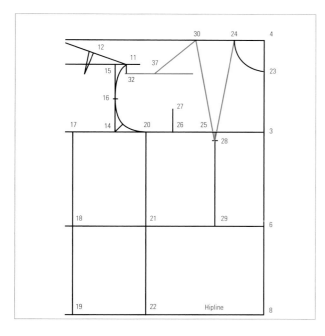

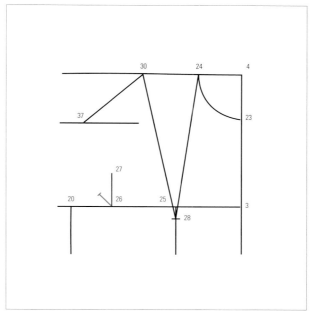

Step 14

- Draw a line from 28 up to 24; this is one dart leg.
- Measure the dart measurement over from 24 and mark as 30.
- Draw a line from 28 up to 30 the same length as the line from 28 to 24; this is the second dart leg.
- Square a line out from 32.
- Draw a line the shoulder length from 30 to touch the line squared out from 32; mark as 37.

Step 15

- Draw a line out from 26 at a 45° angle; make a mark. The length of the line will depend on the size of the sloper you are making:

  sizes 6–8   ⅝in (1.5cm)
  sizes 10–14   ¾in (2cm)
  sizes 16–20   1in (2.5cm)
  sizes 22–24   1⅛in (3cm)

See the conversion chart on page 23 for UK and European sizes.

Step 16

- Draw in the front armhole curve, starting at 37, touching the mark at 27, the mark you made from 26, and around to 20.

Shaping the slopers

You can add shape to your slopers with the addition of darts at the side seam and at the front and back waistline.

- Square a line from 29 down to the hipline and label it as 31.
- Measure over ⅜in (1cm) on the waistline from the side seam toward the back and mark. Measure over ¾in (2cm) from the side seam toward the front and mark.
- Draw two lines from 20 that pass through the new marks on the back and front waistline and back down to 22 at the hipline. This creates the shaping at the side seam.
- The width of the back waist dart is 1in (2.5cm). Make a mark at the waistline ½in (1.3cm) to each side of 18.
- Draw two lines from 17 that pass through the new marks on the back waistline and back down to the end of the dart 5in (12.5cm) below the waistline.
- The width of the front waist dart is 1⅜in (3.5cm). Make a mark at the waistline ⅝in (1.5cm) to either side of 29.
- Draw two lines from the bust point at 28 that pass through the new marks on the front waistline and back down to the end of the dart 3in (7.5cm) below the waistline.

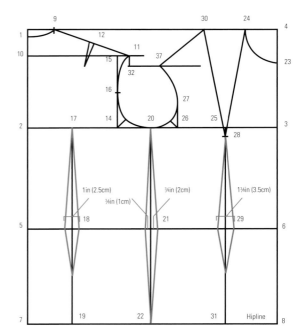

The close-fitting sleeveless sloper

To adapt the fitted sloper into a sleeveless sloper, raise and widen the armhole and adjust the side seam.

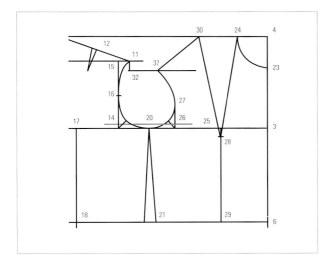

Step 1

- Move the armhole depth line from 2 to 3 up ⅜in (1cm) at 20.

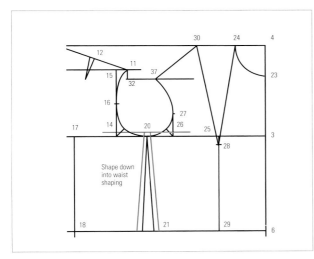

Step 2

- Measure in ⅝in (1.5cm) from the side seam at both sides and redraw the seam into the waistline.

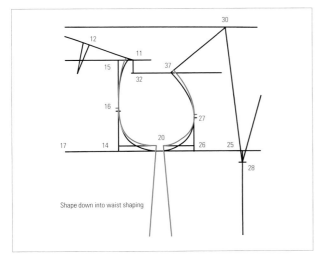

Step 3

- Measure in ⅜in (1cm) from 11 and 37 on each shoulder line and mark.
- Measure up ⅜in (1cm) at 16 and 27 and mark.
- Draw in a new armhole curve through the new marks, finishing at the raised armhole above 20.
- Once you have finished drawing your sloper on paper, you can transfer it to oak tag.

The knit/stretch fabric sloper

Because there are numerous stretch fabrics, with multiple stretch capabilities, you will have to test the stretch of the horizontal "action" stretch and the vertical, or warp, stretch of the fabric. On body fitting garments you have to decide the amount of visual action stretch when the fabric is stretched horizontally and deduct this from the sloper. To do this, refer to the stretch characteristics information in Chapter 1, page 17.

The stretch recovery of the fabric is another important factor to consider. A fabric with poor recovery will need more ease to be added to the sloper than a fabric with good recovery.

If you are working with a variety of knit/stretch fabrics you may have to draft multiple slopers that may have to be re-adjusted after the first fitting.

Use the standard measurement chart with the percentage of stretch deducted.

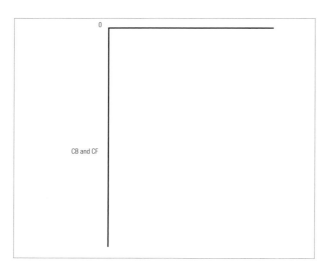

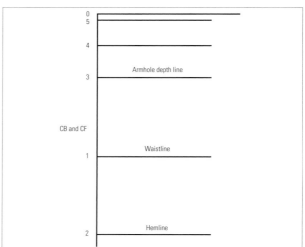

Step 1

- Draw a line down the left-hand side of a piece of paper the length of the measurement from nape to waist plus the measurement from waist to floor. Label it as the center back and center front (CB and CF).
- Label the top of the line as 0.
- Square a line across to the right-hand side of the paper from 0.

Step 2

- Measure down the neck to waist measurement plus ⅜in (1cm) from 0 and mark as 1.
- Square a line across from 1. Label this as the waistline.
- Measure down the finished length of the garment from 0 and mark as 2.
- Square a line across from 2. Label this as the hemline.
- Measure down the armhole depth from 0, less 1in (2.5cm) for fabrics with up to 30% stretch; 1⅛in (3cm) for up to 35–50% stretch; 2in (5cm) for over 50% stretch; mark as 3.
- Square a line across from 3; label as the armhole depth line.
- Divide the measurement from 0 to 3 in half and label it 4.
- Square a line across from 4.
- Divide the measurement from 0 to 4 into five; make a mark one fifth down from 0 and mark as 5.
- Square a line across from 5.

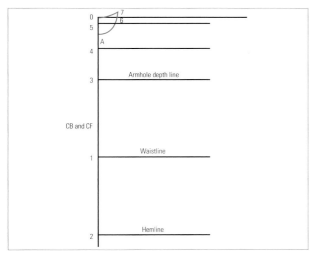

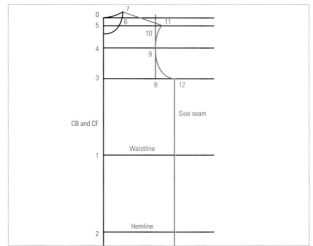

Step 3

- To shape the neckline, measure one sixth of the neckline measurement from 0 less ¼–½in (6mm–1.3cm), depending on the stretch; mark as 6.
- Square a ½in (1.3cm) line up at 6 and mark as 7.
- Draw in the back neck curve from 0 to 7.
- Measure down one sixth of the neckline measurement from 0 less ⅜–½in (1–1.3cm), depending on the stretch; mark as A.
- Draw in the front neck curve from A to 7.

Step 4

- To shape the armhole, measure across from 3 half the back width less ⅞in, 1in, or 2⅜in (2.2cm, 2.5cm, or 6cm), depending on the stretch; mark as 8.
- From 8 square a line up to the line drawn from 4 and mark as 9. Continue up to the line drawn from 5; mark as 10.
- At 10, square a ⅜in (1cm) line out and mark as 11.
- Draw a line from 7 to 11, which is the shoulder line.
- From 3 measure across one quarter of the bust measurement less ⅝in, 1⅛in, or 3⅛in (1.5cm, 3cm, or 8cm), depending on the stretch; mark as 12.
- Square a line down to the hemline from 12. Label this as the side seam.
- Draw in the armhole curve from 12, touching 9 and then round up to 11.

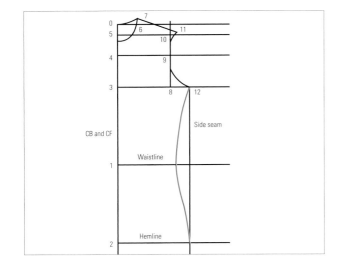

Step 5

- At the waistline, measure in 1⅛in, 1⅜in, or 1⅝in (3cm, 3.5cm, or 4cm), depending on the stretch. Make a mark and redraw the side seam from 12, curving the line through this new mark and back down to the hemline.

The sleeve for the knit/stretch fabric sloper

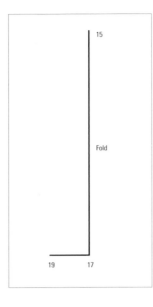

Step 1

- Draw a line down your paper the length of the jersey sleeve plus 1⅛–2⅜in (3–6cm), depending on the stretch; label the top 15 and the bottom 17; label the line as the fold.
- Square a line across from 17 half the wrist measurement less ¼–⅝in (6mm–1.5cm), depending on the stretch; mark as 19.

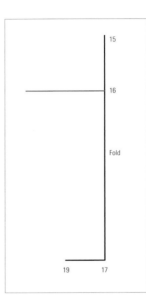

Step 2

- From 15 measure down half the measurement from 0 to 3 plus ⅜in (1cm); mark as 16.
- Square a line across from 16.

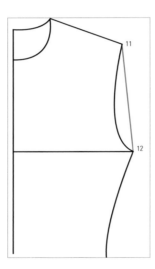

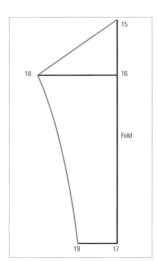

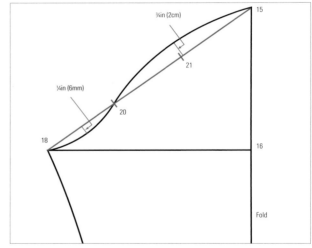

Step 3

- Draw a line from 15, the same measurement as the line from 12 to 11 on the knit sloper plus ⅜in (1cm), to touch the line from 16; mark as 18.
- Draw a concave curved line from 18 to 19.

Step 4

- To shape the sleeve head, start by dividing the line from 18 to 15 into three equal sections; label the first from the underarm point as 20 and the second as 21.
- Divide the line from 18 to 20 in half and measure down ¼in (6mm) and mark. Measure up ¾in (2cm) from 21 and mark.
- Draw a curved line from 18 to 15 touching the marks you have just added, starting with a concave curve from 18 to 20, then reversing the curve from 20 to 15.

Camisoles and slips

Slip dresses have become a signature style for some of today's designers. They resemble the petticoats or full slips that women wore under their outerwear garments in the 1940s to 1980s. Slips are usually close fitting and made from fabrics with stretch, or are cut on the bias so that they skim over the body. Knit fabrics are cut on the straight grain; woven fabrics can be cut on the straight grain if they have some stretch content, but if not are usually cut on the bias. If you are working with a non-stretch fabric you will need to add a small opening that can be created as a design detail.

Full slip with added flare in the skirt

This slip is bias cut with a flared skirt. A back yoke and soft bra cup can be added. For a camisole, follow the directions to redraw the side seam down to the hipline.

- Trace around the close-fitting sloper, ensuring that you have the required length for your slip.
- Draw in the neckline on the front and back pattern pieces. The front neckline can be shaped but the measurement from the bust point up to the neckline should be approximately 2¾–3in (7–7.5cm).
- Make a mark ⅝in (1.5cm) in at the underarm on the side seams on both the front and back pattern pieces.

- Make a mark ¼in (6mm) in along the waistline from the side seam on the front and the back and reshape the side seam from the top to the hipline.
- Delete the front and back darts from the pattern pieces.
- Extend the hemline approximately 2in (5cm) or the desired amount out from the side seam on the front and back. Redraw the side seam from this mark up to the hipline.
- Redraw the hemline to create a smooth curve.
- Mark the bias grainline.
- Mark the lace placement, the center front and center back, and the seam allowances onto the pattern.

2.2

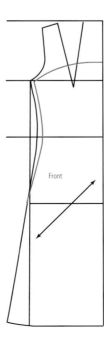

Front

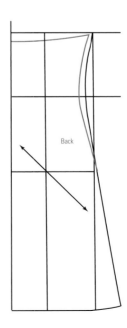

Back

2.2 / Bias-cut slip with flared skirt, and lace detailing on hem and cups.

Adding a yoke and soft cup

- Draw in the back yoke line approximately 2½in (6.5cm) wide.
- Draw in the soft cup so that it matches the back yoke at the side seam and has approximately 2¾–3in (7–7.5cm) of length down from the bust point.
- Cut the front and back yokes from the pattern.
- Tape the front dart together at the neckline so that it forms a dart on the lower edge; reshape the lower edge. If gathers are going to be used for bust shaping add ½in (1.3cm) down from the center of the under-bust dart and reshape the lower edge.

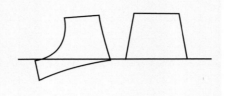

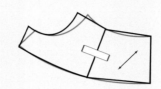

2.3

Closely fitted slip with vertical seams

This slip follows the contours of the body. Flare is added to the side and vertical seams from the hipline down to the hemline; alternatively you can add a split to the vertical seam(s) from the hemline. A soft cup and back yoke can be added to this pattern. For a camisole, finish the pattern at the hipline.

- Draw around the close-fitting sloper, checking that you have the required length for your slip.
- Draw in the new neckline.
- Increase the width of the front and back waist dart by ¼in (6mm) on either side at the waistline. Redraw the dart legs.
- Measure in ¼in (6mm) at the underarm side seam on both the front and back pattern pieces; repeat at the waistline; measure in and mark ⅛in (3mm) at the hipline.
- Redraw the curve of the side seam, on both the front and back, from the new armhole point to the hipline through the new marks.
- Make a mark ¾in (2cm) either side of the side front and back vertical seams at the hemline.
- Redraw the side front and back panel seams up to the end of the waist darts.
- Measure out ¾in (2cm) from both side seams at the hemline and mark.
- Redraw the side seams from the new marks up to the hipline.
- Mark the lace placement, the center front and center back, and the seam allowances on the pattern.

2.3 / Elizabeth Taylor made a statement in this closely fitted slip dress in the 1960 film *Butterfield 8*.

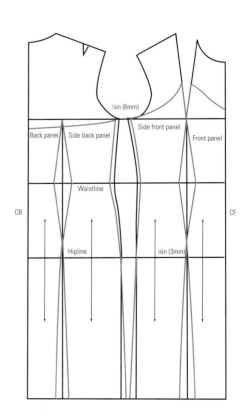

¼in (6mm)

Back panel | Side back panel | Side front panel | Front panel

Waistline

CB

Hipline

⅛in (3mm)

CF

Panties or briefs

In the 1930s panties were tailored to the body, becoming panty briefs that could be worn under the new bias-cut slinky dresses.

Can-Can dancers began wearing "shorts" after a police ordinance was issued in Paris that required women who appeared on stage to wear shorts. The shorts were created by stitching the crotch of the pantaloon together; they were also shortened so that they revealed the thigh. These were the first French knickers, which later, in the 1950s, were mass produced in the new man-made fabrics of the era, such as nylon. They offered freedom of movement, with no visible pantie line (VPL) making them suitable for both day and evening wear.

Waist	
High hip	
Low hip	
Crotch depth	
Crotch length	
Crotch	

Basic brief sloper

The basic brief sloper is the starting point for a variety of brief designs. The basic brief can be altered by lowering the waistline, raising the cut of the leg, and can even be turned into a thong. It is a close-fitting brief sloper but it is easy to add fullness at the leg or waistline (or both) depending on the design. A brief can be made from a stretch or woven fabric cut on the straight grain or bias, in an assortment of fabrics, from fine cottons and silks to synthetics. It can be finished with an elastic waistband that has a logo woven into it, lace, or any other embellishments of your choice.

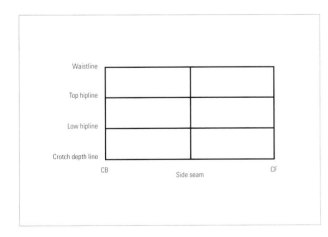

Step 1

- Draw a vertical line down the center of your paper the length of the crotch depth and mark the top and bottom. Add approximately 2in (5cm) to the top of the line and 8in (20cm) to the bottom.
- Draw two horizontal lines at the top and bottom marks. Each line should extend one quarter of the hip measurement either side of the vertical line.
- Square a line down each side from the top to the bottom horizontal line.
- Divide the crotch depth into three; make two marks on the central vertical line and square lines across to the outside of the box.
- Label the top horizontal line the waistline, the bottom line the crotch depth line and the two lines between the top and low hiplines. The central vertical line is the side seam, the line at the left-hand side of the box is the center back, and the line on the right is the center front.

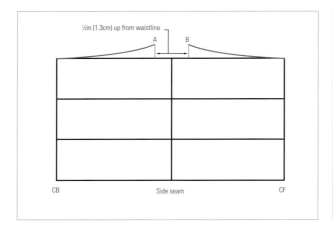

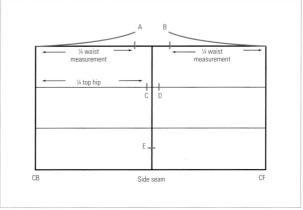

Step 2

- On the waistline at the center front measure across one quarter of the waist measurement and mark. Repeat from the center back.
- Square up ½in (1.3cm) from each mark and make a further two marks; label the mark on the back A and the mark on the front B.
- Redraw the waistline from the center back to A using a curved ruler. Repeat from the center front to B.

Step 3

- On the top hipline from the center back, measure across one quarter of the top hip measurement; mark as C. Repeat from the center front and mark as D.
- Divide the vertical line joining the low hipline and the crotch depth line in half and mark it E.

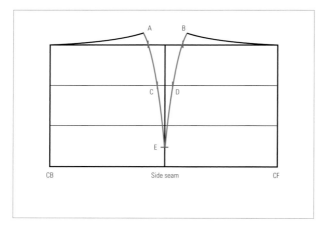

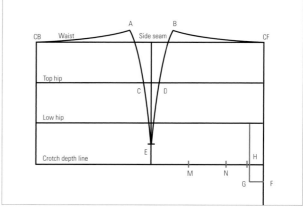

Step 4

- Using a curved ruler, draw in the side seam from A to C and from B to D, finishing at E.

Step 5

- Extend the center front line by one third the full crotch measurement (front crotch); mark as F.
- Square a line in half the crotch width, 1¼in (3.3cm) from F; mark as G.
- Divide the crotch depth line from the side seam to the center front into three equal parts. Measure across 1¼in (3.3cm) along the low hipline; mark, then draw a line down from this point to G.
- Measure in from this line on the crotch depth line by ⅛in (3mm); mark as H.

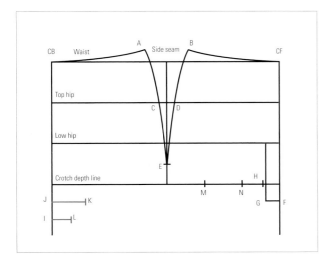

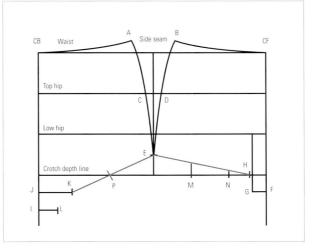

Step 6

- Extend the center back line by two thirds the full crotch measurement (back crotch); mark as I.
- Divide the measurement from I to the crotch depth line in half and mark as J.
- Square in a line from J the width of the crotch; mark as K.
- Square a line over from I half crotch width, 1¼in (3.3cm); mark as L.

Step 7

- Draw in the leg opening from K to E and E to H.
- Divide the line from K to E in half and mark as P.
- Draw a line up from M and N through the line from E–H.

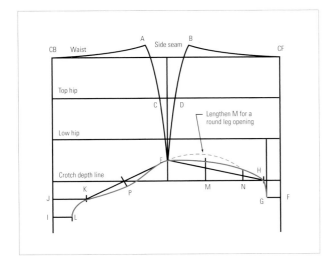

Step 8

- Draw a curved line from L to K.
- Draw a straight line from H to G.
- Square a line down from P and mark:

  extra small – ½in (1.3cm)
  small – ⅝in (1.5cm)
  medium – ¾in (2cm)
  large – ⅞in (2.2cm)
  extra large – 1in (2.5cm)

- Using a curved ruler, draw in the back leg curve from K to E that passes through the measured line down from P.
- On the line up from M and N measure and mark:

  extra small – ½in (1.3cm)
  small – ¾in (2cm)
  medium – 1in (2.5cm)
  large – 1¼in (3.3cm)
  extra large – 1½in (3.8cm)

Note: You can make the length up from M longer than the length up from N if you would like a rounder, higher front leg opening.

- Using a curved ruler, draw in the front leg curve from E to H through these marks.

Hipsters

Hipsters are close fitting, with the waistline sitting on the hipline. The leg can be the same as the brief or it can be high cut. Another name for the hipster is the low-rise brief.

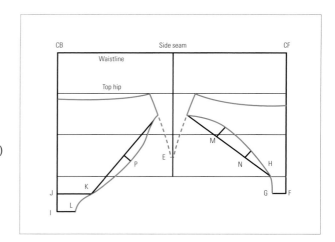

- Follow the instructions for the Basic Brief (see page 39) to create the basic grid for designing the brief.
- On the top hipline at the center front, measure across one quarter of the top hip measurement and mark. Repeat from the center back.
- At the center back, measure down ½in (1.3cm) from the top hipline and mark.
- At the center front, measure down 1in (2.5cm) from the top hipline and mark.
- With a curved ruler, draw in the top of the brief joining these marks on the back and front.
- From the mark on the top hipline, draw a line down to E on both the front and back.

- From a point on this line, which will depend on the height of the hip, draw a line on the back pattern down to K and on the front pattern down to H.
- Repeat Step 8 from the Basic Brief to draw in the front and back leg curves.

Brief with added fullness

Adding fullness to the body of the brief or hipster means that you can finish the waist and leg openings with elastic, giving a pretty ruffled finish. These briefs are now usually low rise or hipster, but for a vintage look cut them to sit at the natural waistline. They are usually made with a separate crotch. They can be made from many fabrics, from sheer tulles and all-over soft lace cotton voiles, to silk, and can be embroidered and embellished.

- Create or choose your sloper.
- Remove the crotch.
- Then slash and spread the front and back sloper to create the fullness required.

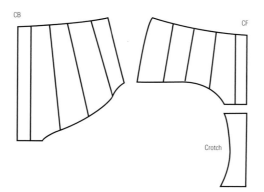

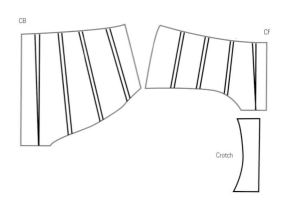

2.4 / Briefs with added elastic on waist and leg openings.

A high-cut leg

The brief can be low-rise or finish on the waistline, which is called a French cut. It has a fuller back, while the high-cut leg gives the wearer the appearance of a longer leg and no visible pantie line.

- Redraw the leg curve from the top hipline down to the crotch.

2.5

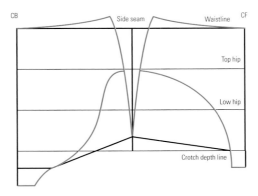

CB   Side seam   Waistline   CF

Top hip

Low hip

Crotch depth line

Bikini brief

The bikini brief hugs the hips, sitting 4in (10cm) down from the waistline. The top is finished with a band of stretch lace or elastic, and some even tie on the side. A swimwear fashion created in the 1960s, it remains one of the most popular styles of brief worn by women today.

- You can alter the brief sloper for a high-cut brief to raise the leg curve still further.

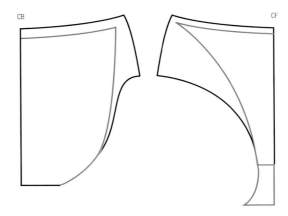

CB   CF

2.5 / High-cut leg brief. The embroidering on the leg openings helps to make legs look longer.

Thong

The thong has been around for centuries, evolving from the loincloth worn by men. In 1974 Rudi Gernreich designed and showed a brief that he called a thong. Before this the thong was mainly associated with exotic dancers. A thong has a "V" shape to the back making it a little wider than a Tanga or G-string; it can also be called a Brazilian brief.

- Start by drawing around the sloper for the basic brief (see page 39).
- Measure and mark 1½in (3.8cm) from the waistline down the center back; 1in (2.5cm) down the side seams; and 1¾in (4.5cm) down the center front.
- Using a curved ruler, redraw the waist curve.
- From the new waistline, measure and mark 1in (2.5cm), or the length you need for your design, down the side seam.
- Draw in the front and back crotch, which is usually 2–2½in (5–6.5cm) in width but can be as little as ½in (1.3cm).
- Draw in the new leg curves on the front and back, from the crotch back up to the marks you made on the side seam.

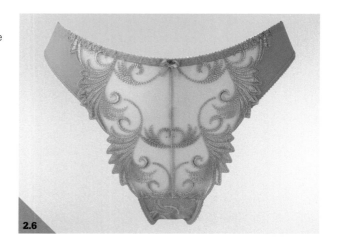

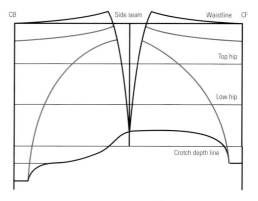

Tanga/G-string

A tanga or G-string can be low-rise, or sit at the waist in front like a brief with a T-shaped back. The tanga is invisible when worn under form-fitting clothing so is the favored brief for models and many celebrities.

- Alter the sloper for the basic brief (see page 39).
- Measure and mark 1½in (3.8cm) from the waistline down the center back; 1in (2.5cm) down the side seams; and 1¾in (4.5cm) down the center front.
- Using a curved ruler, redraw the waist curve.
- Draw in the front and back crotch, which is usually 2–2½in (5–6.5cm) in width but can be as little as ½in (1.3cm).
- On the back, draw a vertical line the width of the crotch to the new waistline; it can be really narrow (e.g., a string).
- On the front, use a curved ruler to draw a line up to the new waistline, finishing at the distance from the side seam required by your design.

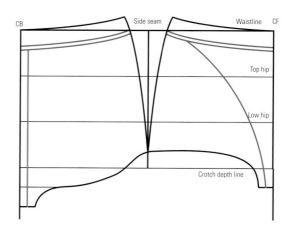

2.6 / Thong or Brazilian. The back is out of sight in this image, but is a narrow, V-shaped strip of material.

Retro thong using stretch lace

The retro thong is high-waisted, cut to flatter and hug the mid-section. Originally made from lace, the modern retro thong is made in a high-tech material, giving the wearer no visible pantie line and no cling when worn under figure-hugging garments.

- Taking the basic brief sloper (see page 39), remove the pattern for the crotch. Measure the stretch of the lace both horizontally and vertically. Remove that measurement from the top hip measurement.
- Redraw the front crotch, which will be cut in cotton or a similar high-wicking fabric, making it 2–2½in (5–6.5cm) in width at the front, narrowing in to ½in (1.3cm).
- Reduce the back crotch to ½in (1.3cm) in width.

2.7

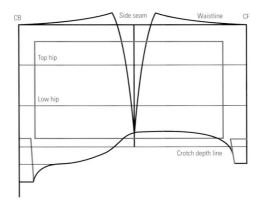

CB   Side seam   Waistline   CF

Top hip

Low hip

Crotch depth line

Slips, panties, and petticoats

2.7 / Retro thong with pink flower detailing and bow.

Boy shorts

Boy shorts resemble men's knit boxer shorts but for women are cut to sit low on the hip. Comfortable and modest to wear, today they are one of the most popular briefs.

2.8

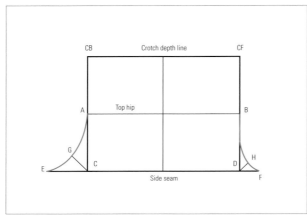

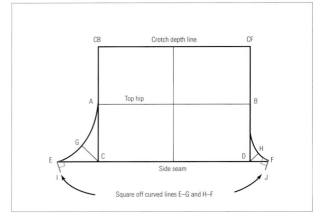

Step 1

- Draw a line down the center of your paper the measurement of the crotch depth. This line will become the side seam.
- Draw a horizontal line at the bottom of this line extending one quarter of the hip measurement either side of the vertical line.
- Square a line up at each end. The left-hand line is the center back and the right-hand line is the center front.
- Divide the crotch depth in half; draw a horizontal line at this point across the box and label where it touches the center back line as A, and where it touches the center front line as B. Label this as the top hipline.
- Label the bottom of the center back line as C, and the bottom of the center front line as D.
- From D, square a line out one third of the full crotch measurement; mark as F.
- From C, square out a line two thirds of the full crotch measurement; mark as E.
- From D draw a line at a 45° angle one quarter of the front crotch measurement; mark as H.
- From C, draw a line at a 45° angle half the back crotch measurement; mark as G.
- Draw a curved line from A to G to E, blending the line from the center back line, and another from B to H to F.

Step 2

- From E square a line down from the curved crotch line 1¼in (3.3cm) long; mark as I.
- From F square a line down from the curved crotch line 1¼in (3.3cm) long; mark as J.

2.8 / Boy shorts with embroidery strips.

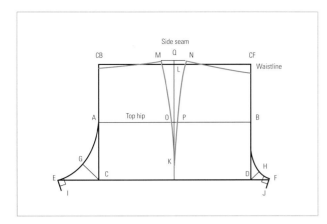

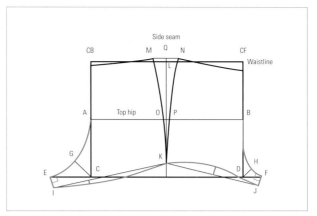

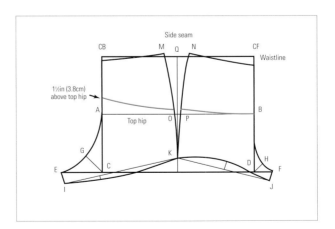

Step 3

- The crotch depth line is now going to be shaped into the side seam. Extend the line at the top by ¼in (6mm) and mark as Q.
- Measure one sixth of the crotch depth up the side seam on the crotch depth line; mark as K.
- On the top line measure over from the center back line toward Q by one quarter of the waist measurement and mark as M; repeat from the center front line and mark as N; mark the top line as the waistline. Measure in from A by one quarter of the hip measurement; mark as O. Repeat from B; mark as P.
- Using a curved ruler, draw in the side seams from M to O and down to K, and from N to P and down to K.
- Again using a curved ruler, draw in the waistline from the center back line, curving up to M, and from N, curving down to the center front line, finishing ½in (1.3cm) below the waistline.

Step 4

- Draw a straight line from I to K, and K to J. This is the leg length.
- Divide the leg length from I to K into three. Measure in from I one third of the leg length; mark and then square a line down ½in (1.3cm) and mark.
- Divide the line from K to J in half; mark and then square a line up ½–1in (1.3–2.5cm) and mark.
- Using a curved ruler, draw a line from I to K, touching the mark you made, and from K to J, again, touching the mark you made.

Step 5

- You can drop the waistline down to the hipline by measuring up from the top hipline on the center back line by 1–1⅝in (2.5–4cm) and drawing a curved line across to the center front line. Alternatively, the leg length can be changed by measuring down on the front and back leg curvature markings.

French knickers

Worn in movies by the Hollywood stars during the 1920s and 30s, these flirty little pants, also known as tap pants, were mass-produced in the 1940s. Today, they are usually made with an elasticized waist, where once they had a side opening with a placket.

2.9

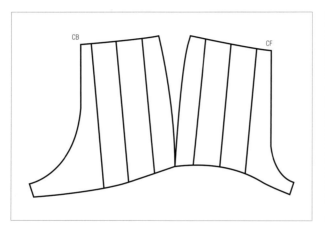

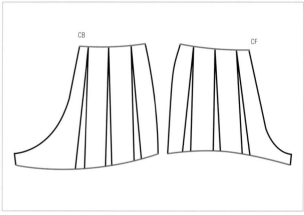

Step 1

- Draw around the boy shorts sloper (see pages 46–47). Divide the sloper into four equal parts and cut up the lines from the leg opening to the waistline.

Step 2

- Slash and spread. The waistline can also be spread open if you wish to use elastic at the waist or left if a placket is going to be added and the waist finished with a binding. Using a curved ruler, redraw in the leg curvature and waistline.

2.9 / French knickers with lace detailing.

Body-shaper leggings

These are worn as a popular form of tight control. They can also include a tummy control panel. When made in a strong stretch fabric you will need to allow for the amount of stretch in the fabric and deduct this from the pattern (see Chapter 1, page 17).

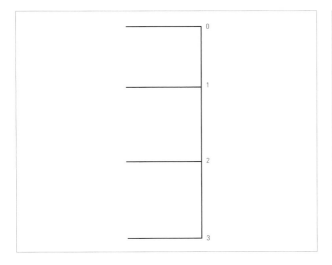

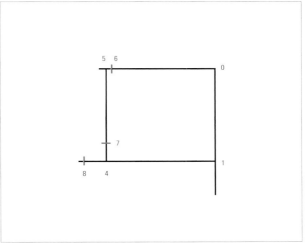

Step 1

- Draw a line down the right-hand side of a piece of paper; label the top as 0.
- From 0 square a line across.
- Measure down from 0 the length of the body rise less ⅜in (1cm); mark as 1.
- Measure down from 0 the waist to floor measurement; mark as 3.
- Square across a line from 3.
- Divide the measurement from 1 to 3 in half; mark as 2.
- Square a line across from 2.

Step 2

- Measure across from 1 one quarter of the hip measurement less ¾in (2cm); mark as 4.
- From 4 square a line up to the line from 0; mark as 5.
- Divide the measurement from 4 to 5 into four; mark the first quarter from 4 as 7.
- Divide the measurement between 1 and 4 into six; measure out one sixth from 4 and mark as 8.
- Measure ⅜in (1cm) from 5 on the line toward 0; mark as 6.

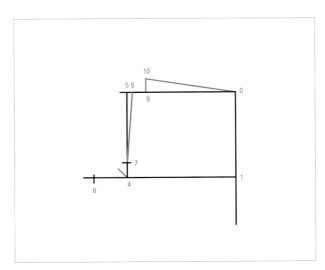

Step 3

- Draw a line from 6 to 7.
- Draw a line out from 4 at a 45° angle and mark. The length of the line will depend on the size of the sloper you are making:

  sizes 6–14   ⅞in (2.2cm)

  sizes 16–24   1in (2.5cm)

See the conversion chart on page 23 for UK and European sizes.
- Measure across 1⅝in (4cm) from 5 toward 0; mark as 9.
- From 9 square a line up 1⅛in (3cm); mark as 10.
- Draw a line from 10 to 0.

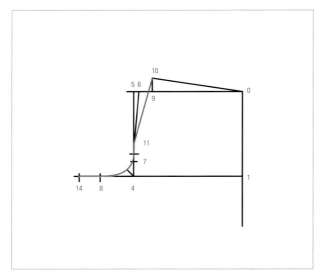

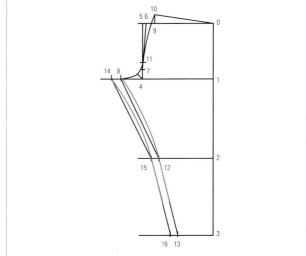

Step 4

- Using a curved ruler, draw a line from 7 to 8, touching the end of the 45° line from 4. This completes the front crotch line.
- Divide the measurement from 4 to 5 into four; measure up one quarter from 4; mark as 11.
- Draw a line from 10 to 11. Make a mark on the line out from 4 at 1⅜in (3.5cm) for sizes 6–14, and at 1⅝in (4cm) for sizes 16–24; mark as 14. (See the conversion chart on page 23 for UK and European sizes.)
- Draw in a curved line from 11 to 14, touching the end of the 45° line from 4. This completes the back crotch line.

Step 5

- Divide the measurement from 1 to 4 into three; taking this measurement, measure across two thirds from 2 and mark as 12.
- Measure out a further 1⅛in (3cm) from 12; mark as 15.
- Divide the ankle measurement in half; make a mark on the line from 3 and label as 13.
- Measure out a further ¾in (2cm) from 13; mark as 16.
- Draw a straight line from 8 to 12. Halfway down this line, square in ¼in (6mm) and make a mark. Repeat from 14 to 15.
- Using a curved ruler, draw a line from 8 to 12 that touches the mark halfway down, and then a straight line from 12 to 13. This is the front inseam.
- Using a curved ruler, draw a line from 14 to 15 that touches the mark halfway down, and then a straight line from 15 to 16. This is the back inseam.

Step 6

- To make a one piece pattern draw a line down the center of your paper.
- Trace the back onto one side of the center line and the front on the other side.
- Add 1in (2.5cm) to the top waistline edge.

Teddies or cami-knickers

In 1910 the garment resulting from the joining together of a camisole and knickers was called a "combination" in the UK. The name changed to cami-knickers with the arrival of a new, briefer garment in the 1920s.

Vintage cami-knickers in the 1920s were made from bias-cut silk or Swiss voile cotton trimmed with lace. Looser fitting, sometimes sheer garments that you stepped into, they became popular in the 1940s when, as part of the war effort, women began to go out to work in pants (trousers). Better known by the 1990s as teddies, or bodies, they could be worn with or without a bra.

Today teddies can be worn as body-shaping garments made from high-tech fabrics or, when made from softer bias-cut fabrics, as sleepwear. The crotch can have a button or snap closure.

The sloper for a teddy can be made by joining the close-fitting sloper and the French knickers sloper at the hipline. A soft bra can also be added to the neckline. The waist can be finished with a drawstring tie to give more definition.

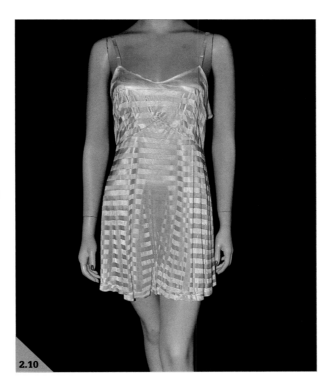

2.10

2.10 / Vintage cami-knickers.

Teddy (cami-knickers)

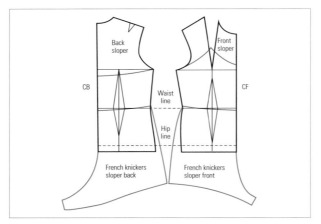

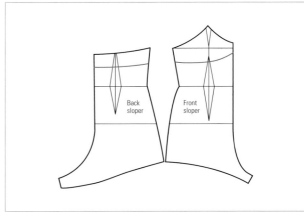

Step 1
- Trace around the front and back close-fitting slopers (see page 33).
- Place the front and back French knickers slopers (see page 48) onto the close-fitting slopers, matching the center front and back lines, the side seams, and the waistlines.
- Draw in the neckline shape of your choice.

Step 2
- To add a bra cup, draw in the shape of the bra cup on the front.
- Matching the length of the side seam on both the front and back, draw in a yoke across the back.

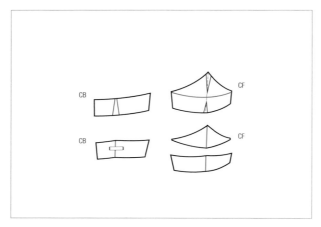

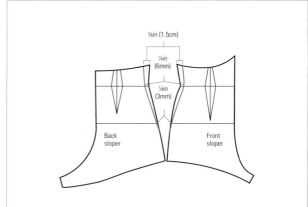

Step 3
- Trace off the front bra cup and the back yoke.
- Cut through the bust line on the front bra cup and tape the darts closed. You now have a two-piece bra cup.
- Tape the dart closed on the back yoke.

Step 4
- On the front and back bodies reduce the side seam by ⅝in (1.5cm) at the underarm (half the amount on each side), by ¼in (6mm) at the waist (half the amount on each side), and ⅛in (3mm) at the hip (half the amount on each side).
- Redraw the side seam.

Body shaper or teddy draft, with or without a bra top

A body shaper can be worn to smooth the contours of the body or to stop a form-fitting garment clinging to the body. A body shaper is a modern girdle. It can also lift the derrière and bust, and smooth the stomach area. Legs can be added to smooth the thigh.

Before you begin you will need to check the amount of stretch and stretch recovery in your fabric (please refer to the stretch characteristics chart in Chapter 1, page 17). You may need to make some adjustments to the knit/stretch fabric sloper measurements for the stretch characteristics of your fabric; it may even be better to draft a new sloper.

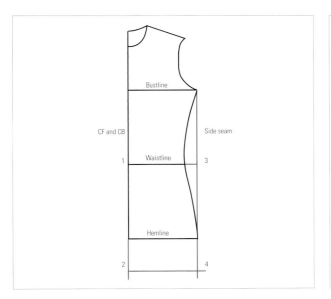

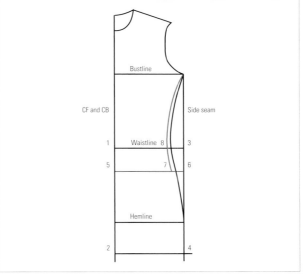

Step 1

- Trace around the knit/stretch sloper (see page 35), allowing extra paper at the bottom for the addition of the crotch.
- Mark the waistline on the center back/front as 1.
- Draw a line down from 1 the length of the body rise; mark as 2.
- Square a line down from the bust line at the underarm to the waistline; mark as 3.
- Square a line from 3 across to the waistline.
- From 2, square a line across and mark as 4.

Step 2

- Divide the measurement from 1 to 2 into four; mark the first quarter down from 1 as 5.
- From 5, square a line across and mark as 6.
- From 6 measure in 1⅛in (3cm) and mark as 7.
- From 3 measure in 1¾in (4.5cm) and mark as 8.
- Using a curved ruler, draw in the new side seam from the underarm point through the marks at 8 and 7.

2.11 / Body shaper or teddy.

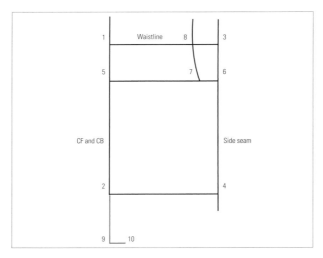

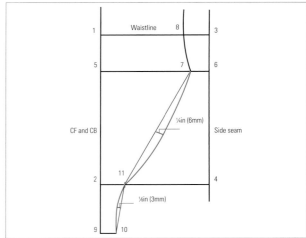

Step 3

- For the back crotch, from 2 measure down one eighth of the bust measurement plus ⅜in (1cm) and mark as 9.
- Square a 1⅜in (3.5cm) line across and mark as 10. This is the back crotch line.

Step 4

- From 2, square a 2⅜in (6cm) line across; mark as 11. This is the gusset line.
- Draw a line from 10 to 11, find the center, and square out a ⅛in (3mm) line.
- Draw a concave curve from 10 to 11, touching the end of the ⅛in (3mm) line. This completes the gusset.
- Draw a line from 11 to 7, find the center, and square out a ¼in (6mm) line.
- Draw a convex curve from 11 to 7, touching the end of the ¼in (6mm) line. This is the back leg curve.

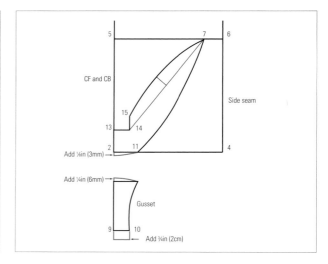

Step 5

- Measure from 2 to 9; divide in half and mark this up from 2; label as 13. From 13 square a ¾in (2cm) line across; mark as 14. This is the front crotch line.
- From 14, square a ¾in (2cm) line up; mark as 15.
- Draw a line from 14 to 7. At the halfway point, square up a ⅝in (1.5cm) line; draw a curve from 15 to 7, touching the end of this line for the front leg curve.

Step 6

- For a separate gusset, trace off the back gusset from 2 to 11 downward. From 2 on the gusset square up ¼in (6mm) and draw a curved line back down to 11.
- From 9 and 10 square down ¾in (2cm) and square a line across.
- On the sloper body, square down ⅛in (3mm) from 2 and draw a curved line back up to 11.

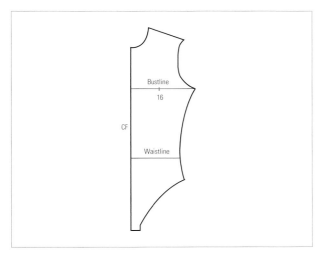

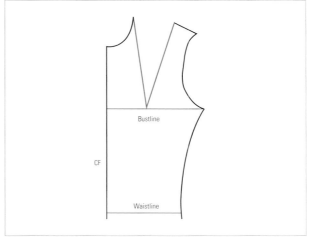

Step 7
- To add a bra top, trace off the new front sloper.
- Divide the bust line in half less ⅜in (2cm), measuring toward the center front; mark as 16.

Step 8
- Draw a line from the neckline at the shoulder neck point down to 16; cut down this line. Spread the shoulder open by 4in (10cm) to create a dart. You will get a crease in the paper below the bustline when you open the dart.

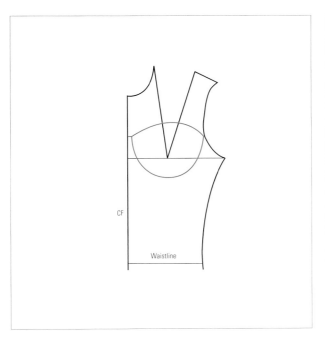

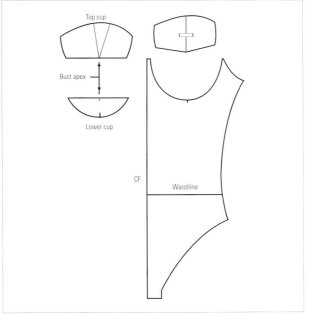

Step 9
- Draw in the bra cup shape and trace off. Reshape the horizontal seam line across the bra cup, if desired.

Step 10
- Cut across this seam line so you have an upper and lower cup. Close the dart on the upper cup and redraw the neckline on the bra cup if it has become distorted.

Petticoats

From the late 1950s until the early years of the 1960s, hiding under every full belted skirt were layers of net petticoats.

The layers of net were gathered onto a yoke at the hip, which was either tied with a drawstring at the waistline or had a placket opening; the number of layers of net depended on how full you wanted the hemline to be. American designer Perry Ellis first allowed the lace edge of a petticoat to show from under the skirts of his sportswear in the 1980s, while John Galliano for Christian Dior brought the petticoat out from under the skirt for his 2009 couture collection.

2.12

2.12 / The petticoat as outerwear in Christian Dior Haute Couture, Autumn/Winter 2009.

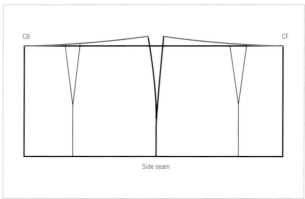

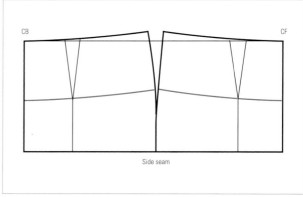

Step 1

- Trace around the close-fitting sloper (see page 32) from the waist down to the hipline. Measure up ¼in (6mm) on both side seams at the waistline and mark.
- Using a curved ruler, draw in a new waistline from the center front and back to the top of the new side seams.

Step 2

- Decide on the length of the yoke and draw a line across both the front and the back.
- Trace off the new front and back yoke pattern pieces.

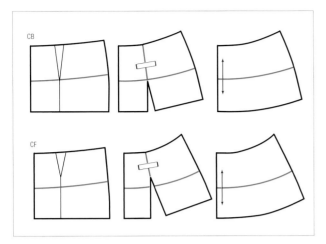

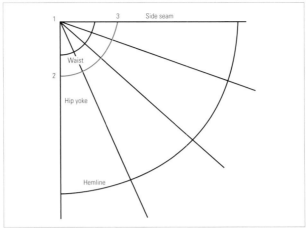

Step 3

- Cut up the line to the bottom of the dart on both the front and back, and tape the darts closed; the cut lines will open.
- Using a curved ruler, redraw the bottom of the new front and back yoke pieces and trace off the new patterns.

Step 4

- To add a circular skirt, draw a line down the left-hand side of a piece of paper; label the top of the line as 1.
- From 1, square a line across. This is the side seam.
- To find the radius of the lower edge of the yoke, measure the circumference of the lower edge of the yoke and divide it by 6.28.
- Measure down from 1 the radius of the lower edge of the yoke along both lines; make a mark on both lines, labeling them as 2 and 3 respectively.
- Draw a curved line to create a quarter circle from 2 to 3.
- Divide the quarter circle in half and in half again.
- Measure down these lines the length of the skirt and draw in the hemline as a quarter circle.

Gathering onto the yoke

The skirt can be gathered onto the lower edge of the yoke. Cut a length of fabric three times the hip measurement by the skirt length.

For a fuller petticoat, divide the skirt length into two or three sections.

- Make each section 1.5 times longer than the last, so that the lowest is almost three times longer than the top section. Mark the sides as Fold and Gathers, as shown.

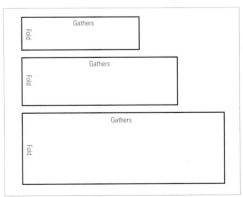

Half-slip

The half-slip is a skirt with an elasticated waist worn under a fitted outer garment. A half-slip was once part of every fashionable woman's lingerie drawer. It can be A-line, or have splits at the hemline. A half-slip can be cut on the bias or on the straight grain, and can be made from a knitted fabric or a woven fabric with added stretch. The hem is usually finished with lace.

- Trace around the close-fitting sloper (see page 32) from the waist down, ensuring you have the required length for your skirt.
- Measure up ¼in (6mm) on both side seams at the waistline and mark.
- Using a curved ruler, draw in a new waistline from the center front and back to the top of the new side seams.

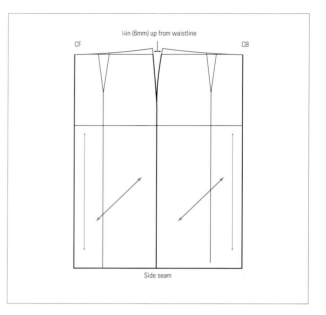

2.13 / Garter (suspender) belt.

2.14 / Garter band with flower embellishment.

Garter belts

The garter (suspender) belt is worn to hold up a pair of stockings. Less commonly in use today, the garter belt can be fun, alluring, and sexy.

- Trace around the front and back yokes of the petticoat from page 56.
- Divide the yokes in half and draw in the shape of your garter belt, making the tabs at front and back the width of the garter clips.
- Elastic can be added to the front at the side seam. Allow for the amount of stretch by removing a panel from the front of the belt.
- Add seam allowance around the belt and finish with a hook and eye closure at the center back. Finally, attach the garter clips.

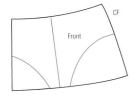

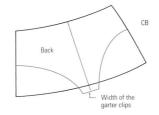

2.13

Garter bands

Garters were once worn to hold up stockings. Today they are a traditional part of a bride's wedding-day ensemble.

- Begin by measuring around the thigh where you want the garter band to sit.
- Cut a 1in (2.5cm)-wide strip of elastic to this measurement.
- Cut a pattern for the casing twice the width of the elastic plus 1in (2.5cm) and seam allowances.

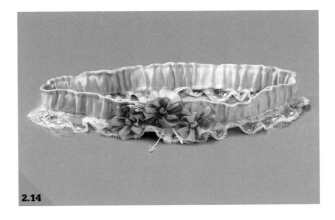

2.14

3 Designing and Pattern Drafting
Sleepwear

Sleepwear can be flirty and sexy, an image conjured up by the wonderful negligee sets once worn by movie stars in the era of the silver screen, or the babydoll sets of the 1960s. The classic pajama has even become fashionable as outerwear, with celebrities like Rihanna being photographed on the red carpet wearing a pair. Today's sleepwear is more about comfort with an element of lounge wear – something to change into after work – but we all still like to have that special piece of sleepwear if only for the feel-good factor.

The fabric for sleepwear should feel soft to the touch. It can be luxurious silk, fine cotton voile, or the old favorite brushed cotton, and is usually combined with lace, ruffles, and frills, or embellished with embroidery. Sleepwear can be cut straight on the grain, or on the bias if using a woven fabric.

A silk georgette and chiffon nightdress, circa 1913.

The looser-fitting sloper (block)

Because sleepwear is made with a looser fit than most other lingerie, the sloper shown and used here has more ease than the close-fitting sloper in Chapter 2. This sloper can be worked from standard measurement charts, or from personal measurements, as explained on page 26.

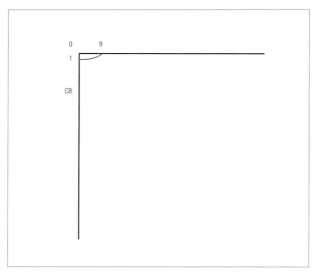 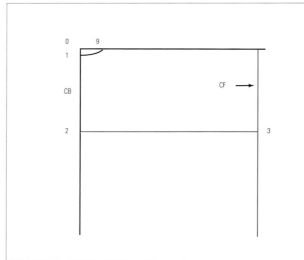

Step 1

Start with the back sloper.

- Draw a line down the left-hand side of a piece of paper the length of the measurement from nape to waist. Label it as the center back (CB).
- Label the top of the line as 0.
- Square a line across to the right-hand side of the paper from 0.
- Measure down ⅝in (1.5cm) from 0; mark this point as 1. Measure across one fifth the neck measurement from 0; mark this point as 9. Draw in the back neck curve from 1 to 9.

Step 2

- Measure down from 1 the armhole (armscye) depth plus 1in (2.5cm); mark this point as 2.
- Square across from 2 half the bust measurement plus 2¾in (7cm); mark this point as 3. For each size above size 14, add ¼in (5mm); a size 18, for example, will be half the bust measurement plus 3⅛in (8cm).
- Square a line up and down from 3. Label this line as the center front (CF).

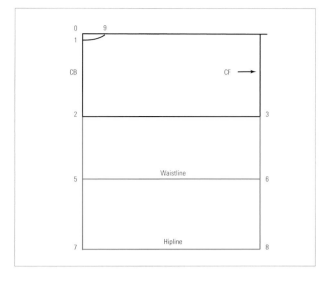

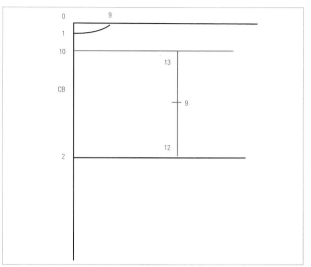

Step 3

- Measure down from 1 the nape of neck to waist measurement; mark this point as 5.
- Measure down from 5 the waist to hip measurement; mark this point as 7.
- From 7 square a line across to the center front; mark this point as 8. This is the hipline.
- From 5 square a line across to the center front; mark this point as 6. This is the waistline.

Step 4

- To begin to plot the detail for the back shoulder area, first measure down from 1 one fifth of the armhole depth measurement less ⅜in (1cm); mark as 10.
- Square a line halfway across the paper.
- From 2 measure across half the back width measurement plus ⅜in (1cm); mark as 12.
- Square up from 12 to the line you drew from 10; mark as 13.
- Divide the line from 12 to 13 in half; mark as 9.

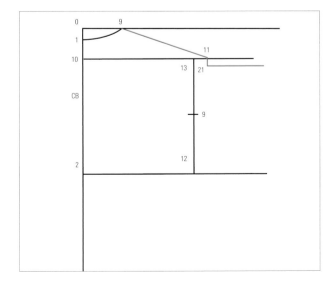

Step 5

- To shape the back shoulder, draw a line from 9 the length of the shoulder plus ⅜in (1cm) and angle it down to touch the line you drew from 10; mark as 11.
- From 11 square a line ⅝in (1.5cm) down from 11; mark as 21.
- From 21 square a line across approximately 4in (10cm) long.

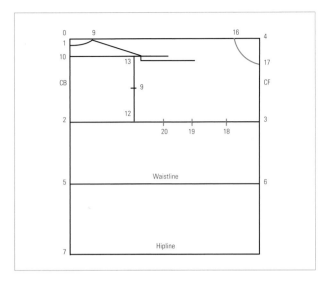

Step 6

- Label the top of the center front line as 4.
- From 4 measure across one fifth the neck measurement less ¼in (6mm); mark as 16.
- From 4 measure down one fifth of the neck measurement; mark as 17.
- Draw in the front neck curve from 16 to 17.
- From 3 measure across half the chest measurement plus ⅜in (1cm); mark as 19.
- Divide the measurement from 3 to 19 in half; mark as 18.
- Divide the measurement from 12 to 19 in half; mark as 20.

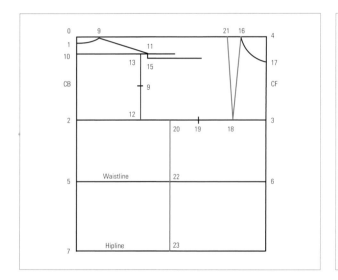

Step 7

- Draw a line down from 16 to 18.
- From 16 measure across half the dart measurement; mark as 21.
- From 21 draw a line down to 18.
- Square a line down from 20 to the waistline; mark as 22. Continue down to the hipline; mark as 23. This is the side seam.

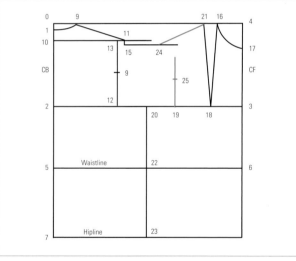

Step 8

- Draw a line the shoulder length plus ¼in (6mm) from 21 to touch the line squared out from 15; mark as 24.
- Square a line up from 19. Divide the line from 3 to 17 in half less ¾in (2cm); mark at this point on the line from 19 and label it as 25.

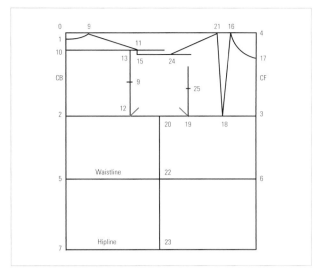

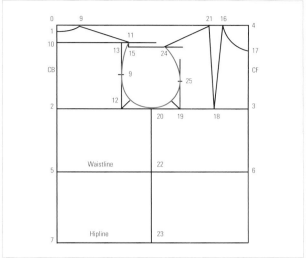

Step 9

- Draw a line out at a 45° angle from 12. The length of the line will depend on the size of sloper you are making:

    sizes 6–8 ⅞in (2.2cm)
    sizes 10–14 1in (2.5cm)
    sizes 16–20 1⅛in (3cm)
    sizes 22–24 1⅜in (3.5cm)

- Draw a line out at a 45° angle from 19. Again, the length of the line will depend on the size of sloper you are making:

    sizes 6–8 ¾in (2cm)
    sizes 10–14 1in (2.5cm)
    sizes 16–20 1⅛in (3cm)
    sizes 22–24 1¼in (3.3cm)

See the conversion chart on page 23 for UK and European sizes.

Step 10

- Draw in the armhole curve, starting at 11, curving down to 9, round to touch the end of the line out from 12, around to 20, touching the end of the line out from 19, up to 25, and finishing at 24.

The sleeve for the looser-fitting sloper

Step 1

- Begin by measuring around the armhole on your sloper from 11 to 24.
- Draw a line down the center of your paper the sleeve length; label the top of the line as A and the bottom as B.
- To start with the back of the sleeve, square a line across from B.

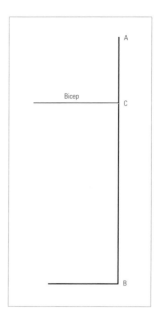

Step 2

- From A measure down one third of the armhole measurement less ¼in (6mm) for sizes 6–14, and ⅛in (3mm) for sizes 16–24; mark this point as C.
- From C square a line across one quarter the armhole measurement for a sleeve cap that is 4–4½in (10–11.5cm) long. This is the bicep line.

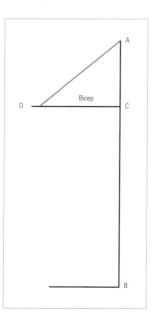

Step 3

- From A draw a diagonal guideline half the armhole measurement down to touch the line squared out from C; mark as D.

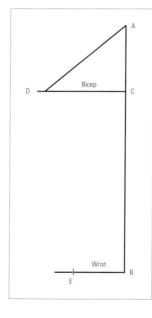

Step 4

- From B measure across half the wrist measurement; mark as E. This is the wrist line.

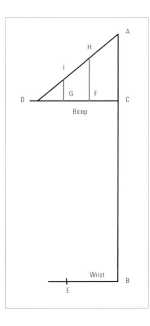

Step 5

- To shape the sleeve cap, divide the line from C to D into three equal parts; label the mark nearest C as F, and the other as G.
- Square a line up from F to touch the guideline from A to D; mark as H.
- Square a line up from G to touch the guideline from A to D; mark as I.

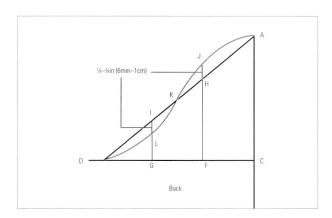

Step 6

- Continue up the line from H for ¼–⅜in (6mm–1cm); mark as J.
- Divide the line from H to I in half; mark as K.
- From I measure down ¼–⅜in (6mm–1cm); mark as L.
- Using a curved ruler, draw a curved line from A to J to K and reverse the curve to continue down to L and D. This is the back armhole curve.

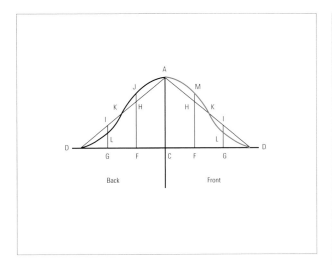

Step 7

- To draw the front of the sleeve, mirror the back of the sleeve through Step 5.
- Continue the line up from H by ¼–⅜in (6mm–1cm); mark as M.
- Divide the line from H to I in half; mark as K.
- From I measure down ¼–⅜in (6mm–1cm); mark as L.
- Using a curved ruler, draw a curved line from A to M to K and reverse the curve to continue down to L and D. This is the front armhole curve.

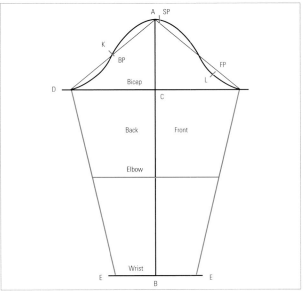

Step 8

- Draw a line from D to E on both the back and front.
- Divide the line from C to B in half less ½in (1.3cm); square a line across to both the back and front and label as the elbow line.
- From A measure across ¼in (6mm) toward the front; mark as the shoulder notch point (SP).

Yokes

Nightgowns and sleepwear need to incorporate extra fullness to allow for comfort and ease of movement. The addition of a yoke will control extra fabric added below the bustline.

Yokes and above-the-bust bands

A nightgown made with a yoke or above-the-bust band is a popular style that can be made any length, from tunic length, to go over the top of a pant, to ankle length. The yoke design can also be used in the design of robes.

The yoke can be used with a sleeve or with shoulder straps. Shoulder straps can be narrow and tied on the shoulder, or wide and gathered onto the band, forming a cap sleeve. Both a yoke and an above-the-bust band can be made from the fashion fabric, lace, or ribbon, or they can be embroidered and heavily embellished using a combination of all three.

3.1

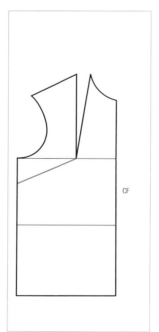

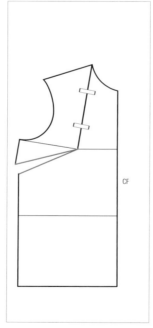

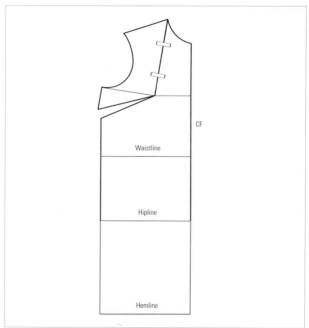

Step 1

- Adapt the looser-fitting sloper, starting with the front. Draw a diagonal line from the bust point down to the side seam, finishing about 3in (7.5cm) below the armhole point.
- Cut along this line and close the shoulder dart; this will open up a dart at the side seam.

Step 2

- Extend the side seam and center front lines to the desired length. Mark in the waistline, hipline, and hemline.

3.1 / Vintage nightdress with lace yoke.

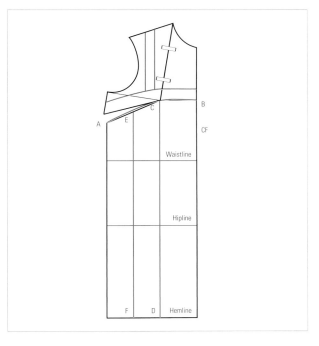

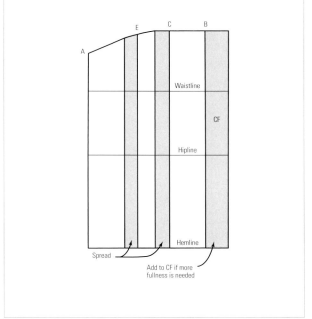

Step 3

- Draw a line along the lower of the two new dart legs, rounding it across the bust point and continuing to the center front line; mark the end of the line on the side seam as A and on the center front as B.
- Draw in a second line parallel to the line from A to B, approximately 2⅜in (6cm) up from the bust point. These two lines will create the yoke.
- Draw a line from the bust point down to the hemline; label the top of the line as C and the bottom as D.
- Starting from the lower dart leg, draw a second line between, and parallel to, the side seam and the line from C to D; label the top of the line as E and the bottom as F. You will slash along these two lines to add fullness to the front of the skirt.
- Divide the shoulder length in half and draw in the shoulder strap of your chosen width on either side of this point.
- Separate the pattern pieces for the front yoke and the strap from the skirt.

Step 4

- For a gathered skirt slash down the lines from C to D and from E to F.
- Spread the pieces apart to create the fullness required. If needed, you can also add extra fullness at the center front line.

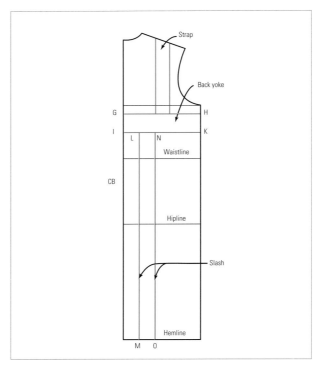

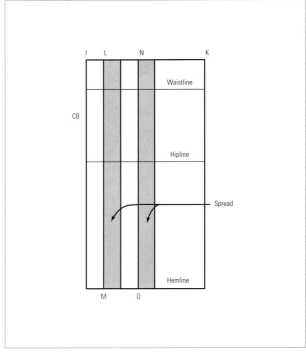

Step 5

- Next adapt the back of the looser-fitting sloper. Draw the back yoke so that it matches the front yoke perfectly at the side seams.
- Draw two lines from the bottom of the yoke along which you will slash and spread the back of the skirt to add fullness. Label the top of one line L and the bottom as M, and the top of the other as N and the bottom as O.
- Draw in the strap to match the position and width of the strap on the front pattern.
- Separate the pattern pieces for the back yoke and the strap from the skirt.

Step 6

- For a gathered skirt, slash down the lines from L to M and from N to O.
- Spread the pieces apart to create the fullness required.

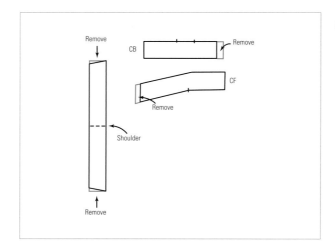

Step 7

- Measure in ¼in (6mm) from the side seam of the front and back yoke pieces and redraw the seam lines.
- Join the back and front shoulder straps at the shoulder seam; measure in on the inside of the strap ¼in (6mm) and mark; redraw the ends of the shoulder straps from the mark to the outside edge of the strap.

A round yoke with a front opening

The rounded yoke can be used with or without a sleeve. Add a button stand and facing to the center front of the skirt for pajama tops and robes. Alternatively, an open-ended zipper can be used instead of buttons down the front of a robe.

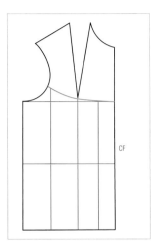

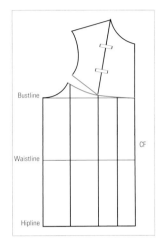

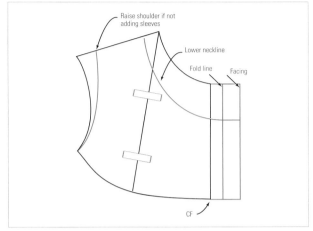

Step 1
- Trace around the loose-fitting front sloper.
- Using a curved ruler, draw in a line from the center front bust line, finishing at a point on the armhole where it begins to curve into the underarm.
- Draw three straight lines from the curved yoke line down to the hemline.

Step 2
- Cut along the curved yoke line until it meets the original bust line; close the shoulder dart with tape.
- Cut along this line to separate the yoke from the skirt.

Step 3
- Using a curved ruler, draw in a lower, wider neckline.
- Add a ⅜in (1cm) button stand to the center front; label the front of the stand as the fold line.
- From the fold line draw a 1in (2.5cm)-wide facing.
- If you are not adding a sleeve, measure in ⅜in (1cm) from the shoulder point and redraw the armhole.

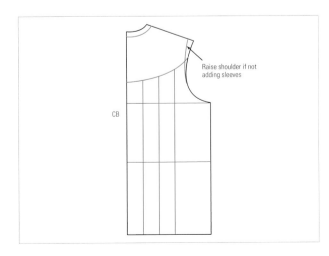

Step 4
- Trace around the loose-fitting back sloper.
- Draw in a curved line from the center back, finishing at the armhole so that it matches the front armhole. The length of the yoke at the center back can be longer or shorter than the yoke at the center front.
- Draw three straight lines from the curved yoke line down to the hemline.
- Lower the back neckline, making sure that it matches the front neckline at the shoulder.
- If you are not adding a sleeve, measure in ⅜in (1cm) at the shoulder point and redraw the armhole.
- Cut along the new yoke line to separate the yoke from the skirt.

A circular yoke

A cicular yoke can be used on nightgowns and robes. It was a popular choice in the 1960s, when it topped full-skirted babydoll nightgowns. The yoke can be left to cap the top of the arm, or it can have a sleeve attached. It can be channel stitched, embellished with embroidery and ribbons, or smocked.

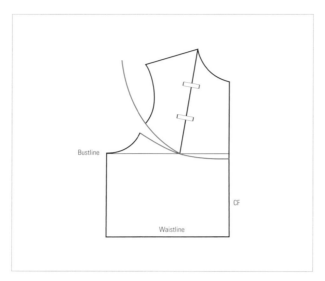

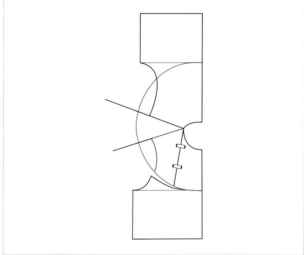

Step 1

- Trace the loose-fitting front sloper onto paper down to the waistline.
- Draw a line representing a quarter of a circle from the center front, which passes through the bust point and finishes above the shoulder line.
- Cut along the line from the armhole to the bust point and tape the shoulder dart closed.

Step 2

- Place the loose-fitting back sloper onto the paper so that the two shoulder neck points line up and you have a continuous neckline from center back around to center front.
- Trace around the back sloper and draw another quarter circle from the end of the line above the front shoulder around to the center back, creating a semicircle.
- Extend both the front and back shoulders out to the semicircle line.
- Cut around the line separating the circular yoke from the skirt.

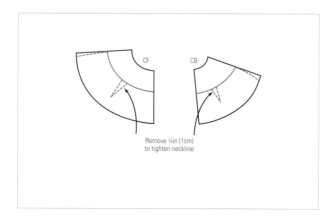

Remove ⅜in (1cm) to tighten neckline

Step 3

- From the neckline, measure down the center back, front, and shoulder seams by approximately 2–2⅜in (5–6cm), or to the midpoint of the shoulder and mark.
- Using a curved ruler, draw in a new neckline, joining the marks.
- If you want the shoulder to curve down toward the arm, measure in ⅜in (1cm) from the new shoulder point and curve the shoulder seam back to the neckline.
- For a tighter-fitting neckline make small ⅜in (1cm)-wide darts into the yoke; cut down the center of each dart and tape closed.

A shaped yoke and short full skirt

This yoke makes a pull-on tunic or babydoll nightgown, with or without a sleeve. You can add scallops to the bottom edge of the yoke, or piping between the yoke and the seam.

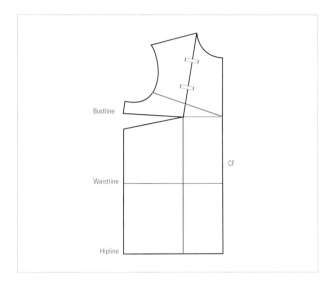

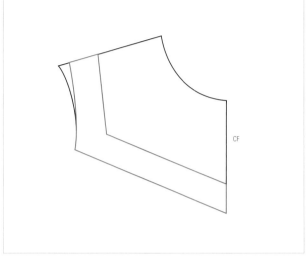

Step 1

- Trace around the loose-fitting front sloper.
- Draw a diagonal line from the bust point down to the side seam, finishing about 3in (7.5cm) below the armhole point.
- Cut along this line and close the shoulder dart; this will open up a dart at the side seam.
- Draw a line from the center front that angles up into the armhole; this is the yoke line. The position of this line is your design decision.
- Draw a straight line from the bust point down to the bottom of the sloper. This will be your slash line.

Step 2

- Cut down the yoke line and remove the pattern piece.
- At the shoulder point measure in ⅜in (1cm) and reblend the curve of the armhole.
- Draw a line parallel to the yoke line at the distance of the desired width for the yoke; continue the line up to the shoulder.

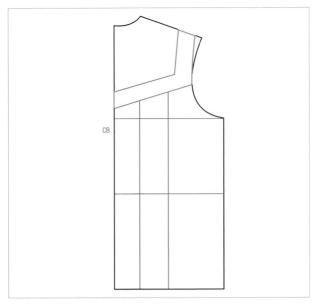

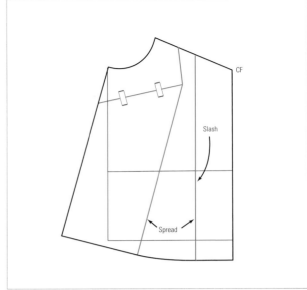

Step 3
- Trace around the loose-fitting back sloper.
- From the center back, draw a straight line across to the armhole for the yoke; this line can be lower or higher than the front.
- At the shoulder point measure in ³⁄₈in (1cm) and reblend the curve of the armhole.
- Draw a line parallel to the yoke line at the distance of the desired width for the yoke; continue the line up to the shoulder. Make sure that the width of the yoke at the shoulder is the same on the front and back.
- Draw two evenly spaced straight lines from the lower edge of the yoke down to the bottom of the sloper. These will be your slash lines.

Step 4
- Returning to the front sloper, to add fullness at the hemline and at the top of the skirt, cut along the slash line. The fullness can be added as tucks or gathers.
- Close the dart at the side seam and tape together.
- Retrace the front skirt pattern pieces onto paper.
- Measure down from the waistline to the desired hem length.
- Spread the two skirt pattern pieces apart to the desired amount of fullness, adding extra fullness to the side of the skirt that curves back into the underarm and out at the hemline.

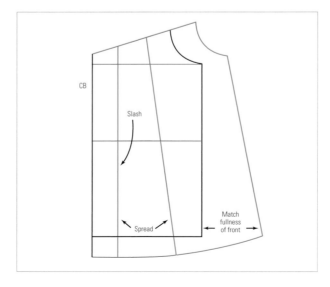

Step 5
- Slash down the line(s) on the back skirt sloper.
- Retrace the back skirt pattern pieces onto paper.
- Measure down from the waistline to the desired hem length.
- Spread the pattern pieces apart for the desired amount of fullness at both the top edge and the hemline.
- Add fullness to the side of the skirt that matches the added fullness on the side front.

A midriff band

Midriff bands are used in sleepwear to control fullness that has been added for comfort and ease of movement. They can be placed just across the front midriff, finishing at the side seam, with the back fullness controlled with a tie, or can continue across the back.

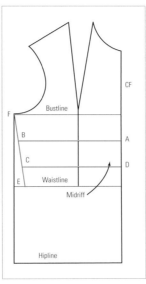

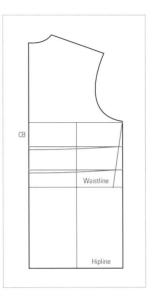

A midriff band can be any length and shape, from a band that finishes on the high hip line to one that is curved lower at the center front or back. It can be attached to a triangle cup, soft bra cup, or bodice that may or may not have a center front or back opening. The band can be made from the fashion fabric, the same fabric in a contrasting color, a different fabric, or a lace trim. A midriff band is the perfect place to add embellishments like embroidery and appliqué; it can also be created using pintucking or smocking.

Step 1

- Trace the loose-fitting front sloper onto paper.
- From the side seam at the waistline, measure in 1in (2.5cm); mark as E.
- Label the armhole point as F and draw a line from E to F.
- On the center front measure up from the waistline to where you want the midriff to start. This can be as little as ¾in (2cm). Mark as D.
- From D square a line across to the line from E to F; mark as C.
- From D, measure up the center front the width of the midriff band, approximately 2⅜in (6cm); mark as A.
- From A, square a line across to the line from E to F; mark as B. Alternatively, you can shape this line at the center front by raising it ⅜in (1cm) and curving it back down to B.
- For a back midriff follow the same steps. Then, at the center back, measure down ⅜in (1cm) at both the top and bottom lines of the midriff and mark; draw a curved line from the marks back up to the side seam.

3.2 / Vintage nightdress with midriff band.

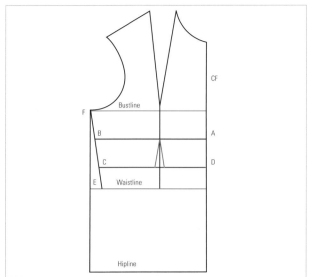

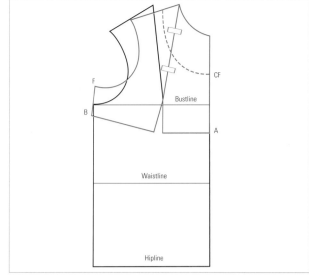

Step 2

- To shape the midriff band, make a dart by measuring out on each side of the line extending down from the bust point ⅜in (1cm) at the waistline; draw in the dart. This works well when the midriff finishes at the front sides and does not extend to the back.

Step 3

- Cut along the top line of the midriff band separating the bodice from the band.
- Slash up the center line to the bust point and tape the shoulder dart closed.
- Lower and widen the neckline, or add a front opening.

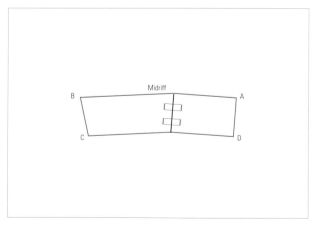

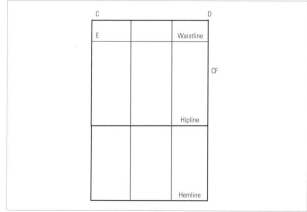

Step 4

- Cut along the lower line of the midriff band, separating it from the skirt.
- Close the dart on the band and tape it together.

Step 5

- Trace the skirt onto paper.
- From the waistline measure down the center front and side seam the desired length and draw in the hemline.
- To add fullness, draw straight lines down the length of the skirt.

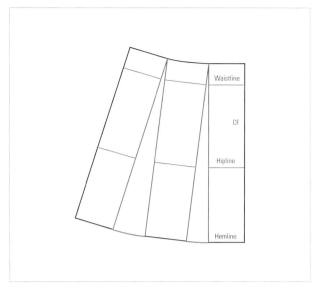

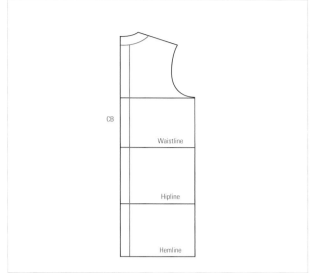

Step 6

- Slash and spread apart along the lines for the desired fullness at the hemline.
- The top of the skirt can also be spread if you want to gather or tuck the skirt onto the midriff band.
- Using a curved ruler, redraw the hemline into a smooth curved line.

Step 7

- For the back trace around the loose-fitting back sloper.
- From the waistline measure down the center back and side seam the desired length and draw in the hemline.
- Lower the neckline, making sure that the new necklines match on the front and back shoulders.
- From the center back line at the neckline measure across approximately 2in (5cm); mark and draw a straight line down to the hemline.

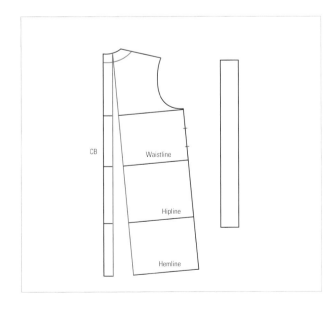

Step 8

- Slash down this line and spread open to the desired amount of fullness at the hemline.
- Add fullness at the side seam to match that added to the front skirt.
- Mark the position of the midriff band on the new side seam with notches; this will be the position of the tie belt.
- Draw a tie belt the width of the front midriff band and the desired length.

A bias-cut gown with a midriff band and a cowl neckline

This gown is cut on the bias to enable the cowl neckline to drape, and has a shaped midriff band, or yoke.

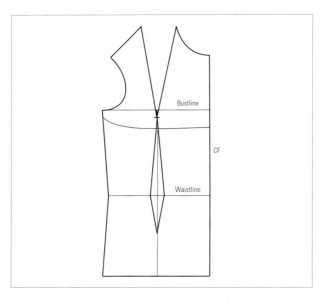

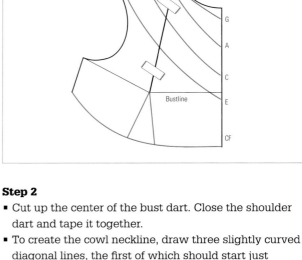

Step 1

- Trace around the close-fitting front sloper.
- For the bodice, measure down approximately 1in (2.5cm) from the bust line and draw a curved line from the center front over to the side seam, finishing approximately 2in (5cm) below the armhole point.
- Cut across this line, separating the bodice from the skirt.

Step 2

- Cut up the center of the bust dart. Close the shoulder dart and tape it together.
- To create the cowl neckline, draw three slightly curved diagonal lines, the first of which should start just below the bustline, from the center front up to the shoulder seam; label the line nearest the neckline A at the center front and B at the shoulder; repeat for the other lines, labeling them C–D and E–F respectively.
- Label the top of the center front line at the neckline as G. From G, draw another line to B.
- Cut across the line from B to G and remove this section of the pattern.

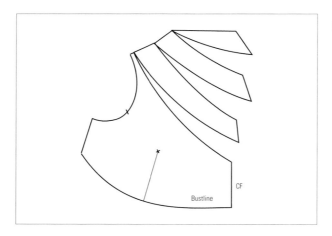

Step 3

- Slash along the lines from the center front line, finishing approximately ⅛in (3mm) from the shoulder seam.
- Spread each of the lines at least 1in (2.5cm) apart. (The farther apart the lines are spread, the deeper the cowl.)

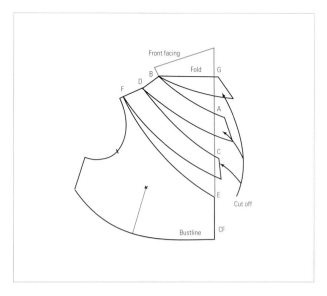

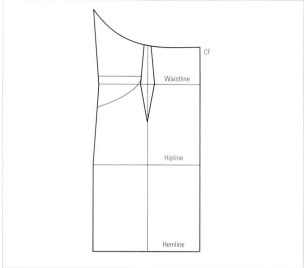

Step 4

- Take another piece of paper large enough to be able to retrace the bodice and draw a straight line down the center of the paper. This is the new center front line.
- Place the center front of the slashed pattern on this new line and trace around the new bodice pattern, removing the sections of the slashed pattern that extend beyond the new center front line.
- Extend the center front line up at least 3in (7.5cm) beyond the top of the slashed pattern for the facing. Complete the facing by drawing a line that will taper the facing back slightly toward the shoulder neck point. Finally, square a line back down to the shoulder neck point at B.

Step 5

- Trace around the skirt onto paper.
- From the waistline, measure down the center front and side seam the desired length and draw in the hemline.
- On the side seam, measure up ¾in (2cm) from the waistline; mark and square a line over to the edge of the dart.
- Using a curved ruler, draw a line back down to the side seam, finishing between 2–3in (5–7.5cm) down from the waistline. This creates a gusset and shapes the waist down to the top hip.
- Cut along the lines of the gusset to separate it from the skirt.

Step 6

- Close the front dart by cutting through the center of the dart from the top of the skirt to the hemline; tape the dart closed.
- Redraw the hemline using a curved ruler.

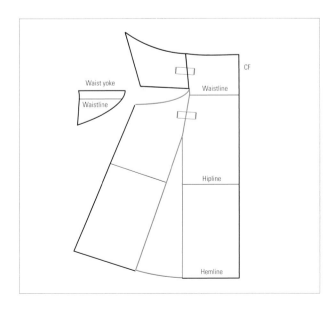

Sleeves

Sleepwear can feature a wide variety of sleeves, from long sleeves finishing in a cuff, full flutter or puff sleeves, to kimono or raglan sleeves. They can be finished with ribbon ties, elastic, or buttons, and can be embellished with smocking and embroidery.

3.3

Raglan sleeve

A raglan sleeve extends from the underarm to the neckline, including the shoulder. It is a loose-fitting sleeve that is comfortable to wear, making it a popular option for sleepwear.

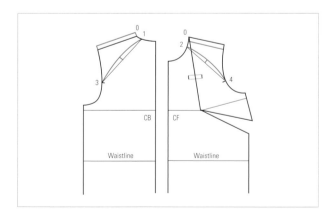

Step 1

- Begin by tracing around either the close-fitting or loose-fitting front and back slopers.
- Add ³⁄₈in (1cm) to the back shoulder and remove ³⁄₈in (1cm) from the front shoulder. Label the new shoulder neck points on the front and back as 0.
- On the back, measure 1¹⁄₈–2in (3–5cm) down the neckline from 0; mark as 1.
- On the front, measure 1¹⁄₈– 2in (3–5cm) down the neckline from 0; mark as 2.
- Draw a line from 1 down to the notch point on the back armhole; mark as 3.
- Draw a line from 2 down to the notch point on the front armhole; mark as 4.
- Divide both lines in half and then measure up approximately ¹⁄₄in (6mm) from this point and mark.
- Draw a curved line from 1 to 3 through this new mark, and from 2 to 4 through the new mark.
- Cut down the curved lines on both the front and back.

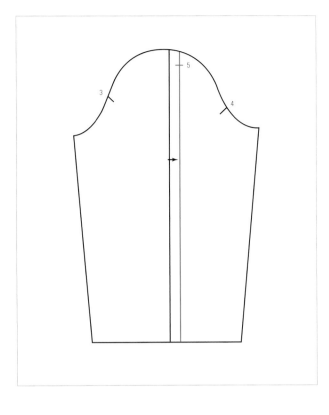

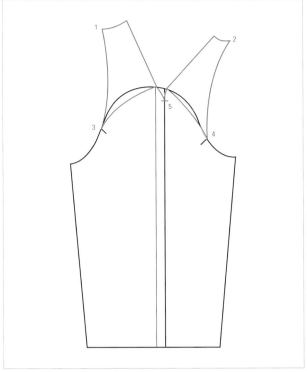

Step 2

- Trace the sleeve sloper from page 67 onto paper.
- Draw a line down the sleeve that is ⅜in (1cm) forward of the sleeve center line toward the front of the sleeve.
- Measure down the line ¾in (2cm); mark as 5.
- Move the front notch point up 1⅛in (3cm); re-mark as 4.
- Mark the back notch point as 3.

Step 3

- Place the back bodice shoulder section that you removed in Step 1 onto the back of the sleeve head, matching 3.
- Place the front bodice shoulder section on the front of the sleeve head, matching 4.
- Redraw both the front and back shoulder lines, curving them back to 5.
- Trace off the new raglan sleeve.

Raglan flutter sleeve

A raglan flutter sleeve has a smooth sleeve head and a full, flowing hemline. The sleeve is usually elbow length or slightly above. The raglan shoulder gives a looser fit to the flutter sleeve.

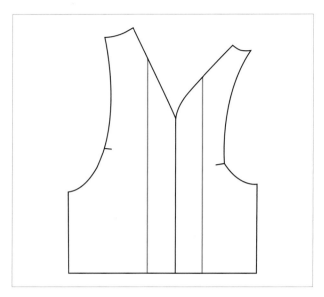

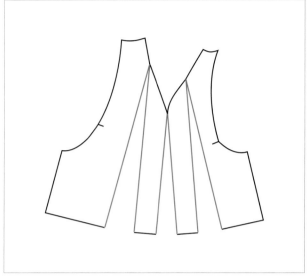

Step 1

- Trace off the raglan sleeve onto paper.
- Draw a line approximately 2in (5cm) either side of the center line.

Step 2

- Slash up these two lines and the center line to approximately ⅛in (3mm) from the shoulder line.
- Spread the sleeve apart to the required fullness.
- Using a curved ruler, redraw the lower edge of the sleeve.

Step 3

- Retrace your sleeve onto paper, adding all markings, notch points, and seam allowance.

Dropped shoulder with a puff sleeve

A puffed raglan sleeve can be gathered at both the neckline and the lower edge. The shoulder of a puffed raglan sleeve can be dropped for an off-the-shoulder effect as shown in the following directions. Both the neckline and lower edge can then be gathered and finished with bias-cut binding or smocking, or the lower edge can be finished with a small band of elastic. A puffed raglan sleeve can finish at the elbow or can be designed as a short cap sleeve.

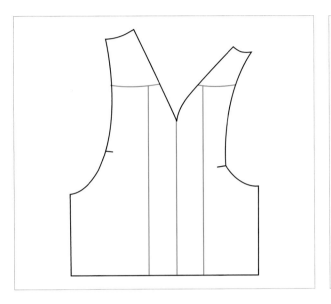

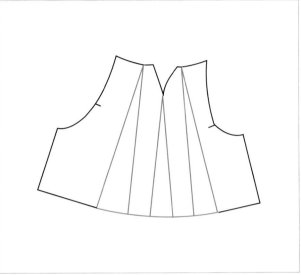

Step 1
- Trace off the raglan sleeve onto paper.
- Draw a line approximately 2in (5cm) either side of the center line.
- Draw a line across from the shoulder line to the armhole at the level of the sleeve head on both the front and back sleeve. This is the new neckline.

Step 2
- Remove the sleeve head above the new neckline.
- Slash up these two lines and the center line to approximately ⅛in (3mm) from the neckline and spread apart to the required fullness.
- Extend the sleeve to the required length and redraw the curve of the lower edge of the sleeve.

Step 3
- Using a curved ruler, redraw the neckline edge across the front and back sections, removing the dart.
- The neckline can be adjusted to fit the armhole edge on the front and back bodice of your chosen style.
- Add the seam allowance around the sleeve, notch points, and all markings.

Note: for a fuller neckline, cut through the neckline on the lines and spread the sleeve apart from the neckline to the lower edge.

Kimono sleeve

The kimono sleeve is cut in one piece with the bodice.

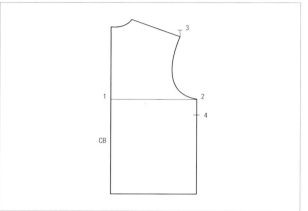

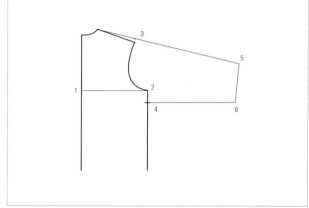

Step 1

- Trace around the loose-fitting back sloper.
- Mark in the armhole depth line; label the end of the line on the center back as 1 and at the armhole as 2.
- Measure up ⅝in (1.5cm) from the shoulder point; mark as 3.
- From 2 measure down one quarter of the armhole depth; mark as 4.

Step 2

- Draw a line from the shoulder neck point across to 3. Continue the line to complete the sleeve length; mark as 5.
- From 5 square a line down half the wrist measurement plus 1in (2.5cm); mark as 6.
- Draw a line from 4 to 6.

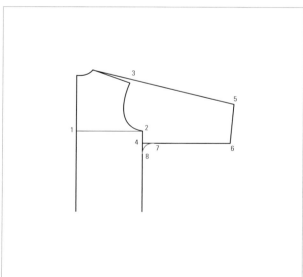

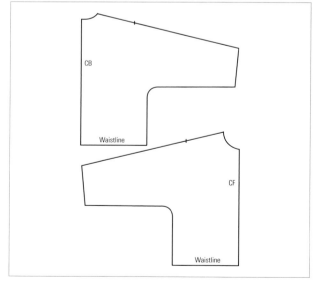

Step 3

- To make the curve at the underarm, from 2 measure down 2¾in (7cm); mark as 8.
- From 4, square a 2¾in (7cm) line across; mark as 7.
- Draw a curved line from 8 to 7.

Step 4

- Repeat from Step 1 for the sleeve front.
- Retrace the front and back slopers and add the notches.

Set-in sleeve

A set-in sleeve is a sleeve that is set into the armhole of the bodice. All the manipulations shown here can be created using the close-fitting, loose-fitting, or knit sleeve sloper.

Set-in sleeves can be created in different styles, including the bishop sleeve, flutter sleeve, puff sleeve, and cap sleeve.

Bishop sleeve

A bishop sleeve is a long, full sleeve finished with a cuff.

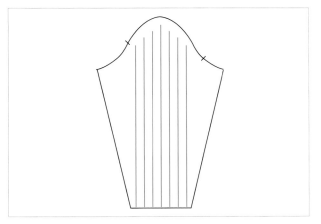

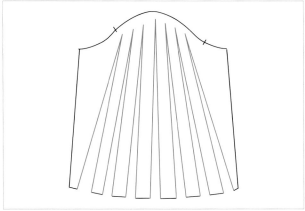

Step 1

- Trace around the sleeve sloper.
- Draw between 5 and 7 evenly spaced lines down the length of the sleeve, starting approximately 1in (2.5cm) down from the top of the sleeve.

Step 2

- Slash up the lines and spread each 1–2in (2.5–5cm) apart at the bottom of the sleeve.

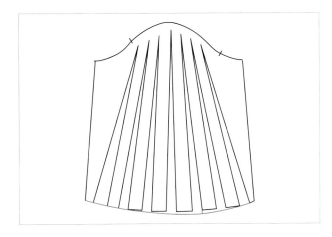

Step 3

- Measure across three quarters of the new sleeve width from the back of the sleeve along the bottom edge; square a line down ¾in (2cm).
- Draw in the hemline of the sleeve so that it curves down to touch the bottom of the line.

Step 4

- Retrace the sleeve onto paper for the finished pattern and add seam allowances.

Flutter sleeve

A flutter sleeve is short, full, soft, and romantic. It is a short variation of the bishop sleeve.

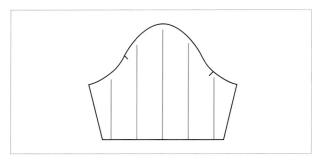
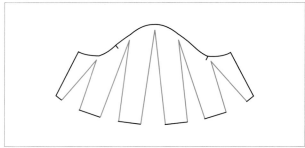

Step 1

- Trace around the sleeve sloper.
- Measure down from the bicep line the desired length and draw in the bottom of the sleeve.
- Draw between 5 and 7 evenly spaced lines down the length of the sleeve, starting approximately 1in (2.5cm) down from the top of the sleeve.

Step 2

- Slash up the lines and spread each 1–2in (2.5–5cm) apart at the bottom of the sleeve.

Step 3

- Retrace the sleeve onto paper for the finished pattern and add seam allowances.

Puff sleeve

A puff sleeve has fullness at both the cap and the hemline, which can be gathered into a cuff or an elastic casing.

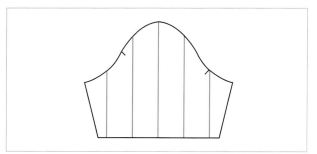

Step 1

- Trace around the sleeve sloper.
- Measure down from the bicep line to the required length of the sleeve and draw a line marking the hemline.
- Draw between 5 and 7 evenly spaced lines down the sleeve.

Step 2

- Slash down these lines and spread each 1–1½in (2.5–3.8cm) apart, depending on how full you want your sleeve.

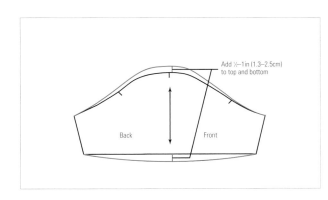

Step 3
- Add ½–1in (1.3–2.5cm) to the top of the sleeve cap.
- Redraw the sleeve cap, rounding the line up to take in the new extended sleeve cap.
- At the bottom of the sleeve, extend down at the center ½–1in (1.3–2.5cm) and redraw in the bottom of the sleeve with a curved line.
- Add seam allowances.

Full sleeve head

This sleeve has fullness in the sleeve head only, with a fitted bottom or hemline.

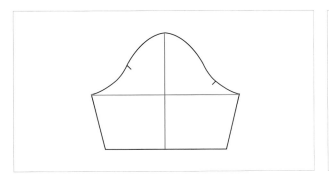

Step 1
- Trace around the sleeve sloper.
- Measure down 3–5in (7.5–12.5cm) from the bicep line for the required length of the sleeve. Draw in the hemline.

Step 2
- Cut down the center line of the sleeve from the top of the sleeve cap to the bicep.
- Cut along the bicep line to approximately ⅛in (3mm) from each end.
- Spread until you have the required fullness in the sleeve head.

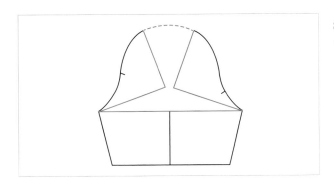

Step 3
- Retrace the sleeve onto paper for the finished pattern.

Cap sleeve

As the name indicates, this sleeve consists of the sleeve cap only.

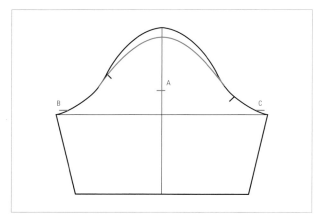

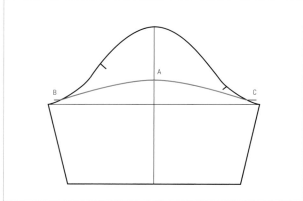

Step 1

- Trace around the sleeve sloper from the bicep line to the top of the sleeve cap.
- Shorten the height of the cap by ⅜in (1cm) to remove the ease in the sleeve head.
- Redraw the sleeve cap.
- Measure 1–2in (2.5–5cm) up the center line from the bicep line; mark as A. This is the length of the sleeve.
- Measure ¾in (2cm) up from the bicep line at each side of the sleeve and mark as B and C.

Step 2

- Draw in the hemline with a curved line from B, touching A and across to C.

Step 3

- Retrace the sleeve onto paper adding all markings, notch points, and seam allowances.

Collars

The mandarin and Peter Pan are two types of collar that are often used on sleepwear. Ruffles and frills are also a good choice to decorate a neckline, either on their own or around the edge of a collar.

3.4

Peter Pan collar

A Peter Pan collar sits flat to the neckline. It was designed for a costume worn by Maude Adams, who played Peter Pan in the 1905 Broadway production of *Peter and Wendy*. A Peter Pan collar can be finished with piping, or a ruffle made of fashion fabric or lace. It can also be embellished with embroidery.

- Place the front and back sloper shoulders together. There will be a ¾in (2cm) overlap at the armhole edge.
- Draw your desired collar shape.
- Trace off the collar onto paper, marking the shoulder with a notch point.
- Add seam allowances around the collar.

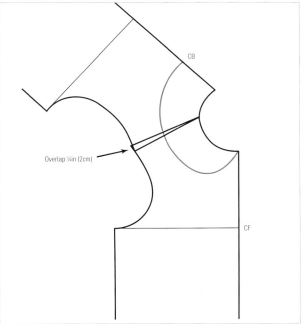

CB

Overlap ¾in (2cm)

CF

3.4 / Nightdress with a Peter Pan collar, finished with a lace ruffle.

Mandarin collar

A mandarin collar is a stand-up band that is between 1–4in (2.5–10cm) high. It can be finished with piping, or a ruffle of fashion fabric or lace. It can also be embellished with embroidery or smocking.

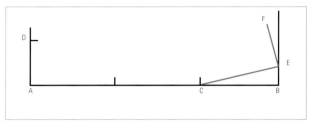

Step 1

- Measure around the neckline edge from center front to center back.
- Draw a line the length of this measurement; label the left-hand side as A and the right as B.
- Divide the collar into three equal parts and mark. Label the mark closest to B as C. The other mark is the shoulder point notch.
- Square a line up from A the collar height; mark as D.

Step 2

- Square a line up from B.
- From B measure up ¼in (6mm); mark as E.
- Draw a line from C to E.
- From E draw a line at 90° to the line from C to E, the measurement of the collar height; mark this point F.

Step 3

- Draw a curved line from D to F, parallel to the line from A to E.

Step 4

- Add seam allowances and all markings.

Godets

Godets can be added to any hemline. A godet is usually a triangular-shaped piece of fabric that is added between seams or into slits on a hemline of a skirt or sleeve. They can be made any length, and different lengths can even be combined on the same garment.

The wider the godet, the more fullness you are adding to the hemline. The shape of the hemline can also be changed if the godet is cut with a point hanging lower than the hemline, creating a handkerchief hem. Godets can be made in contrasting fabric to the rest of the garment, or in a contrasting color.

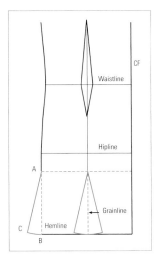
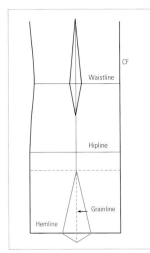

Step 1

- Work out the length of the godet, measuring up from the hemline; mark as A. Mark B at the hemline.
- Extend the hemline out half the width of the desired godet. Measure down from A to B. Taking this measurement, measure down from A towards the extended hemline; make a mark and label it as C.
- Draw a line from A to C and curve the hemline back down to B. (A–B and A–C should, therefore, be the same length.)
- You can also shape the hemline into a pointed instead of a curved shape.
- Add the grainline, which should be vertical from the top of the godet to the hem.

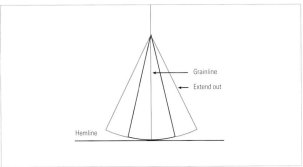
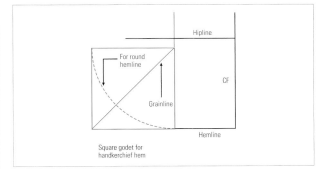

Step 2

- Fold a piece of paper in half and place on the center line of the godet. Trace off the godet shape, ensuring that the pattern is symmetrical.
- To add fullness to the godet, extend the hemline out, making sure that this extended line remains the same length as the center line of the godet.
- Cut around the godet.
- Open the pattern and draw a line down the fold. This is the grainline.
- Add seam allowances, notch points, and all markings to the godet.

- For a handkerchief hemline, cut a square of fabric for the godet. The hemline can be rounded or left pointed.

Pajamas

What better way to stay cozy at night than to snuggle up in a pair of cotton flannel pajamas? The word pajamas comes from the Hindi word pājāma, meaning "leg covering." They were first worn by men and boys who had been introduced to them by missionaries and colonials returning from the East around 1870.

The pajama pant can be long and full, a legging, Capri length, or shorts. The pajama top can be the traditional shirt with long or short sleeves, a pull-over-the-head tunic top, or a tank (vest). Pajamas can be made in luxurious silks and cottons or jersey knits, and can be embellished with piping, embroidery, lace, or ribbons.

Classic pajama shirt

Begin by drafting the pattern using the loose-fitting sloper for the classic pajama shirt.

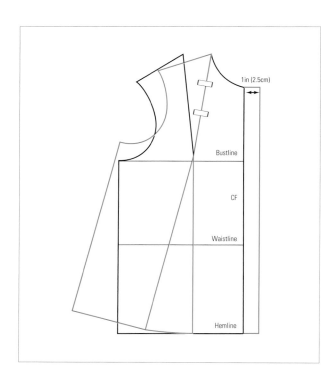

Step 1
- Trace around the loose-fitting sloper front.
- Draw a vertical line down from the end of the dart to the hemline.
- Cut up the vertical line and close the shoulder dart. The dart fullness will be transferred to the hemline.
- Redraw the side seam as a vertical line from the underarm down to the hemline.
- Draw a line 1in (2.5cm) out from the center front line for the button extension and square lines back to join it to the neckline and hemline.

Step 2
- Retrace the front onto paper.
- To add a front facing, mirror the front neckline and continue down the shoulder for 1–1½in (2.5–3.8cm).
- Measure out 2¾in (7cm) at the hemline.
- Draw a line joining the shoulder down to the hemline.
- Add seam allowances.

Step 3
- Trace around the back loose-fitting sloper without adding any shaping.
- Add seam allowances.

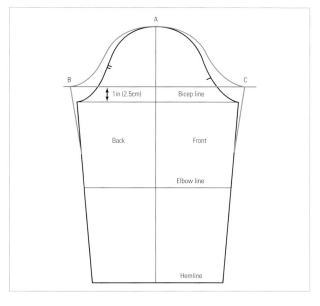

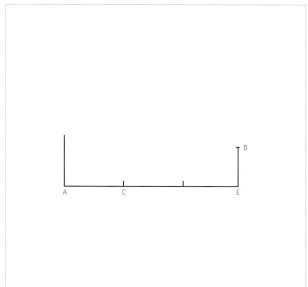

Step 4

- Trace around the loose-fitting sleeve sloper.
- Measure up 1in (2.5cm) from the bicep line and square a line across.
- Place the sloper on top of your sleeve and pivot it up from the shoulder point A so that the underarm of the sleeve is touching the new line at the back; mark as B.
- Pivot the sloper from A so that the underarm of the sleeve is touching the new line at the front; mark as C.
- Draw a line from B to C.
- Blend a line from B down to the underarm seam and repeat from C.
- Add seam allowances.

Step 5

- Measure the front and back neckline from the center front line around to the center back.
- Draw a line the length of this measurement; label the left-hand side as A and the right-hand side as E.
- Divide the collar into three equal parts and mark. Label the mark closest to A as C.
- Square a line up from E the collar width of 1½ –3in (3.8–7.5cm); mark as D.
- Square up a line from A.

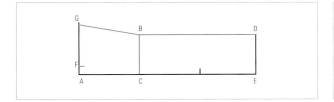

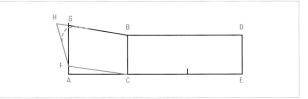

Step 6

- From C square up the collar width; mark as B.
- Draw a line from B to D.
- Measure up from A ¼in (6mm); mark as F.
- From F measure up the collar width; mark as G.
- Draw a line from G to B.

Step 7

- From G measure out ½in (1.3cm) at the same trajectory as the line from B to G; mark as H.
- Draw a line from H to G.
- Draw a line from H to F, and from F to C.
- For a rounded collar point, draw a curved line around the point at H.
- Retrace the collar and add seam allowances.

Classic pajama pant

Pajama pants are cut loose for comfort. Begin by drawing the front.

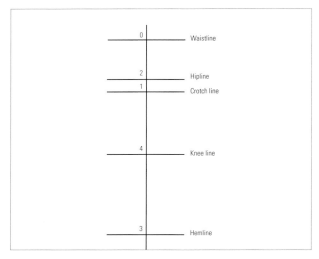

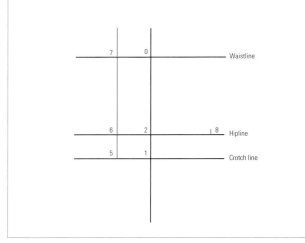

Step 1

- Draw a line down the center of the paper the pant leg length; label the top as 0 and the bottom as 3.
- Below 0 square a line out to each side for the waistline; below 3 square a line out to each side for the hemline.
- From 0 measure down the body rise plus ⅜in (1cm); mark as 1. Square a line out to each side as the crotch line.
- From 0 measure down the waist to hip measurement; mark as 2. Square a line out to each side as the hipline.
- Divide the line 1–3 in half less 2in (5cm); mark as 4. Square a line out to each side of 4 as the knee line.

Step 2

- From 1 measure across one twelfth the hip measurement plus ⅝in (1.5cm); mark as 5.
- From 5 square up a line to the line from 2; mark as 6. Continue the line up to the line from 0; mark as 7.
- From 6 measure out one quarter of the hip measurement plus ⅜in (1cm); mark as 8.

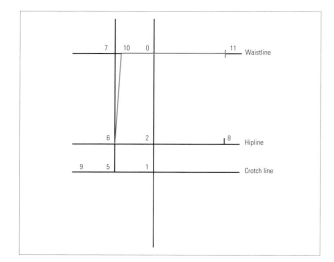

Step 3

- From 5 measure out one sixteenth of the hip measurement plus ⅜in (1cm); mark as 9.
- From 7 measure out ⅜in (1cm); mark as 10.
- From 10 measure out one quarter of the waist measurement; mark as 11.
- Draw a line from 10 to 6.

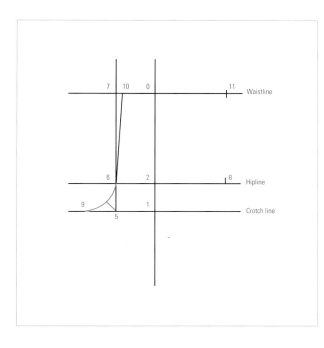

Step 4

- Draw a line at a 45° angle from 5. The length of the line will depend on the size of sloper you are making:

  sizes 6–14 1⅜in (3.5cm)

  sizes 16–24 1½in (3.8cm)

See the conversion chart on page 23 for UK and European sizes.

- Draw the curve from 6 to 9, touching the end of the line out from 5.

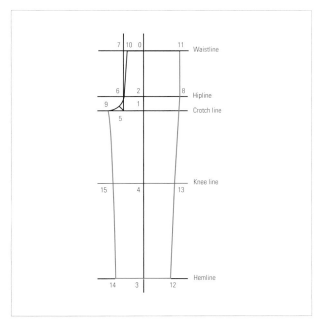

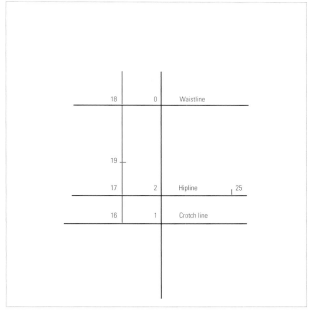

Step 5

- The leg width at the front hemline is approximately 8in (20cm). Measure out 4in (10cm) either side of 3; mark as 12 on the side seam and 14 on the inseam.
- Draw a line from 11 to 8; continue down to 12.
- Draw a line from 9 to 14.
- From 4 square a line out either side; where it joins line 8–12, mark as 13; where it joins line 9–14, mark as 15.
- Halfway down the line 9–15 mark ¾in (2cm) in; with a curved ruler redraw the line 9–15 through the mark.

Step 6

- For the back of the pant, repeat Step 1.
- From 1 measure across one twelfth the hip measurement plus ⅝in (1.5cm); mark as 16.
- From 16 square up a line to the line from 2; mark as 17. Continue up to the line from 0; mark as 18.
- Halfway between 16 and 18 mark 19.
- From 17 measure out one quarter of the hip measurement plus ¾in (2cm); mark as 25.

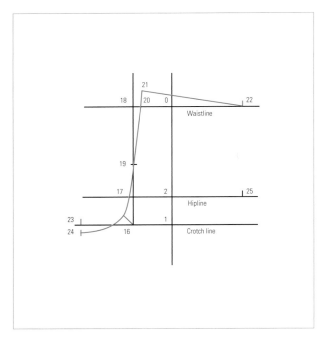

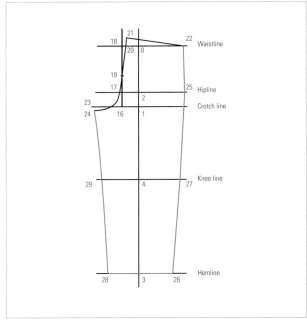

Step 7

- From 16 measure half the measurement from 5 to 9 on the front crotch line and mark as 23.
- From 23 square down ⅛in (3mm) and mark as 24; from 18 measure out ¾in (2cm) and mark as 20.
- Draw a line from 19 to 20; continue up ¾in (2cm) from 20 and mark as 21.
- Draw a line from 21 one quarter the waist measurement, angling it down to touch the line from 0; mark as 22.
- Draw a line at a 45° angle from 16; the length will depend on the size you are making:
    sizes 6–14 1¾in (4.5cm)
    sizes 16–24 2in (5cm)
See the conversion chart on page 23 for UK and European sizes.
- Draw the curve from 19 to 24, touching the end of the line out from 16.

Step 8

- The leg width at the back hemline is approximately 9in (23cm). Measure out 4½in (11.5cm) on either side of 3; mark as 26 on the side seam and 28 on the inseam.
- Draw a line from 22 to 25; continue down to 26.
- Draw a line from 24 to 28.
- From 4 square a line out either side; where it joins line 25–26 mark as 27; where it joins line 24–28 mark as 29.
- Halfway down line 24–29 mark ⅜in (1cm) in; with a curved ruler, redraw the line 24–29 through the mark.
- Retrace the front and back pant, adding all markings and seam allowances.

Drawstring-neckline top and shorts

The neckline for a drawstring is widened in the draft so that it can be pulled into gathers, or gathered and finished with a binding. The lower edge can also be finished with ruffles. The pant sloper can be turned into shorts with a casing for elastic or a drawstring.

3.5

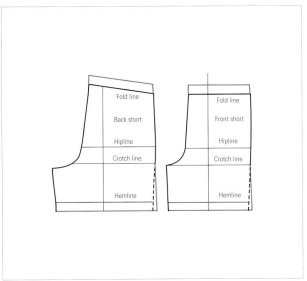

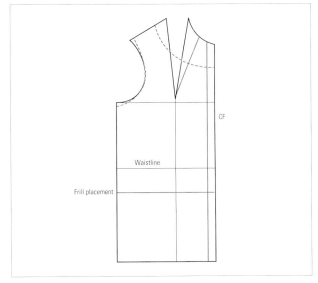

Step 1

- For the shorts, trace off the front and back pajama pant sloper (Step 5 from page 95, and Step 8, opposite).
- Straighten the line from the crotch line on the side seams so it is at 90°, and measure down on both front and back 1½in (3.8cm) on the inseam and 2in (5cm) on the side seam, or the desired length.
- Add a 1in (2.5cm) hem to the bottom of both front and back legs.
- Add a 1in (2.5cm) facing at the waistline on both front and back.

Step 2

- For the top, trace off the front and back loose-fitting slopers.
- Divide the front neckline measurement in two; mark and draw a line to the bottom of the shoulder dart.
- Divide the neckline measurement between this line and the center front; mark and draw a line from the neckline to the hemline.
- Draw in a new neckline that is both wider and lower.
- Lift the armhole on the shoulder ⅜in (1cm) and lower the underarm of the armhole ⅜in (1cm). Using a curved ruler, draw in the new armhole.
- To mark the frill placement, draw a line from center front to the side, 3–4in (7.5–10cm) below the waistline.

3.5 / Nightdress with drawstring neckline.

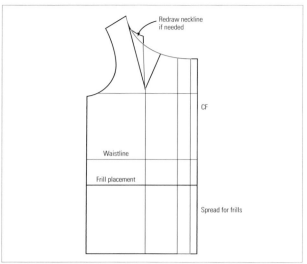

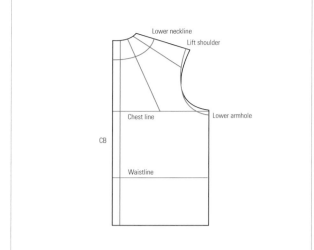

Step 3

- Slash down the new line from the neckline to the bottom of the shoulder dart, and close the shoulder dart.
- Cut along the new neckline and armhole line.
- Slash down the line from the neckline to hemline and spread the front the desired amount for the gathers.

Step 4

- For the back, draw a line from the neckline to the hemline approximately 1in (2.5cm) in from the center back line.
- Divide the neckline in half and draw a diagonal line at this point from the neckline down to the chest line.
- Divide the remaining neckline in half and draw another diagonal line out to the armhole.
- Draw in a lower and wider neckline that matches the front at the shoulder.
- Lift the shoulder at the armhole ⅜in (1cm) and lower the underarm ⅜in (1cm).

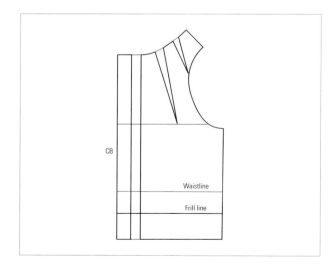

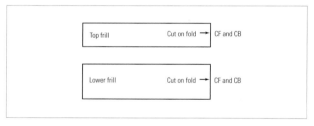

Step 5

- Slash down the three lines and spread as for the front. Draw a line at the high hip for the frill placement.

Step 6

- To create the pattern for the frill, measure across both the front and back frill placement lines and draw a line twice this length.
- Decide the frill width and draw a rectangle for the frill; mark one end as the center front and back lines; mark to cut on the fold. Label as the top frill.
- Draw a second rectangle the same length but at least 1in (2.5cm) wider; mark one end as the center front and back lines. Mark to cut on the fold; label as the lower frill.

Negligees and peignoirs

The first negligees appeared in France in the 1700s; they were long and heavy, and designed purely for utilitarian purposes. Negligees were then in vogue from the 1940s through to the 1970s; they were made from sheer, semitranslucent fabrics trimmed with lace, ribbons, and even feathers.

Peignoirs are long outergarments, usually sheer and made of chiffon. A peignoir is meant to be worn with no underwear, whereas the negligee is made to be worn over underwear or a gown. The peignoir was originally worn as a dressing gown when combing and dressing the hair.

3.6

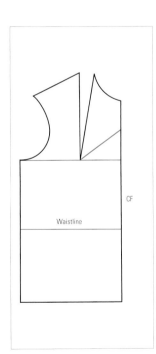

CF

Waistline

Step 1
- Trace around the front and back loose-fitting slopers.
- On the center front measure halfway between the neckline and bust line; mark and draw a line down to the bottom of the shoulder dart.

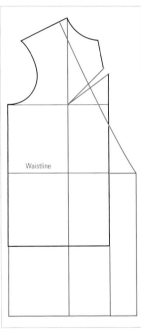

Waistline

Step 2
- Slash down from center front to bust point; close the shoulder dart.
- Lengthen the side seam and the center front line as desired; draw in the new hemline.
- Draw a vertical line from the shoulder neck point to the hemline.
- Square out 6in (15cm) lines from the waistline and new hemline.
- Draw a line from the new extended hemline up to the new extended waistline.
- Lower the neckline at the shoulder line and from this point draw a line down to the extended waistline to create the new neckline.

3.6 / A negligee with lace detailing and sash.

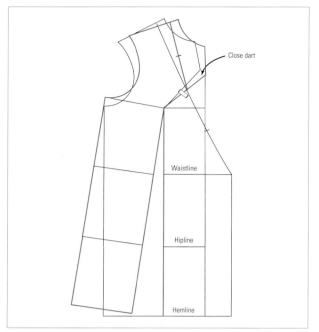

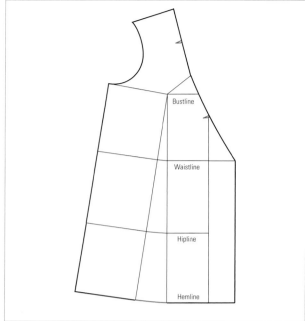

Step 3
- Slash up the line from the hemline to the bottom of the shoulder dart; open out the dart while closing the new dart from the bustline.
- Divide the new neckline in half from the now closed dart up to the shoulder and mark; repeat from the dart down to the waistline and mark.

Step 4
- Make a small ⅜in (1cm) dart in the paper at each of these marks.

Step 5
- Close the darts and tape down.

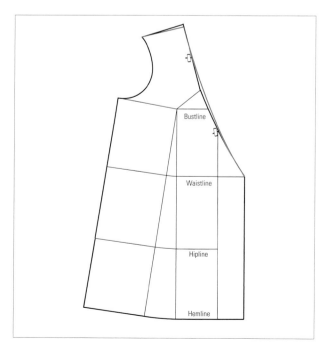

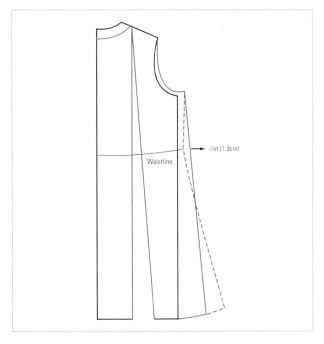

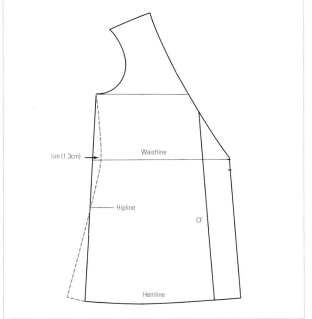

Step 6

- Lengthen the back so it matches the front.
- Divide the back in half at the waistline; square a line up to the shoulder line and down to the hemline.
- Slash up this line and spread to the desired amount of fullness.
- Mark ½in (1.3cm) out from the waistline at the side seam.
- Draw a line from the underarm to touch the mark on the waistline and back out to the hemline, adding extra fullness at the hemline if required.

Step 7

- Retrace the front onto another sheet of paper.
- Mark ½in (1.3cm) in at the waistline at the side seam.
- Add all markings and seam allowances. Mark the front bow closure placement. Add your choice of sleeve.

4 Construction Techniques
Slips, panties, petticoats, and sleepwear

Most lingerie and sleepwear sold today has to be serviceable, easy to launder, and easily replaceable. The selling price will determine how the piece is constructed and the choice of fabric and embellishments. At the lower end of the market garments will be quickly serged together and manufactured mainly from knitted cottons and man-made fabrics with a few added embellishments. Higher-end designer, heirloom, and couture lingerie and sleepwear will be made from silks and fine cottons and linens, both woven and knitted. Some of the wovens may be bias cut. These garments will be constructed using French and flat fell seams, with appliquéd lace, rouleau buttonhole loops, and straps made using a mix of machine- and hand-stitched construction techniques. The techniques used in such higher-end designer lingerie and sleepwear have not changed over the decades.

This designer adjusts the waist of a negligee with highly embellished sleeves.

The bias cut

Cutting on the true bias will give your garment more elasticity, drape, or flexibility than a garment cut on the straight grain. Because lingerie and sleepwear garments are made from lighter-weight fabrics, cutting them on the true bias makes the most of the added stretch or elasticity that is characteristic of these fabrics, allowing them to follow the contours of the body softly.

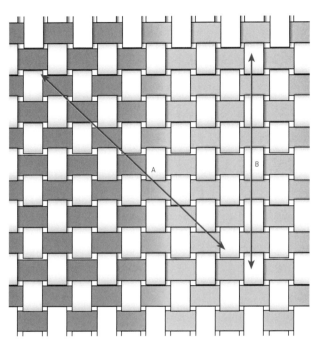

Woven fabric is made up of vertical threads on the straight grain, also known as warp threads, and horizontal threads on the cross grain at 90 degrees to the warp threads, also known as weft threads. The bias is found at 45 degrees to these warp and weft threads. Use a set square or draw a small 1in (2.5cm) square with chalk following the grain lines on your fabric, then draw a line diagonally across the square at a 45-degree angle to find the bias.

Fabric grain
A: Bias grain
B: Straight grain

The bias and the cross grain

The bias is sometimes referred to as the cross grain, but technically the cross grain is the horizontal grain (weft) of the fabric from selvage to selvage edge, so try not to become confused.

Using the bias cut

Take your time and double check that your pattern is placed on the true bias of the fabric. If it is slightly off, the finished garment may distort or pull unattractively on the body. Also, leave extra seam allowances down the side seams as they will pull in and the garment will stretch in length. This happens because the weft and the warp yarns/threads have different tensions. Once the garment pattern pieces are cut, attach weights evenly along the hem and hang from a coat hanger for up to two days so that the bias will fully stretch out.

Seams and seam finishes

Seams take a lot of stresses and strains in both lingerie and sleepwear.
Because lingerie is constructed from fine, soft, sometimes sheer fabrics,
the choice of seam is important.

The seam has to be flat and well finished because of its proximity to the skin; it should not rub or chafe. It can be hidden or sandwiched between two pattern pieces, such as at the crotch, or be visible and decorative, or double stitched for strength. The finish of the seam is important because you do not want it to show through onto the right side of the garment, or to break down, thus destroying the seam line and ultimately the garment. This is why the three main seams and finishes found in lingerie and sleepwear are the French and flat fell seams, for the higher end of the market, and the serged (overlocked) seam, for lower-priced garments.

French seam

A French seam is a narrow seam with the seam allowance folded in half. It is a seam within a seam, so there are no raw edges. It is used on lightweight fabrics such as sheer chiffons, georgettes, organdies, lace, and satin charmeuse. The French seam is used to finish both high-end lingerie and sleepwear.

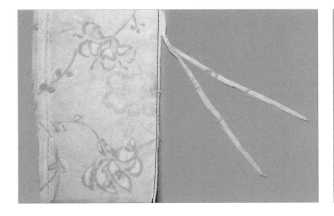

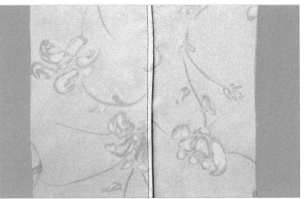

Step 1

- Using a stitch length of 2.5–3mm, move the sewing machine needle over to one side, if it is possible to do this on your machine, so that the stitching will be closer to the fabric edge. With the wrong sides of the fabric together, sew down the length of the seam half-way into the seam allowance and press. Cut the seam allowance away so that you have approximately ⅛in (3mm) left.

Step 2

- Fold the fabric down the seam line, bringing the right sides of the fabric together and enclosing the seam allowance. Starting the stitching about five stitches down from the top of the seam, stitch back toward the fabric edge then down the length of the seam allowance. Back tack for about five stitches to finish.

Step 3

- Press the seam flat.

Flat fell seam

A flat fell seam also encloses the raw edges of the seam allowance. It is a strong seam, with two rows of stitching showing on the right side of the fabric and one row of stitching showing on the wrong side. The flat fell seam is made on the right side of the fabric, and it can be made with or without the felling foot that is available for most sewing machines. This seam can be used on most fabric weights.

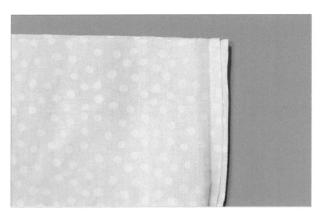

Step 1

- Use a stitch length of either 2.5 or 3mm. Place one piece of fabric on the table, right side down; lay the other fabric piece right side up on top, with the fabric edge approximately ¼in (6mm) in from the lower fabric edge, staggering the seam allowance.

Step 2

- Fold the extra seam allowance back over the top seam allowance and press flat along the fold line.

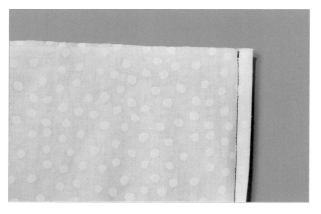

Step 3

- Stitch down the middle of the seam allowance, catching the raw edge of the lower seam allowance.

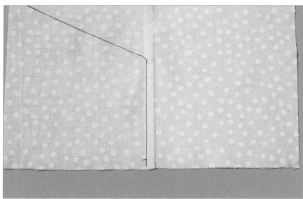

Step 4

- Open the fabric so that it is laying flat on the table and press the seam allowance flat so that the raw edges are hidden. Keeping the stitching close to the folded line, stitch down the length of the seam, back tacking both of the seam ends.

Plain seams finished with zigzag stitch

Plain seams that are pressed open and flat are not used in lingerie because the raw edges of the fabric have to be finished in some way and this sort of finishing can add bulk, or shadow through fine, lightweight fabrics. A plain seam that is not pressed open but has the raw edges serged together is, however, used for lingerie at the lower end of the market. If you do not have access to a serger, zigzag the seam allowance together and then cut off any remaining seam allowance.

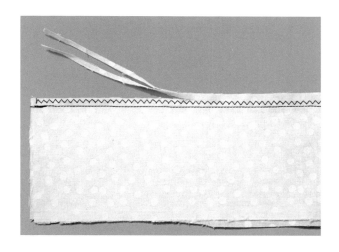

Serged plain seams

Running the seam through a serger is a quick way to produce lingerie, especially with a knit fabric. The serger will both sew and finish the seam, which will be strong and stretchy, and should look good on both sides if the tension is set correctly.

The looper threads on a serger are looped with the needle thread(s). Use a three-thread serger to maintain stretch – the fourth thread runs down the middle of the other three, locking them, and will reduce the amount of stretch. Set the stitch width at ¼in (6mm) and cut all seam allowances to this width before you start. Be careful when pressing a serged seam; the bulk can create lines on the right side.

Fine zigzag seam for knit fabrics

If you do not have a serger, use a small zigzag stitch for your seams. The zigzagging gives the seam some elasticity so the stitches will not "pop" when the seam is stretched.

Using a 2.5mm stitch length, a zigzag stitch width of 1mm (refer to your sewing machine manual for the correct stitch width for your machine), and a ball-point needle with a size suitable for your fabric weight, stitch down the seam allowance on your fabric.

Finish by pressing the seam allowances flat and open and zigzag-stitching on top of the original stitching down the seam, with a width of 3mm and a stitch length of 2.5–3mm.

Hems and hem finishes

The lingerie hem needs to be kept small and soft. The choice of fabric, and whether the garment is bias, straight of grain, or a knitted fabric, are important factors in your final choice of hem or hem finish.

Cover stitch hems on knit fabrics

Some sergers include a cover stitch for hemming, or you can use a cover stitch machine. The cover stitch produces two to three rows of stitching on the right side of the fabric and a flat lock stitch on the wrong side. Cover stitching is a quick and easy way to hem the knit or stretch fabric garments found in lingerie.

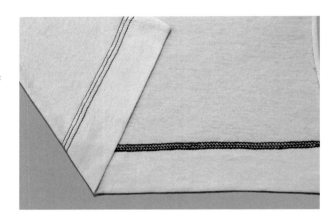

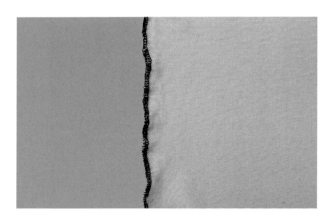

Lettuce-edged hem

Begin by altering the differential feed (tension) on your serger. Place the fabric to be hemmed under the foot of the serger so that the edge of the fabric is sitting up against the cutting blade. As you run the edge of your fabric through the serger, keep it under tension by stretching the edge out as it passes through to create a frilly lettuce-edged hem. The machine will cut any extra fabric away as you serge, giving a clean, neat edge to the hem.

Narrow rolled hems

Narrow rolled hems are used on sheer or very lightweight fabrics. The hem can be rolled and stitched by hand, or machine stitched with a rolled hem foot that is available for most sewing machines.

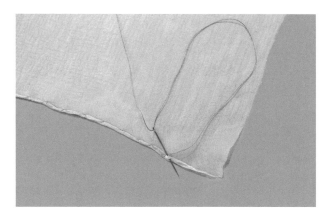

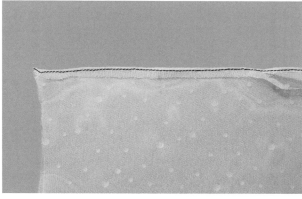

Step 1

- To hand sew a rolled hem, roll the raw hem edge of the fabric between your index finger and thumb to create a small length of rolled hem and slip stitch it in place. Repeat this process down the length of the hemline.

Step 2

- To create a machine-rolled hem, fold over approximately ¼in (6mm) of the raw edge of the fabric to the wrong side and stitch with a 2.5mm stitch length as close to the folded edge as possible.

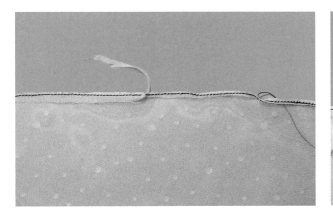

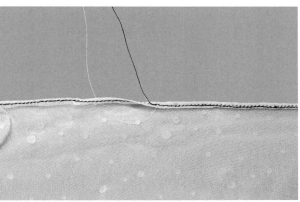

Step 3

- Cut the excess fabric off close to the stitching line; be careful to cut only the excess, not the garment fabric.

Step 4

- Roll the hem again over the line of stitching, and stitch in place.

Bound, ribbon, and lace edges

Neck and armhole edges in sleepwear can be finished with a bias-cut binding,
ribbon, or narrow edging lace. These can all be made from a contrasting color, print,
or fabric, giving an interesting design detail to both woven and knit fabric garments.

Bias-bound edge

Most sewing machines have a binding foot attachment
available to help make and attach the binding in one step,
or you can buy a tool or machine for making bias tape
(binding). With both you thread in a bias-cut fabric strip and
it folds the seam allowances inward along both sides as
you pull it out. The difference between the two is that the
machine folds the tape with heat, while the manual tool
requires you to press the tape as it emerges.

Seam allowance
For lingerie and
sleepwear a bound seam
allowance is usually ½in
(1.3cm) for armholes,
necklines, sleeve hems,
and plackets.

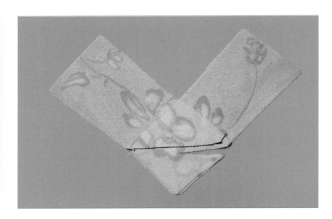

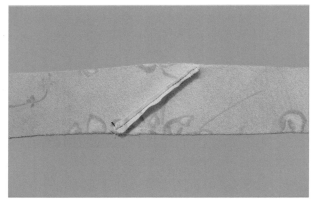

Step 1
- Cut a bias strip of fabric for the binding twice the
  width of the seam allowance of the garment plus
  an additional ½in (1.3cm), which will be divided
  between ¼in (6mm) seam allowances on each side of
  the binding. You may have to join one or more strips
  together to get the length required. To do this, place
  the bias strips at right angles right sides together,
  matching the lengthwise grain one on top of the other,
  and stitch; trim to leave a ¼in (6mm) seam allowance.
  Press the seam allowances open.

Step 2
- Pin the bias-cut strip with right side to the wrong side
  of the garment, keeping an even tension, starting from
  a shoulder point or underarm. Attach the bias strip
  using a 2.5mm stitch length, back tacking to secure the
  stitching only when the ends meet.

Step 3
- Press the seam allowance and bias strip flat away from
  the garment edge.

Step 4
- Fold the unsewn edge of the bias strip in toward the
  edge of the seam allowance and press.

Step 5
- Bring the folded edge of the bias strip over to the right
  side of the garment so that it encloses the raw edge
  of the seam allowance and just overlaps the line of
  stitching. Pin in place and stitch along the folded edge
  of the bias strip to finish attaching it to the garment.

Ribbon edging

Ribbon can be used to hem or finish the edges of an all-over lace, tulle, or sheer-fabric garment. It is also a great way to finish the edge of a flounce or frill. Consider using a contrasting colored ribbon to provide interest to a hem or edge of a garment.

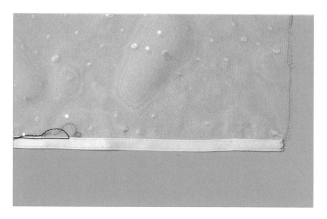

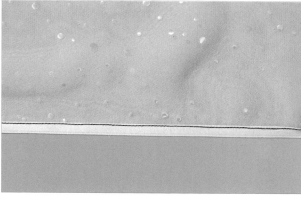

Step 1
- With the right side of the ribbon facing up and the wrong side of the garment facing you, place the ribbon so that one edge is lying along the raw edge.

Step 2
- Attach the ribbon by stitching along the inner edge, being careful to stay on the edge of the ribbon.

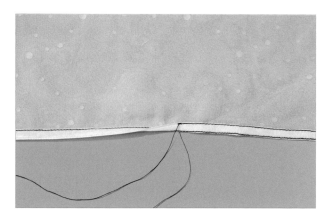

Step 3
- Fold the ribbon to the right side of the garment so that it encloses the raw edge of the fabric; stitch down the unstitched side of the ribbon to finish the edging.

Working with lace

Lace is used extensively in lingerie, sleepwear, and foundation garments. It has no grainline but does have a specific pattern, and the position of that pattern on the finished garment needs to be carefully considered before cutting or sewing.

Photocopying your lace and using the paper version as a template is a good and inexpensive way to make sure that the pattern on the lace matches symmetrically on both left and right sides of the pattern pieces before cutting out.

You may also want to try using spray starch on the back of the lace and pressing it to give it some stability and strength before cutting.

Mitered lace corners

The corners of an edging lace can be mitered so that there is no interruption to the scalloped or finished edge.

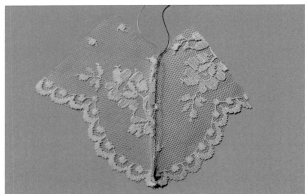

Step 1
- Measure the lace along the garment edge past the corner to be mitered by the width of the lace. Mark the length on the outside edge of the lace, then fold the lace back on itself at the mark. Draw a line at 45° from the mark back to the inside edge of the lace. Mark a ¼in (6mm) seam allowance outside this line with a second line. Cut down this second line. When you open out your lace a "V" shape will have been removed.

Step 2
- Fold the lace back on itself and stitch together along the first line from the corner to the outer edge. Depending on the lace pattern and width, either trim the excess lace or press it open and flat.

Step 3
- Stitch the lace in place along the garment edge to the mitered corner; keep the sewing machine needle down in the fabric, lift the presser foot, and turn the fabric under the needle until your stitching line is facing you; continue to stitch the lace to the garment's edge.

Selecting and attaching appliqué lace

Appliqué lace is a motif sewn onto a garment either by hand or machine, or by using a combination of the two techniques. Lace motifs can be purchased separately or cut from the pattern of an all-over lace fabric. Every lace will offer many motifs for a range of design possibilities: a single flower, a leaf or scroll, or a group of flowers, for example. You can also finish a raw edge around a neckline or sleeve opening using this technique, selecting motifs from the same or another piece of lace.

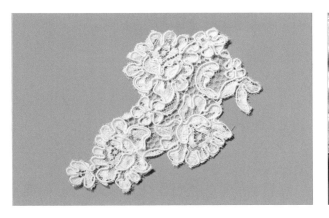

Step 1

- Photocopy your lace and then cut out the motifs from the paper so that you can work out the design of the appliqué before cutting. Spray-starch the back of the lace before carefully cutting out the choice of motif. Cut away as much of the net as possible from around the motif.

Step 2

- Place the lace motif to be appliquéd on the fabric and pin in place, being careful to pin in areas where you are not going to be stitching. Using a wide, see-through foot on your sewing machine and thread color to match the lace, zigzag stitch around the motif with the stitch length set at 2mm and the width at 1.5mm depending on your sewing machine. Working free motion by dropping the feed dogs on the machine and using the darning foot makes it easier to follow the outline edge of the lace. You can also attach motifs by hand using a small blanket stitch around the edge of the motifs.

Working motifs around a neckline

If you are setting individual lace motifs around the top edge of a camisole or neckline of a bra, set each motif under a little tension before stitching so that when the fabric is cut away from behind they will lay flat.

Step 3

- Carefully cut the fabric away from behind the lace, leaving a small ⅛in (3mm) seam allowance.

Appliquéing a lace edge onto lace

The lace you are using may have scalloped edges down both sides and mirrored motifs as with a galloon lace, for example; alternatively the lace fabric may be finished with two different edges. This can leave you with some pattern pieces that will not have the same finished edge, or will have no finished edge at all. You will therefore need to cut a separate piece of lace edging from any leftover pieces of lace and apply it to the mismatched edges.

Step 1
- Place the garment piece that you are going to appliqué flat on a table. Match the motifs on the edge of this piece to the motifs on the edge of a piece of leftover lace. Mark the position of the matched motifs on the piece of leftover lace, then carefully cut along the edge, cutting around the motifs if they are part of the lace edge.

Step 2
- Place the new lace edge on the garment edge, matching motifs, and pin. If you are appliquéing along a neckline or hemline, the shape of the pattern pieces may mean that the lace motifs will not sit flat; you will have to cut into them to lengthen or shorten the distance between motifs or overlap them slightly. Reposition the lace until it lies flat when pinned in place.

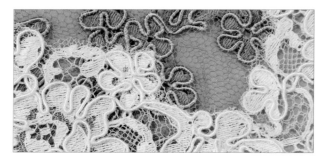

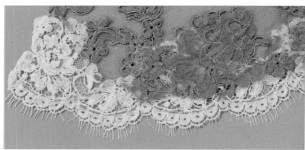

Step 3
- Drop the feed dogs on your machine and attach the darning foot. Using a small zigzag stitch width of 1.5mm, slowly attach the lace motifs using a darning-like motion around the edges. If necessary, join any cut lace motifs.

Step 4
- On the wrong side of the garment cut away the excess lace motifs, leaving a small ⅛in (3mm) seam allowance.

Joining lace with French seams

If you are working with a soft net lace with scattered motifs you can use a narrow French seam to join the seam lines.

Joining lace with appliqué seams

In couture or high-end lingerie an appliqué technique is used to join the seams in which a lace pattern is matched from one side of the seam to the other. The motifs that sit on or directly beside the seam are cut with both pattern pieces. These lace motifs are then overlapped and stitched together either by hand or machine, creating a meandering seam as the stitching works its way around the motifs in the pattern.

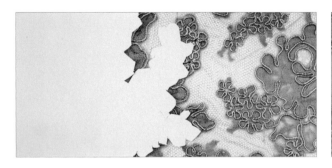

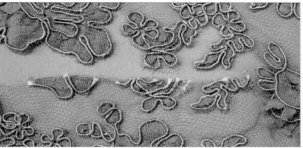

Step 1

- Make a paper photocopy of your lace. Place your pattern pieces on the paper photocopy and match up the lace motifs at the seams. You can even trace around the pattern pieces and re-cut your pattern using the printed photocopy, adding the lace motifs to be overlapped in the seams to each pattern piece. This works really well if you are making more than one garment design using the lace.

Step 2

- Carefully cut the pattern pieces out, cutting around the motifs that will overlap, checking that they match with the motifs on the other pattern piece.

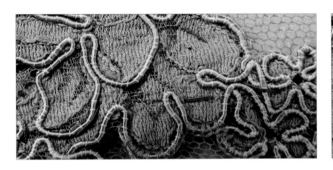

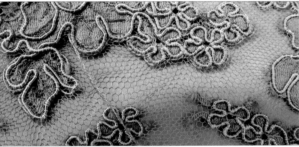

Step 3

- Place the seam together, overlapping and matching the motifs down the seam line. Baste (tack) around the lace motifs for the length of the seam.

Step 4

- Hand stitch around each motif using a small blanket stitch to sew the seam together, or use the sewing machine with a free-motion technique.

Step 5

- Cut away the excess lace motif from behind, leaving a small ⅛in (3mm) seam allowance.

Joining seams with appliqué by hand and machine

If the lace has more net than motif pattern, a mix of both hand and machine stitching can be used.

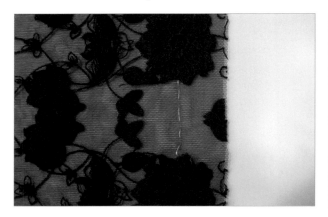

Step 1

- If there are large areas of net between the motifs on the lace, cut the lace pattern pieces out (see Step 1 on page 113). Pin the seam together between the motifs and baste down the net seam line to hold in place.

Step 2

- Cut into the net seam allowance on each side of the motif. Push the seam allowance under between the motifs. Fold the seam back on itself.

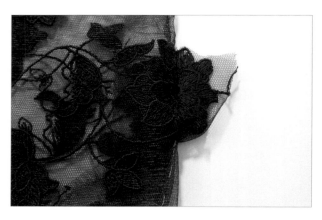

Step 3

- Machine stitch just outside the line of basting stitches using a 2mm stitch length.

Step 4

- Lay the piece flat and hand stitch around the motif edges using blanket stitch, or machine stitch them with a 1.5mm-wide zigzag stitch.

Step 5

- Remove the excess lace from the back of the seam, keeping a small ⅛in (3mm) seam allowance.

Rouleau tie extending from a bound neckline

The edge of a neckline or sleeve may be finished with a bound edge that continues into a rouleau buttonhole loop or ties.

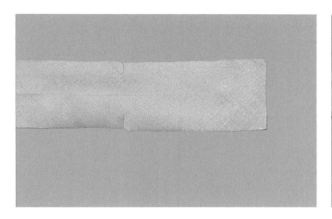

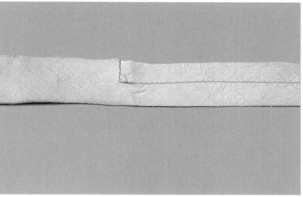

Step 1

- Measure the neckline or hemline to be bound, then add the length of the ties or button loop to this measurement. Cut a bias strip of fabric the required length. Mark the position of the neckline on the bias strip.

Step 2

- Make the rouleau tie or buttonhole loop by folding the bias strip in half, right sides together, and stitching down the length of the bias strip only, starting at the position of the neckline and stitching toward the end of the strip.

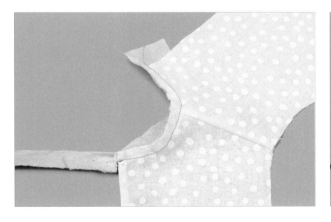

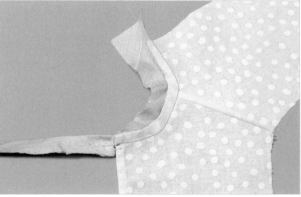

Step 3

- Pin the bias strip to the wrong side of the garment neckline or hemline and stitch in place along the seam line, making sure the start of this stitching matches up with the stitching down the rouleau.

Step 4

- Press the seam allowance flat onto the bias binding strip; fold the seam allowance up or down toward the edge of the neckline or hemline seam allowance and press.

When to use pins or tape
When working with some lace fabrics, nets, and tulle you will find it easier to use a narrow, clear fusible tape to hold the seams together rather than using pins as the pins will drop out of the looser weave structure.

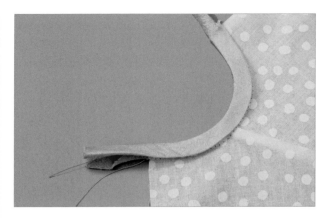

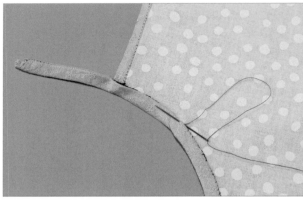

Step 5
- Fold the bias binding strip in half so that it is enclosing the neckline or hemline seam allowance and just covering the first row of stitching and press.

Step 6
- Turn the rouleau ties or buttonhole loop to the right side. Pin the bias binding strip around the neckline or along the hemline and stitch in place, keeping the stitching close to the folded edge from the beginning of the loop or from the beginning of one rouleau tie around to the beginning of the other rouleau tie. The binding can also be finished by hand using a blind hem stitch.

Placket closures

Small placket closures are made on some items of lingerie or sleepwear for ease of access. They can be made in a contrasting colored fabric to add design interest.

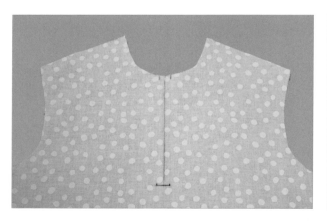

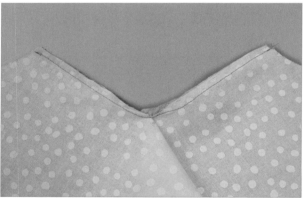

Step 1
- Mark the placement of the placket closure on the garment pattern piece. Cut a bias strip 1½in (3.8cm) wide and twice the length of the placket closure plus 1in (2.5cm) and press in half. Cut down the placket closure marking on the garment pattern piece. Lay the pattern piece flat right side up and spread the slash open.

Step 2
- Place the right side of the bias strip on the wrong side of the slash and pin in place. Stitch along the length of the slash line, attaching the bias strip.

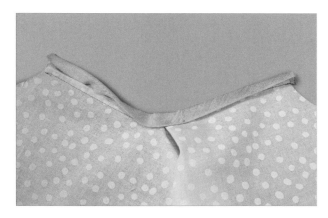

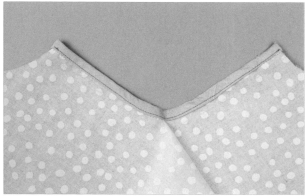

Step 3

- Press the seam allowance down onto the bias strip, fold up the seam allowance on the other side of the bias strip, and press.

Step 4

- Fold the bias strip in half, right sides together, enclosing the slashed seam allowance, and stitch close to the folded edge, just covering the first row of stitching.

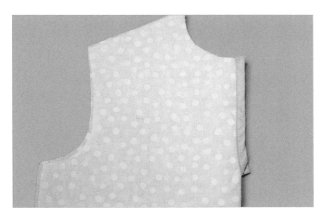

Step 5

- Place the placket flat, with right sides together, and stitch diagonally across the top of the placket.

Step 6

- Fold the top edge of the placket under so that the back of the placket closure extends outward.

Back neck facing

Facings are usually only used on the back neckline in sleepwear, while the front neckline is bound. The facing is not interfaced. The back neck facing is cut long at the center back to add strength and support across the back of the garment. The outer edge of the facing is stitched to the garment to hold it in place, and for comfort.

- Fold a piece of paper in half.
- Place the back loose-fitting sloper bodice (see pages 62–65) underneath the paper, with the center back line lined up with the fold line of the paper.
- Trace onto the paper across the shoulder and neckline to the center back line.
- Measure 9⅜–10in (24–25cm) down the center back line and mark.
- Measure out 2½in (6.5cm) from the shoulder neck point along the shoulder line and mark.
- Use a French curve to connect the two marks and draw in the back neck facing.
- Add seam allowances before cutting out, and place a notch point at the center back neckline edge.

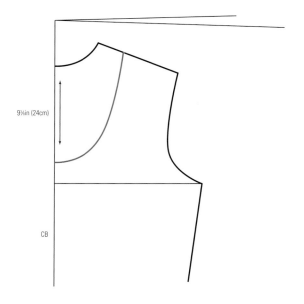

9⅜in (24cm)

CB

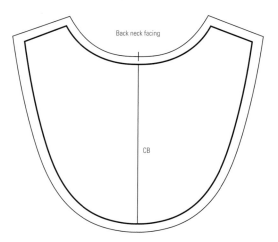

Back neck facing

CB

Bias hem facing

Bias hem facings are used to finish the lower edge of a garment. Because these facings are bias cut they can also easily be shaped into a band around the top of a camisole or nightdress.

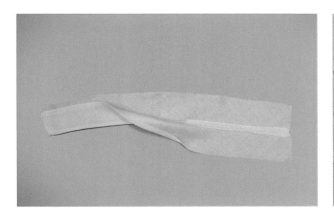

Step 1

- Cut two bias strips the required length and width, remembering to include seam allowances. Stitch the two facings together along the lower edge; press the seam open.
- Turn the facing to the right side, fold in half and press the seam flat; fold the top of the front edge seam allowance under and press.

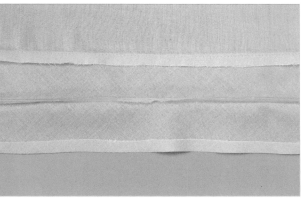

Step 2

- Place the right side of the band onto the wrong side of the hemline and pin in place. Stitch using a 2–2.5mm stitch length, being careful not to stretch either the hem or the facing as you stitch.

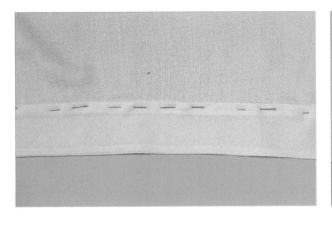

Step 3

- Press the seam allowance into the bias facing. Pin the folded front edge of the bias facing along the stitching line on the front of the garment so that it just covers the stitching.

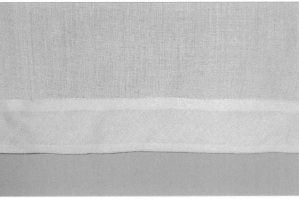

Step 4

- Stitch close to the folded edge with a stitch length of 2–2.5mm to finish attaching the facing to the garment's hem.

Making the crotch

The crotch is attached to the brief with a technique that conceals the seam lines while creating a double layer of fabric in the crotch area. The crotch is usually cut from a cotton knit fabric, whatever the fashion fabric of the brief.

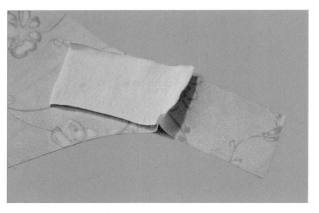

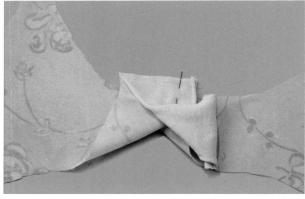

Step 1
- Cut a pattern piece for the crotch from cotton knit and cut out the brief in fashion fabric, including another piece for the crotch. Place the two crotch pieces together, sandwiching the brief back, so that the back seam is aligned on all three pieces, the right side of the fashion fabric crotch is to the right side of the brief back, and the right side of the cotton knit crotch is to the wrong side of the brief back. Match the notches and pin in place. Stitch across the back seam line with a stitch length of 2.5mm.

Step 2
- Pin the fashion fabric crotch to the brief front with right sides together, so that the front seam is aligned.
- With the wrong side of the brief facing up, twist the cotton knit crotch piece around to sandwich the brief front between fashion fabric crotch and cotton knit crotch, as in Step 1. Pin in place, matching notch points, and stitch the front seam line.

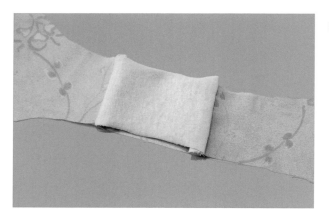

Step 3
- Pull the brief to the right side through the leg opening and press both the front and back crotch seams.
- Finish the brief by using a French seam or a serger to stitch the side seams before attaching the elastic trim around the leg opening.

Elastic casings

This is a nice finish to the top of a pajama pant or brief. A casing can also be added to the back of a garment and elastic inserted to shape the back when the front is finished with a midriff or hip yoke.

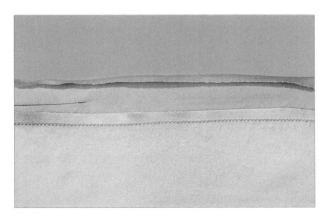

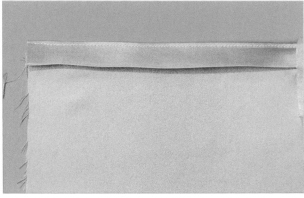

Step 1
- Cut a bias casing the required length, by the width of the elastic to be inserted plus ⅛in (3mm) ease and ⅜in (1cm) seam allowance down each side. Stitch the ends of the casing with right sides together, if it is going around the top of a pant or brief. Fold the seam allowances back onto the casing and press. With right sides together pin the casing to the back top edge of the garment and stitch in place.

Step 2
- Fold the casing to the right side of the garment, press, and edge stitch around/along the top of the casing, close to the edge.

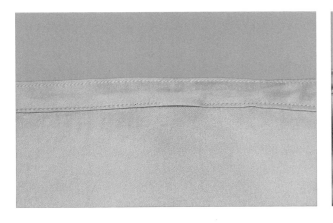

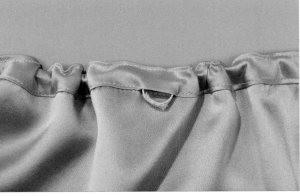

Step 3
- Pin the lower edge of the casing to the garment, making sure that it is laying flat and is not twisted. Stitch around the lower edge of the casing, leaving an opening through which to insert the elastic.

Step 4
- Insert the elastic into the casing using a bodkin. Stitch the ends of the elastic together before stitching the opening in the casing closed.

5

Designing and Pattern Drafting
Foundations

Like a building, at times clothing needs to be built over a frame or have a solid foundation. You might want to distort the body shape, for example, perhaps making the waist smaller or exaggerating the hips, which is when a framework comes in useful. A framework can also be used to give a gown an inner structure on which an outer silhouette can be balanced. Foundations that were once hidden under outer garments, worn by both men and women, have come to the surface and we also now see them as fashionable outerwear or accessory pieces.

It is the cut of the foundation and the correct placement of the boning that will give you the shape you desire. Extra control panels can also be added into foundations to both lift and shape. Hip panels can help give an hourglass silhouette, while extra bust panels can lift or flatten the bustline or help with the fit of a heavy bustline.

The design of the foundation will depend on how it is going to be used; as a support foundation hidden inside a garment, as underwear, or as outerwear. Fabric, length, shape, and strength will also be important factors to consider. Today's foundations are a mix of knitted fabrics, powernet, and woven fabrics, all of which can have differing amounts of stretch added with the inclusion of spandex (elastane) or Lycra® spun into the fiber. The choice of boning is also an important factor to consider; some boning is flexible in both directions and is, therefore, not strong enough if you want to lace a corset tightly – see Chapter 1, page 16, to learn more about the different types of boning available.

Jean Paul Gaultier is renowned for creating underwear as outerwear. Here a white satin bustier from his Spring/Summer 2001 couture collection shows the boning very clearly.

Foundation styles

5.1

5.2

Corset

A corset covers and shapes the torso, including the hips. It may or may not cover the breasts or have added hip panels. A corset usually has lacing down the back and a busk opening in the front.

Basque

A basque will enhance the torso but will not shape the body in the same way as a corset. A basque has fewer bones than a corset and is made from a softer, thinner fabric. It will always have cups.

5.3

Bustier

A bustier covers the breasts but finishes at or just above the waistline, making it shorter than both a corset and a basque. A bustier may or may not have cups and will give more shape to the body than a basque. Open-ended zippers and lacing that can resemble corset lacing can be used as closures on a bustier.

5.1 / Corset (Jean Paul Gaultier Spring/Summer 2014).

5.2 / Basque.

5.3 / Bustier.

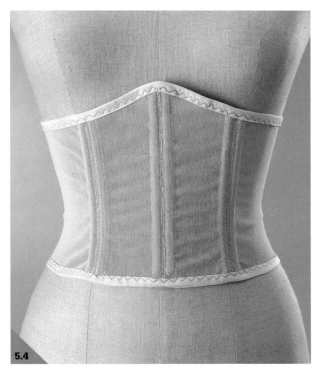

Waspie

A waspie is a wide belt worn around the waist to physically make the waist smaller. It is boned and may have a back-laced closure and a front busk opening. A waspie can also have panels of powernet fabric.

Pannier

A pannier sits on the hip, flattening out both the front and back of a skirt while fanning it out on the sides. The pannier was at its most extreme in the mid-eighteenth century, extending the skirt out several feet on each side, creating a curious, flat silhouette when worn with the high-waisted dresses of the era.

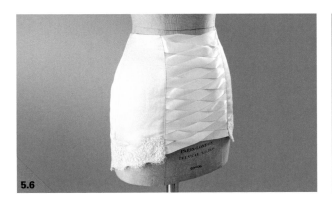

Girdle

The girdle is designed to enhance and control a woman's figure from the upper thighs to the waist; some styles incorporate a bra. These garments were considered essential by most women from the 1920s through to the 1960s. Today it can be seen worn as a dress.

Bustle

The bustle survived into the twentieth century as a skirt support to give the wearer the desired fuller shape below the waist at the back of a garment. Today, bustle foundations are found in bridal and evening wear.

5.4 / Waspie.

5.5 / Pannier (Jean Paul Gaultier 2013).

5.6 / Girdle.

5.7 / Bustle, circa 1875.

Four-panel princess line sloper

Because the princess line sloper (block) hugs the body it is the perfect style to use for many foundation garments, whether they are created as the inner support structure of a gown or as a standalone garment.

5.8

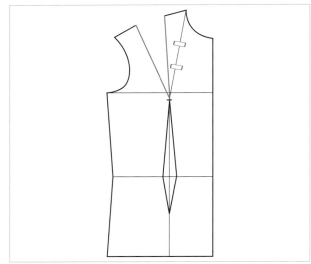

Step 1

- Place the close-fitting front and back slopers (see page 32) on a piece of paper with the side seams facing each other; trace around both slopers.
- Divide the front shoulder in half.
- Draw a line from this point down to the bustline; cut down the line.
- Close and tape the original shoulder dart together.

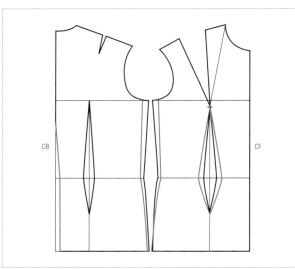

CB   CF

Step 2

- At both the front and back side seams measure in and mark ⅝in (1.5cm) at the underarm, ¼in (6mm) at the waistline, and ⅛in (3mm) at the hipline.
- Draw a new side seam through these marks.
- At the waistline, measure in ⅜in (1cm) at the center back and mark.
- Draw in a new center back line from the mark straight down to the hipline, curving back out from the waistline to the center back line approximately midway between the waistline and underarm line.
- At the waistline measure out ⅜in (1cm) on both sides of the front waist dart and redraw the dart up to the original end point and down to the original end points.

5.8 / Princess line corset featuring rather dangerous-looking studs.

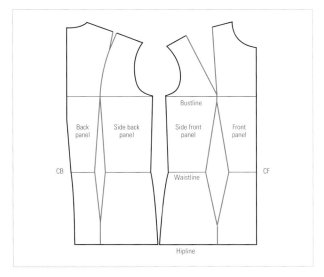

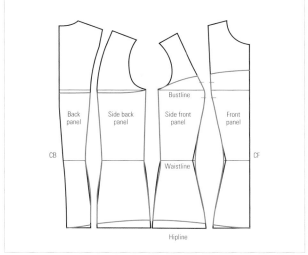

Step 3

- Separate the center front from the side front by cutting down the line forming the front leg of the shoulder dart and down the front side of the waist dart to the hipline; mark as the front panel.
- Cut away the remaining darts on the side front panel.
- Repeat on the back by cutting down the line forming the back leg of the shoulder dart, following a curved line down to the top of the back waist dart, then along the back of the waist dart to the hipline; mark as the back panel.
- Cut away the remaining darts on the side back panel.
- This gives you a basic four-panel princess line sloper.

Step 4

- Trace around all four panels onto paper. For a princess line foundation sloper draw in the shape of the neckline from center front across to center back.
- Draw in the hemline shape from center front across to center back to curve and fit comfortably on the hips.
- Mark in notch points 1½–2in (3.8–5cm) above and below the bust apex on both the side front and front panels.
- Round out the darts at the waistline on the front and back panels.

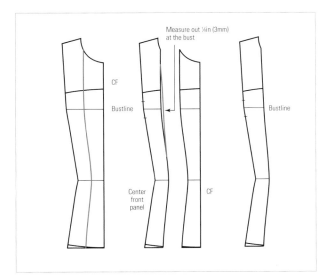

Step 5

- For a larger bust divide the front panel into two from a midway point on the neckline down to the hemline, following the shape of the princess seam line.
- On this new center front panel, measure out ⅛in (3mm) at the bustline and reshape the panel following the line of the original panel. Splitting the front panel also helps to separate the breasts.

Reshaping the panels for a close-fitting garment

The panels can be reshaped to follow the curve of the rib cage, which gives an even closer-fitting garment. The panels can also be reshaped for different effects, such as flattening the bust or adding shape to the hips.

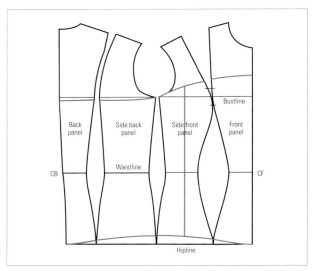

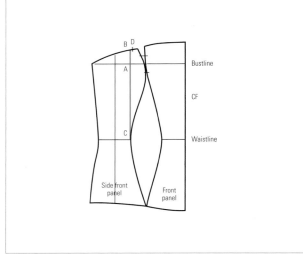

Step 1

- Trace around all four princess line sloper panels. Tape the side back panel to the side front panel at the top and bottom of the side seam; tape the front panel to the side front panel at the bustline and lower edge; tape the back panel at the top and bottom to the side back panel.
- Divide the side front panel in two with a line from the neckline or top edge down to the hemline.
- Cut away the pattern above the neck and below the hemline.

Step 2

- From the outside of the front waist dart draw a line up from the waistline on the side front panel; mark as A where it crosses the bustline, B at the top or neckline, and C on the waistline.
- Measure the width of the dart created between front panel and side front panel at the neckline or top edge.
- Measure this distance over from B toward the center front on the neckline or top edge; make a mark and label as D.

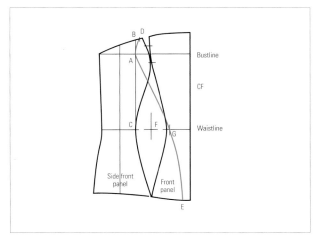

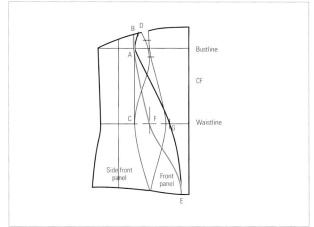

Step 3

- Measure the width of the dart between the front and side front panels at the waistline.
- Divide this measurement in half and mark as F.
- Measure in ¼in (6mm) on the front panel at the waistline; mark as G.
- With a curved ruler redraw the side of the front panel starting at D, through to the bustline at A, and then reversing the curve down to G.
- At the hemline measure across approximately 1in (2.5cm) from the center front; mark as E.
- Using a curved ruler draw a line from E up to the waistline at G. This creates a new front panel.

Step 4

- Using a curved ruler draw a line down from B to F, gradually reversing the curve and continuing down toward E.

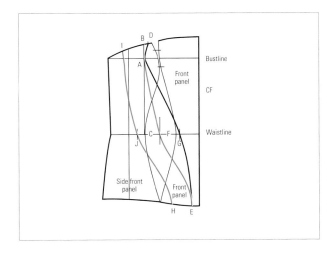

Step 5

- At the top of the line dividing the side front panel in two that you drew in Step 1, measure back 1in (2.5cm) toward the underarm; mark as I.
- From C at the waistline measure across ½in (1.3cm) toward the side seam; mark as J.
- From E on the hemline, measure approximately 1½in (3.8cm) toward the side front panel; mark as H.
- Using a curved ruler, connect I to J, then reverse the curve and continue to H. This creates the new middle front panel.

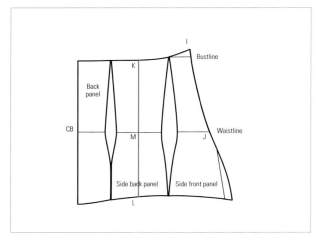

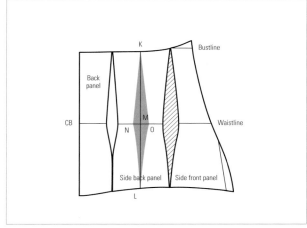

Step 6

- Retape the old side front panel to the side back panel so they lie flat; a dart or gap will form on the side seam at the waistline.
- Draw a line dividing the side back panel in half; mark the top of this line as K, M on the waistline, and L on the hemline. This creates a side back panel and a new middle back panel.

Step 7

- Measure the width of the gap between the side back panel and the side front panel at the waistline.
- Divide this measurement in half and mark this distance on either side of M; label the mark on the center back side as N and the mark on the center front side as O. This transfers the dart from between the side front and side back panels to the middle of the side back panel.
- Draw a line from K to N to L and K to O to L to create the new dart.

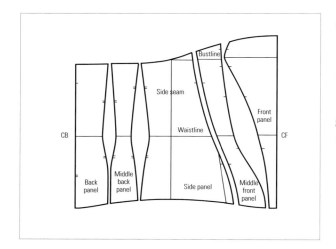

Step 8

- Relabel the panels as back panel, middle back panel, side panel, middle front panel, and front panel.
- Mark notch points on each panel before cutting the panels apart.

Step 9

- Retrace the panel pieces onto paper, adding seam allowances.

Manipulating the sloper to add both bust and hip panels

In the 1900s, or Belle Époque, women distorted their bodies into the fashionable "S" bend shape. This corset, based on a design from that era, can be laced tightly to give a smaller waistline, while the hips can be exaggerated with frills or by creative pattern cutting.

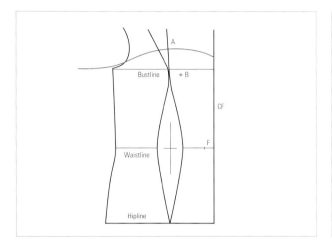

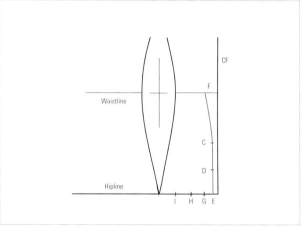

Step 1

- Align the four pieces of the princess line sloper (see page 129) so the pieces touch at the neckline and hipline. Trace the pieces onto a piece of paper.
- Draw in the shape of the neckline, beginning at the center front and finishing at the center back. Add more shape at the center front to create a heart-shaped neckline if desired; mark the top of the dart on the center front panel as A.
- Measure across 2¾in (7cm) from the center front line toward the bustline; mark as B.
- Measure in 1⅛in (3cm) from the center front line at the waistline; mark as F.

Step 2

- Divide the measurement from waistline to hipline in half; at this halfway point, measure in ⅜in (1cm) from the center front line; mark as C.
- Repeat this measurement on the hipline; mark as E.
- Measure across ⅝in (1.5cm) from E toward the side seam; mark as G.
- Measure across from G a further ¾in (2cm); mark as H.
- Measure across from H a further ⅞in (2.2cm); mark as I.
- Make a mark halfway between C and E; mark as D.
- Using a curved ruler, draw a line from F to C continuing with a straight line that passes through D to E.

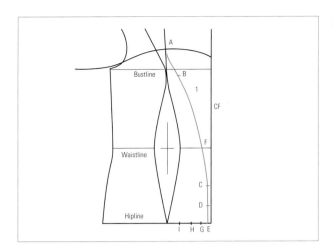

Step 3

- Using a curved ruler, draw a line from A to B, then gently reverse the curve through B to meet the top of the line you drew in Step 2 at F.
- Label this as Panel 1.

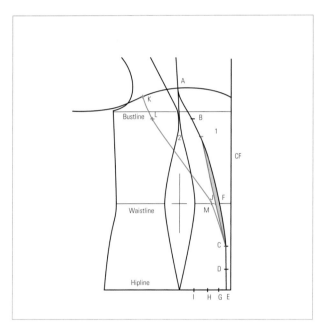

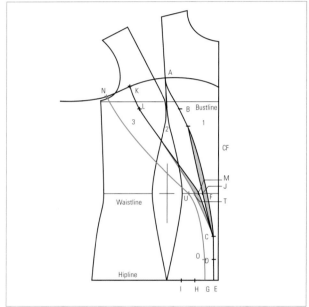

Step 4

- Measure across 2in (5cm) from the bustline toward the underarm; mark as L.
- Measure across 2¾in (7cm) on the neckline of the side front panel; mark as K.
- Measure in ¼in (6mm) from F on the waistline; mark as J.
- Measure in from J a further ⅝in (1.5cm); mark as M.
- Measure 1in (2.5cm) down the line from B and make a mark; from this mark draw a line that passes through J to C. This will form a dart.
- Using a curved ruler, draw a line from K to L, then gradually reverse the curve to continue down through M to C. This will form the second front panel that will shape the bust. Label this as Panel 2.

Step 5

- On the neckline measure across 2⅜in (6cm) from K toward the side seam; mark as N.
- At the waistline measure across ¼in (6mm) from M toward the side seam; mark as T.
- From T draw a straight line up to touch the line from K to M and down to C to form a dart.
- From T measure across ¾in (2cm) toward the side seam; mark as U.
- From D measure across ¾in (2cm) toward the side seam; mark as O.
- Using a curved ruler draw a line down from N to U and then gently reverse the curve continuing down through O and finishing at G. Label this as Panel 3.

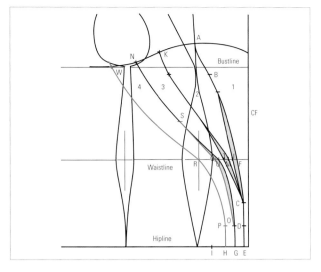

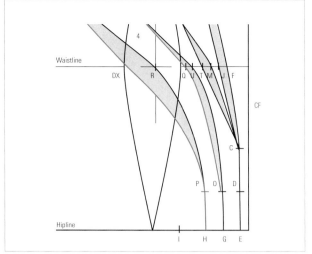

Step 6

- On the neckline measure across 2⅜in (6cm) from N; mark as W.
- Measure across ⅜in (1cm) from U toward the side seam; mark as Q.
- From U measure up 4⅝in (11.8cm) along the side of Panel 3; mark as S.
- Draw a line from S passing through Q to O; this will form a dart.

- From Q measure across ¾in (2cm); mark as R.
- From O measure across ¾in (2cm); mark as P.
- Using a curved ruler draw a line down from W to R and then reverse the curve, continuing down through P to H.
- Mark the side front panel at the waistline DX.
- Using a curved ruler, draw a line from W to DX and then reverse the curve down through P and H. Label this as Panel 4.

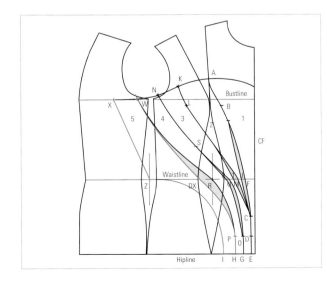

Step 7

- From W measure across 2in (5cm); mark as X.
- Divide the gap between the side front and back panels of the original slopers in half at the waistline; mark as Z.
- Draw a straight line from X to Z.
- Using a curved ruler, draw a convex curve from Z to I. Label this as Panel 5.

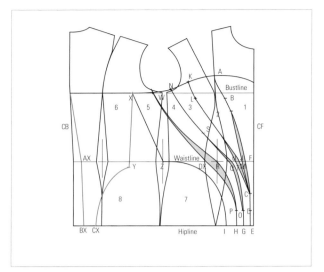

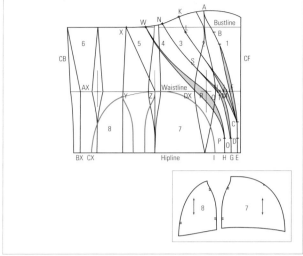

Step 8

- Shape the center back panel; at the center back waistline measure in the width of the gap between center back and side back panels on the slopers and mark as AX; it should be approximately 1in (2.5cm).
- Measure across 3⅜in (8.5cm) from AX along the waistline toward the side seam and mark.
- Draw a line from X the same length as the line X–Z, passing through the waistline; mark as Y.
- Measure ¾in (2cm) across the hipline from the center back line; mark as BX.
- From BX measure across a further 1⅝in (4cm); mark as CX. Using a curved ruler draw a convex curve from CX to Y. Label this as Panel 6. Label the center back line.

Step 9

- Draw a curved line from Z down to the hipline that follows the shape of the side seam on the side front panel. Draw a curved line down from Y that follows the shape of the side seam of the side back panel to finish the front and back hip yokes; mark as Panels 7 and 8.

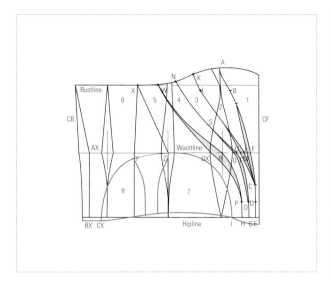

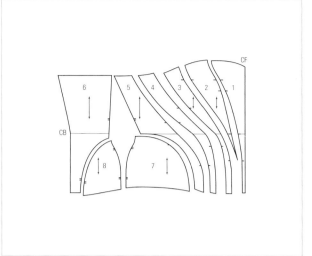

Step 10

- You can shape these lines if you want a fuller hip yoke that stands away from the body.
- Shape the hemline. At the center front measure ⅜in (1cm) down from the hipline and mark.
- From the hipline measure up ⅜in (1cm) on the line up to Z and mark.
- Measure down from Y the length of the new line from Z and mark.
- At the center back measure down ¼in (6mm) and mark.
- Using a curved ruler, draw a line connecting all the marks to create the new hemline.

Step 11

- Mark notch points and grainlines on each panel.
- Cut the panels apart and redraw, adding seam allowances.
- Retrace the panel pieces onto paper, including the seam allowances.

A corset with shoulders

Corsets, basques, and bustiers are not always strapless. Having a shoulder means you can now add a cap sleeve, or one that extends longer. It also means you can add a collar, which will give the corset the tailored look of a jacket.

Even adding just a shoulder strap gives you more design and embellishment options. Adding a shoulder to a modern corset takes it from being an undergarment to being an amazing outer garment.

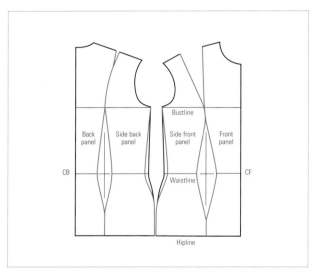

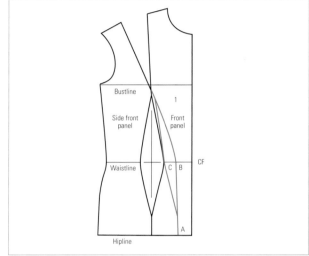

Step 1

- Use the close-fitting sloper from Chapter 2, page 32.
- Reshape the darts as shown in Step 2, page 128, but do not reshape the side seams.
- At the waistline measure in ⅜in (1cm) on each side seam and mark.
- Redraw the side seam, curving it in to the mark on the waistline and rounding back out for the hips. This will give you the hourglass silhouette of Christian Dior's New Look.
- Divide the sloper into four panels.

Step 2

- On the hipline, measure across 1⅝in (4cm) from the center front line; mark as A.
- On the waistline measure in 1⅝in (4cm) from the center front line; mark as B.
- Draw a line connecting A to B and continue up to the end of the shoulder dart, making sure you have a smooth line from the shoulder to the hipline.
- Measure the width of the gap between the front and side front panels.
- Measure across from B one third of this measurement toward the side seam; mark as C.
- Draw in a dart that starts at the same level as the top of the gap, down through C, to finish level with the end of the gap. Label this as Panel 1.

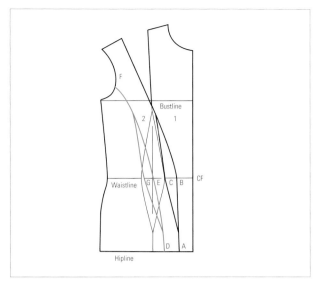

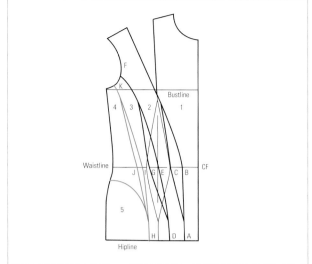

Step 3

- From A measure across ¾in (2cm) toward the side seam; mark as D.
- From C measure across ¾in (2cm); mark as E.
- From E measure across one third of the width of the gap between the front and side panels; mark as G.
- Measure 3⅜in (8.5cm) from the underarm point around the front armhole; mark as F.
- Using a curved ruler draw a line from E down to D.
- Draw in a dart starting at the same level as the top of the gap, passing through G and finishing level with the end of the gap. Label this as Panel 2.

Step 4

- Divide the underarm from F to the side seam in half; mark as K.
- From G measure across 1⅛in (3cm); mark as I.
- From I measure across one third of the width of the gap between the front and side panels; mark as J.
- From D measure across 1⅛in (3cm); mark as H.
- Using a curved ruler, draw a line from I to H.
- Draw in a dart starting at the same level as the top of the gap, passing through J and finishing level with the end of the gap. Label these as Panels 3 and 4.
- Using a curved ruler draw a line from the side seam to join the line from J at the end of the gap to create the hip panel. Label this as Panel 5. If you want to extend and exaggerate the hip further then you will need to adjust the hip panel as a separate pattern piece.

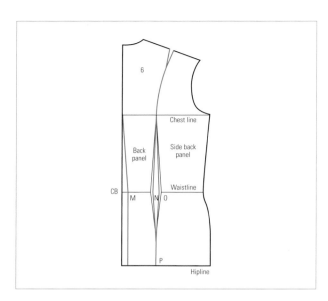

Step 5

- Measure the width of the gap between the back and side back panels at the waistline.
- On the waistline of the back panel measure in half this distance; mark as M.
- Draw a line from the center back line at the chest line down to M.
- Square a line down from M to the hipline.
- On the waistline at the gap between the back and side back panels, add one quarter of the measurement of the original gap to both sides; mark this on the back panel as N and on the side back panel as O.
- Draw a line down from the bottom of the gap between the two panels to the hipline and label the end as P.
- Draw a line from the end of the back shoulder dart, passing through N down to P.
- Draw a line from the end of the back shoulder dart, passing through O down to P. Label this back panel as Panel 6.

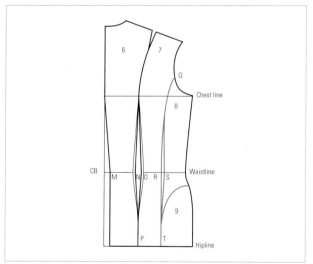

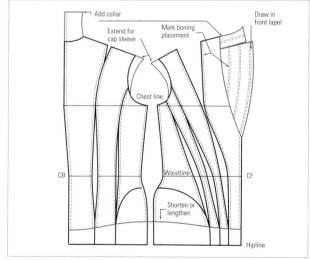

Step 6

- On the waistline, measure the distance from the side seam to O.
- Divide the measurement in half; mark as S.
- From S measure in ⅜in (1cm); mark as R.
- Divide the back armhole measurement in half; mark as Q.
- From R draw a line down to the hipline; mark as T.
- Using a curved ruler draw a line connecting Q with R to T and Q with S to T. Label these new panels as Panels 7 and 8.

- Draw in the optional back hip panel from T around to the side at the same height as the front hip panel. Label it as Panel 9.

This gives you a tight-fitting corset with shoulders. You can then shorten the length, and add cap sleeves, a collar, and a front lapel.

A corset made with an off-the-shoulder neckline, with or without a sleeve

This corset can be worn as outerwear or as the foundation for a gown. Taking away the shoulder and extending the center front panel into a band that sits around the top of the arm gives a very pretty neckline, framing the shoulders. The corset sloper in the following instructions has been changed into a bustier, but the choice of length is optional.

Begin by tracing off the pattern opposite onto paper, aligned so all the panels are touching.

5.9

5.9 / Corset with an off-the-shoulder neckline (Christian Lacroix Autumn/Winter 2002).

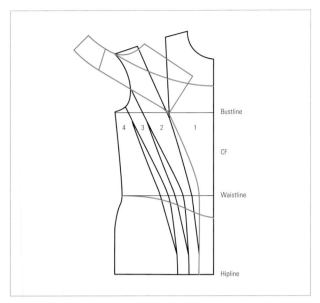

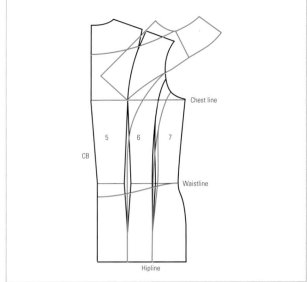

Step 1

- Cut across the bustline of the center front panel from the center front line to within approximately ⅛in (3mm) of the edge.
- Manipulate the piece until the neckline touches the shoulder point of Panel 2.
- Extend the line from the shoulder point half the width of the front sleeve head.
- Draw in the curved neckline from the extended shoulder, extending the center front line up to meet the neckline.
- Decide the width of the shoulder band and square down a line from the extended shoulder point. Using a curved ruler, draw a line that joins the side of the center front panel. Label this as Panel 1.
- Decide the length of the corset and draw in the hemline.

Step 2

- On the center back panel cut across the chest line to within approximately ⅛in (3mm) of the edge.
- Manipulate the top piece until the side of the panel is sitting along the top of Panel 6.
- Extend a line out from the top of the neckline half the width of the back sleeve head.
- Draw in the curved back neckline and redraw the center back line up to meet the neckline.
- Draw a curved line up from the waistline to join the line at the top of Panel 6.
- Draw a line the width of the shoulder band down from the extended shoulder point and draw in the underside of the band back to the top of Panel 6.
- Divide the measurement of the armhole from Panel 6 to the underarm point in half and mark.
- Divide the waistline in half between Panels 6 and 7 and mark.
- Draw a curved line from the mark at the armhole to pass through the mark on the waistline and continue down to the hipline between Panels 6 and 7.
- Move the dart onto the outer side of this line.
- Draw in the hemline so it matches the front at the side of Panel 7.

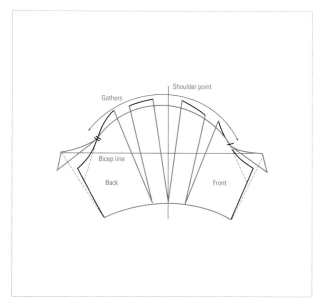

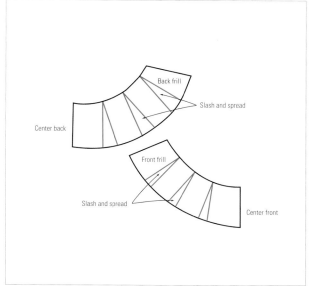

Step 3

- If you are adding a sleeve and want a full sleeve head like that shown in the photograph on page 141, begin by tracing around the sleeve sloper in Chapter 3 (see page 67).
- Decide the length of the sleeve and cut the sleeve out.
- Divide the sleeve head in half between the front notch point and the shoulder point and draw a line down to the hem. Repeat from the back notch point. Draw a line down from the shoulder point to the hem. The sleeve head is now divided into four.
- Slash down the three lines from the sleeve head to approximately ⅛in (3mm) from the hem.
- Draw a vertical line on another piece of paper and add a bicep line at right angles. Position the slashed sleeve on top of the cross shape so that the center and the bicep lines are aligned.
- Open and spread the slashes an equal amount and tape in place.
- Make a slash on either side of the sleeve from a point just beneath the armhole up to the notch points on the sleeve head; open until the curve of the underarm touches the bicep line; tape in place.
- Lower the top of the sleeve head by half the width of the shoulder band and draw in the new sleeve head.
- Redraw the sides of the sleeve and the curved hemline.

Step 4

- If you would like to finish the lower edge of the corset with a frill, copy the shape of the lower edge of both the front and back panels onto paper.
- Decide the length of the frill, draw it in and cut it out.
- Slash and spread the lower edge to the required fullness.
- Tape onto paper and trace around the shapes.
- Mark in all notch points, grainlines, boning placement lines, and seam allowances.

A corset lengthened into a dress

The corset can be lengthened into a dress by extending from the hipline to the desired hem length, or by attaching a skirt to the lower edge.

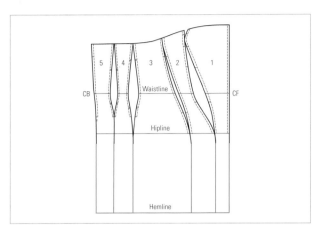

5.10

Step 1

- Trace off the corset sloper from page 132.
- Redraw the hipline.
- Lengthen the center front line from the hipline down to the desired skirt length. Draw a line down from the side hipline the same length as the center front line.
- Square a line across the front panels to the center front line. Label as the hemline. Repeat on the back panels.

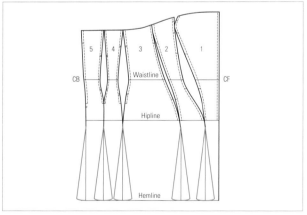

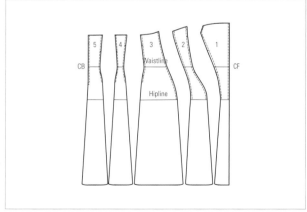

Step 2

- Add fullness to the hemline by marking an equal distance out on each side of each panel; keep all distances equal so they remain balanced.
- Draw a line from the hipline on each panel down to the hemline and mark.
- Mark and redraw the hemline for each panel.

- Mark all notch points, and add seam allowances and boning placement lines to each panel; cut out the pattern pieces.

5.10 / Corset lengthened into a dress (John Richmond, Spring/Summer 2007).

A corset with a crotch

A corset can be made with a crotch; the crotch line can be a thong or follow the crotch line of a full brief. The center of the crotch on a corset can be made to open and is usually finished with snaps.

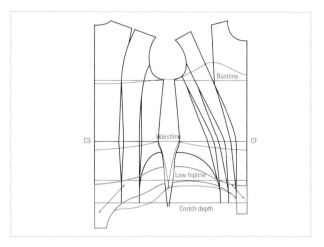

5.11

Step 1

- Trace off your choice of corset sloper, redrawing the hipline if necessary.
- Decide on the crotch you want to add. Using that sloper from Chapter 2 (see pages 39–45), place the lower hipline of the brief sloper on the hipline of the corset, matching center front and back lines. Because of the shape of the corset panels the brief sloper may not extend across to the side panel. If this is the case, draw in the difference.
- Trace around the brief slopers from the hipline.

Step 2

- Reshape the front and back leg and crotch at this point, if required, and cut the pattern piece apart, keeping the original hemline of the corset.
- Retrace the pattern pieces onto paper, adding seam allowances, notch points, boning placement lines, and labeling all pattern pieces.

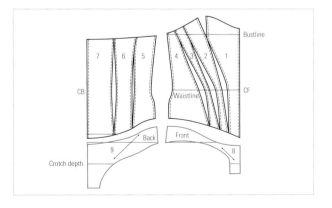

5.11 / Corset with a crotch (Jean Paul Gaultier, Spring/Summer 2010).

Boning placement

There is no right or wrong way to place boning; ultimately where you place it will depend on the cut of your corset or foundation.

If you are making an historic garment, then you need to bone in line with images of corsets from the era. If you are working with a fashion-forward design, then try different placements on the muslin (toile) and make the final decision at the fitting. The boning placement can be changed to help push the breasts up and forward, balance a heavy skirt, or help to hold the volume. Boning can also be added to a sleeve or collar. Curving the boning placement lines forward toward the center front gives the illusion of slimming the waistline and creates a garment that is comfortable to wear.

You can also consider adding close rows of cording (see pages 166–68). The cording can be placed horizontally or on an angle to form a zigzag pattern, which can look decorative while also adding structure to your garment. Cording is a good way to add support to the top of the back panel when it is set at an angle between the boning, or to help hold the shape of the body in the underarm area. Rows of cording can also be used curving across a deep front neckline with shoulder straps, or where the garment has a shoulder, eliminating the need to add boning in this area.

The quickest and easiest bone placement is to add ¼in (6mm)-wide boning on either side of every seam on a multipaneled corset. If you are lacing down the center back, add boning on both sides of the eyelet placement. The seam allowances will become your boning casings and you will only have to add one casing for the boning on the inner side of the eyelets. Remember that if the cut and fit of the garment you are boning is wrong, no amount of added boning or cording will help.

Marking the boning on the pattern pieces

All the boning channel lines and cording lines have to be transferred to the fabric. To do this, carefully run a needle point tracing wheel along all the boning channel placement lines, using a curved ruler for accuracy. If you place the pattern piece on a padded surface before you start you will be less likely to tear the paper.

Pin the pattern pieces onto your choice of fabric, coutil, or cotton canvas and rub chalk over the paper pattern pieces. The chalk should go through the needle holes and transfer all the markings to the fabric.

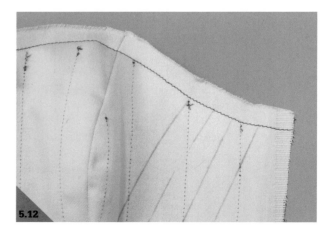

5.12 / Boning from the inside.

5.12

Waspies

The waspie was the fashionable undergarment to wear under Christian Dior's New Look of 1947; it can take inches off the waist.

Today the waspie is still seen on the catwalks, but now it is worn as a wide belt over garments instead of under. Essentially, the waspie is a wide belt that begins under the bustline and finishes at the high hipline, and may or may not have garters (suspenders) attached to its lower edge. A waspie can have a front opening, be laced down the center back, or can be closed by a combination of the two. The panels can be made from powernet and woven fabric, with boning placed down either side of the panel seaming.

- Trace off the basic four-panel princess line sloper (see page 129) onto paper, from the bustline to the hipline.
- Draw in the shape for the top of your waspie; this can be shaped up at the center front to finish on the bustline, or it can be straight.
- Draw in the hemline, remembering that a waspie should be approximately 5–6in (12.5–15cm) wide, usually finishing above or at the high hip.
- Draw lines to divide the side front and side back panels in half.
- Evenly distribute the amount of stretch from your powernet fabric at the waistline on either side of each line.
- If your center back will have a laced closure, measure in ⅜in (1cm) at the center back waistline and make a mark.
- Draw a line from the top of your waspie down to the hemline that connects to this mark.
- Mark in the boning placement lines, eyelets if using, and all seam allowances.

5.13

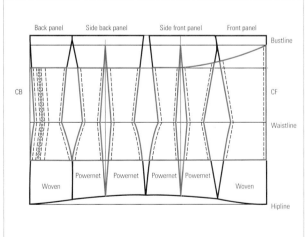

5.13 / Waspie (Christian Dior Fall/Winter 2009).

Girdles

There was a time when every woman wore a girdle to slim and elongate the body. Some girdles include a built-in bra and shoulder straps, while others start at the waistline.

5.14

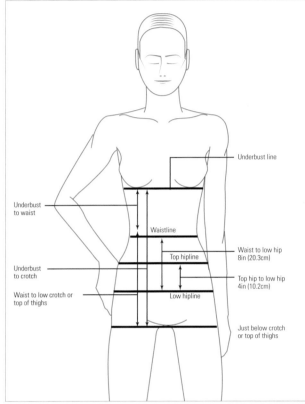

A closure can be added to the front, back, or side panel in the form of a zipper or hooks and eyes. The girdle can be stepped into and pulled up the body, hence the nickname "roll-ons". A girdle is created with panels of strong powernet for most of its figure-shaping body panels, and can have a woven fabric center front panel that may or may not have boning. Garters sewn onto the hemline to hold up stockings are now optional or made so that they can be removed. Today the girdle has become outerwear, when lengthened into a fashionable form-fitting dress.

The full girdle

Before you can start to draft the pattern you will need to calculate the amount of stretch in both the weft and the warp of your powernet (see page 17). You are also going to draft a bra cup and both the front and back full bra band (see pages 213–15).

Step 1

- Measure the body but do not add any ease. It is best to take these measurements over a tight-fitting garment with side seams because you are going to measure across the front from side seam to side seam and then repeat on the back.
- The measurements shown opposite give the calculations needed if the amount of stretch found in the powernet is 1in (2.5cm) starting with an 8in (20cm) unstretched square = approximately 0.8, so 0.8 will be the amount deducted from around the body on the pattern pieces.

5.14 / Girdle with diamond-shaped panel, 1955.

Body measurements

| Waist | 28in (71cm) |
| | Less 0.8 x 28in = 22.4in (0.8 x 71cm = 56.8cm) |

| Top hip | 36in (91.4cm) |
| | Less 0.8 x 36in = 28.8in (0.8 x 91.4 = 73.1cm) |

| Lower hip | 38in (96.5cm) |
| | Less 0.8 x 38in = 30.4in (0.8 x 96.5cm = 77.2cm) |

| Underbust | 31in (78.7cm) |
| | Less 0.8 x 31in = 24.8in (0.8 x 78.7cm = 63cm) |

Front (half the round-the-body measurement)

| Waist | 14in (35.6cm) |
| | Less stretch = 11.2in (28.4cm) |

| Top hip | 18in (45.7cm) |
| | Less stretch = 14.4in (36.6cm) |

| Lower hip | 19in (48.3cm) |
| | Less stretch = 15.2in (38.6cm) |

| Underbust | 15.5in (39.4cm) |
| | Less stretch = 12.4in (31.5cm) |

When the across the front and back waist, top, and lower hip measurements are added together, they should be the same as your first three full-body measurements (waist, top hip, and lower hip).
Now measure the lower crotch or top of thighs
35in (89cm)
Less stretch = 0.8 x 35in = 28in (71cm)
Divide this measurement in half = 14in (35.5cm).
Divide in half again = 7in (17.5cm).

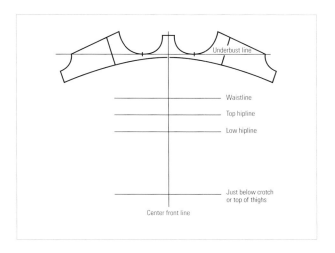

Step 2

- Draw a line down the center of a piece of paper with enough room on either side to accommodate both the front and back bra band; this is your center front line.
- Match the center line of the front bra band to the top of this line and trace around the pattern for the front bra band.
- Match the side seams of the front bra band to those of the back bra band and trace around the back band.
- Draw the underbust line through the notch or balance points at the bottom of the cups.
- Measure down from the underbust line to the waist, mark, draw a horizontal line through the center line, and label it as the waistline.
- Measure 8in (20cm) down from the waist to the lower hip and mark; draw a horizontal line at this point through the center line and label it as the low hipline.
- Halfway between the waist and the low hipline draw a horizontal line across the center line; label as the top hipline.
- Measure down from the under bustline to the lower crotch and mark; draw a horizontal line through the center front line and label it as the lower crotch or top of the thighs.

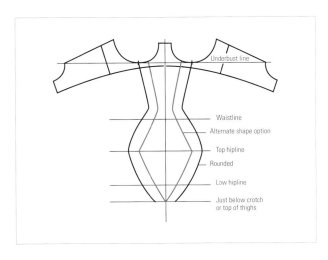

Step 3

- Draw in the shape of the non-stretch front control panel; this can be curved. Starting at the cup notches or balance points, or at either side of the bra bridge, draw two lines down toward the waistline, shaping out with a straight line to the top hipline, and then back toward the center line at the crotch to form a diamond shape over the tummy.

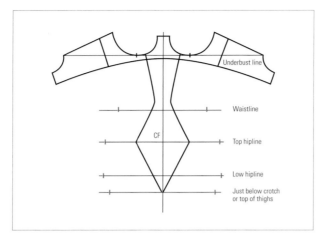

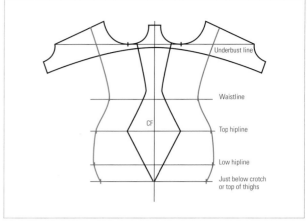

Step 4

- At the center front waistline measure out one half the front waist measurement on each side and mark.
- At the center front top hipline measure out half the front top hip measurement on each side and mark.
- At the center front low hipline measure out half the front lower hip measurement on each side and mark.
- At the center front lower crotch line measure out half the crotch line measurement on each side and mark.

Step 5

- Using a curved ruler draw in the side seams through all the marks from the top of the band down to the lower crotch line.

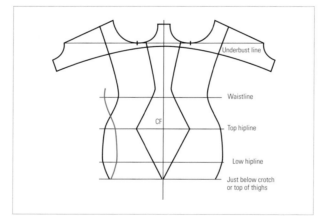

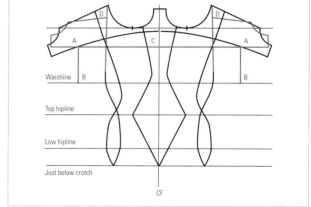

Step 6

- Copy the shape of the side seam from waistline down to the crotch line from the opposite front side seam, to check the two sides match perfectly.
- Use this to draw in the back side seam from the crotch line up to the waistline.

Step 7

- Mark A halfway along the back band lower edge on each side. Draw a line from A straight down to the waistline; mark as B.
- Measure A–B; mark this measurement up from the waistline on the center front line; mark as C.
- Draw a horizontal line from C to pass through A.
- Redraw the back bra band so the bottom sits on this line with side seams matching. Mark the top as D.
- From D draw a line to the new lower band line and down to the waistline, curving it out to connect to the side seam line drawn in Step 6.

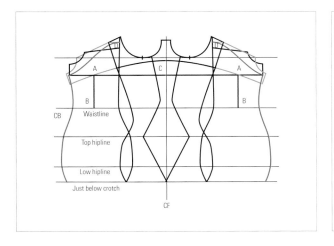

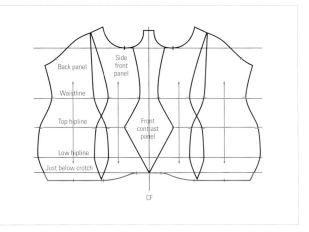

Step 8

- Reshape the top of the back neckline so it connects to the top of the front bra band at the side seam.
- From the back side seam measure across half the waist measurement at the waistline and mark.
- From the back side seam measure across half the top hip measurement at the top hipline and mark.
- From the back side seam measure across half the lower hip measurement at the lower hipline and mark.
- From the back side seam measure across half the crotch measurement at the crotch line and mark.
- Using a curved ruler draw a line down that connects all the marks and label as the center back.

Step 9

- If you are attaching straps, mark in the back strap placement. You can find this point by copying it off the back bra band.
- Shape the hemline of the girdle so it is shorter in the front and curves down to the side seam and across to the center back. The length of the girdle at the back is optional, but you want it to sit under the bottom.
- Divide the back and front girdle hemline in half and mark the garter placement points. You can add a third garter placement just forward of the front side seam – or as many as you like, as long as they are all evenly spaced.

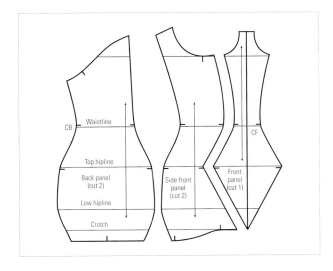

Step 10

- Finish your draft by tracing out the pattern pieces, adding all notch points and seam allowances, labeling the pattern pieces, and marking the grainline before cutting out. Finally, make a draft of the three-piece bra cups (see page 194) in the correct size to fit into the front band used in Step 2.

High-waisted girdle with a front control panel and lace inset down both sides

A girdle can finish under the bustline so that it smooths the midriff area as well as the waist and hips. It can also be closed with a zipper at the side seam. The center front control panel can be decorated with ribbon, which can give added support, and edged with inset lace and fagoting.

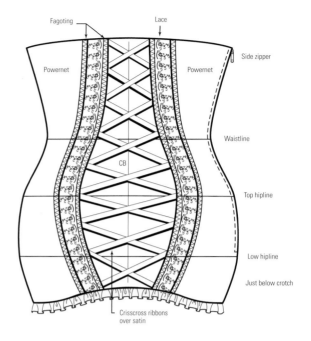

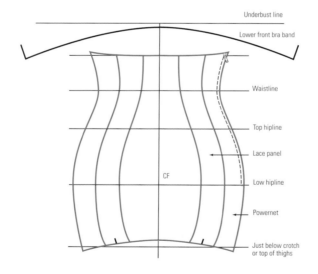

- Trace around the full girdle sloper (see Step 9 on page 151) onto paper.
- Redraw the bottom edge of the front bra band and extend this line out on both sides to the center back line; this will act as a guideline. The top of the girdle can be as high as the bottom edge of the bra band, or you can decide to lower the top edge of the girdle down 2–3in (5–7.5cm) from the bottom edge of the bra band.
- Shape the hemline, making allowance for a ruffle or lace if used.
- Draw in the shape of the front control panel; draw in the width of the lace insets, remembering to allow for the width of the fagoting if used.
- Mark in the zipper placement from the top line down to the low hipline on the left side.
- Mark in the garter placements and ribbon decoration.
- Label all the pattern pieces and mark all notch points and seam allowances.

A roll-on to the waistline with elastic inserts

Elastic inserts can be added at the hemline of the girdle to add comfort when sitting and walking, especially if it is cut to sit low on the top of the thigh.

Follow the directions for the full girdle (see pages 148–51) from the waist down to the crotch. Decide on the shape of the center control panel and draw it in.

- Measure across 2–2½in (5–6.5cm) on the side front panel hemline, the width of the elastic insert, and make a mark.
- Draw a curved line out from the low hipline down to the mark on the hemline.
- Trace off the elastic insert pattern piece.
- Add seam allowances to the side front panel.

- Alternatively, add the elastic insert to the bottom of the front panel. The elastic insert in the front panel can be cut higher and to the width of the whole panel if you are intending to make the girdle into a longer garment, or even a skirt. Follow the instructions for inserting the elastic into the bottom of the front side panels.

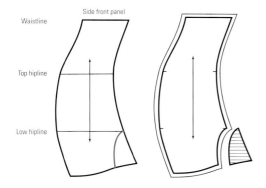
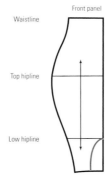
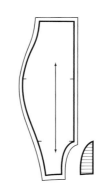

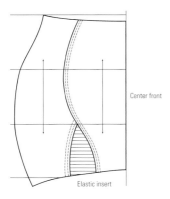
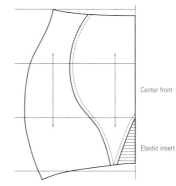

Adding boning placement lines to a girdle

Boning can be added to the center front control panel of a girdle for more structured support. Since the 1950s, however, girdles have become more sophisticated as more high-tech stretch fabrics have become available, replacing the need for boning.

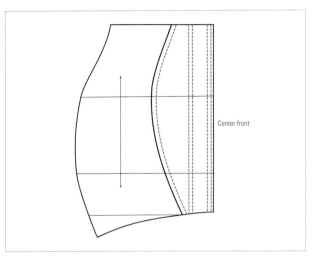

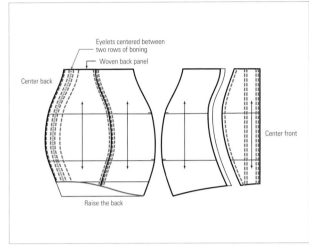

Step 1

- Taking the full girdle pattern (see page 151) draw a line down the center front from the neckline or bra cup, depending on the shape of the front panel, or from the waistline. If you are creating a roll-on, draw a line ⅜in (1cm) out on either side of this center front line.
- Divide the front panel in half on both sides of the center front line and draw a further parallel line down the length of the panel at this point.
- Measure across ⅜in (1cm) from this line and draw in a second parallel line.
- Depending on the shape of the panel, a third boning placement can be added into the seam allowance where the front panel attaches to the side front panel.

Step 2

- For added control, the back panel of the girdle may be made from a woven fabric and have a laced back closure. For comfort, shorten the back at the hemline and add boning on either side of the eyelets.

Adding control panels

Girdles can have added control panels to give additional control at the waistline. These panels crisscross the front panel for extra firm control in the tummy area and to lift the bottom. They are made from powernet as an extra panel layer, or as a band that wraps completely around the body or body part to reshape or control the figure. These control bands are added in addition to the woven boned front and back panels on all-over stretch roll-ons. If a control panel is added to the front of a garment only, and does not continue around to the garment back, the front band will distort the garment back by stretching and pulling it around to the front, removing the extra added support.

- On the side front panel make a mark halfway between the waistline and the underbust line.
- Measure up 2in (5cm) from the side front top hipline and mark.
- On both the front and back side seams measure up 1⅝in (4cm) from the waistline and mark; measure down 2in (5cm) from the waistline on both the front and back side seams and mark.
- Measure up and down 3in (7.5cm) from the waistline on the center back and mark.
- Using a curved ruler, draw a line from the two marks above and below the waistline on the side front panel to the marks above and below the waistline on the side front panel side seam.

- Again using a curved ruler, draw a line from the marks on the back side seam to the marks on the center back above and below the waistline.
- Measure up 3in (7.5cm) from the low hipline on the front of the side front panel and mark; measure up 1in (2.5cm) from the just below crotch line and mark.
- Measure up 1in (2.5cm) from the just below crotch line at the side front panel side seam and mark; measure up 2in (5cm) from this mark and mark. Measure up ⅜in (1cm) from the just below crotch line, and down 1⅛in (3cm) on the center back line, and mark. Measure up 1in (2.5cm) from the just below the crotch line on the back side seam and mark; measure up another 2in (2.5cm) from this point and mark.
- Draw two curved lines from the two marks above and below the low hipline on the front of the side front panel, to the just below crotch line and the mark above this line at the front side seam.
- Draw two curved lines from marks above and below the just below crotch line on the center back, to the marks above the just above crotch line at the back side seam.
- Trace the new pattern pieces for the waist and hip control panel onto paper, joining the front and back pieces together at the side seam so there is one continuous pattern piece.

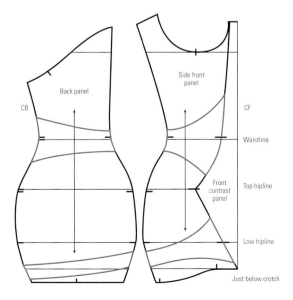

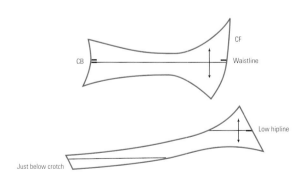

Designing a crinoline or cage

A crinoline or cage remains a popular choice of foundation to support a full-skirted gown. Unlike net petticoats (see pages 56–57), these have rows of boning that can be attached through both horizontal and vertical casings to give a caged effect.

The word crinoline originally described a mixed fabric made of stiff cotton, linen, and horse hair that first appeared around the 1830s and was used to make skirt supports. A hooped metal cage was introduced and patented in 1856 and was worn by women of every social standing. Designers today have taken the cage from under the skirt and designed it to be worn over a skirt to make a dramatic statement.

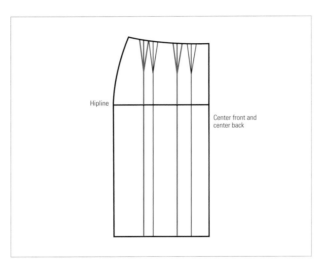

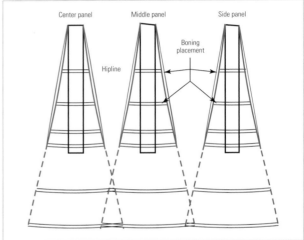

Step 1

- Trace around the close-fitting sloper from waist to hipline, extending the hemline as required. Draw two lines from waist to hemline to divide the front and back pattern pieces into three equal parts. Move the front darts to these lines to keep the waist shape. For an elasticized or drawstring waist, omit the dart shaping.
- Cut down each line to create six panels; three front and three back.

Step 2

- Depending on the required fullness of the crinoline at the hemline, divide the hemline measurement by 6, then again by 2, to find the amount of fullness to be added to each side of the panels. Mark this measurement out on either side of each panel. Draw a line from the waist to the hemline mark on each side of all panels. If less fullness is wanted at the hipline, shape the panels from the hipline down to the hemline only.
- Draw the first boning placement at the hipline, the second placement line approximately 10in (25cm) beneath, and a third boning placement line 10in (25cm) beneath that. Measure up 2in (5cm) from the third boning placement line and add another boning placement line for support in the knee area. Mark in the boning placement line at the hemline and measure up 10in (25cm) for the final boning placement line.

Designing a bustle

The bustle is still a popular choice of foundation to wear under the back skirt of a wedding gown.

As the hoop faded from fashion around the mid-1800s, the fabric from a full skirt began to be draped and bunched up at the back. To support all this fabric a foundation similar to a crinoline had to be worn, made from several layers of flounced horse hair canvas attached at the waist. The bustle became even bigger when straw-filled pillows separated by bands of steel were sewn into the back of skirts, lining them all the way down to the floor.

- To make a small bustle, measure across the center back petticoat panel at the waistline and double this measurement.
- Starting with the bottom layer, draw a rectangle 10in (25.5cm) deep by the doubled back panel measurement; round the sides at the bottom.
- Draw another layer 8in (20cm) deep and the same length as the bottom layer; again, round out the sides at the bottom edge.
- Continue to add layers, with each layer 2in (5cm) narrower than the last until the last layer is 2in (5cm) deep.
- Draw a waistband 1in (2.5cm) wide by the waist measurement plus 1in (2.5cm) for the fastening. Alternatively, the bustle can be attached to the back waistline of a petticoat.

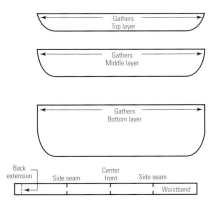

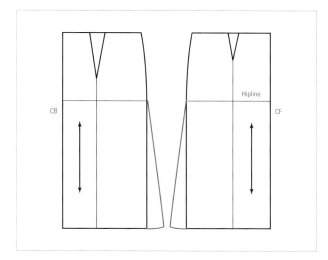

Step 1

- Trace around the close-fitting sloper from the waist to the hipline. Extend the front and back pattern pieces the required length; extend the hemline out 2in (5cm) or more from the side seam for fullness, and mark. Draw a line from the hipline to the hemline mark.
- Measure down the center front from the hipline to the hemline. Use this measurement to measure down the new side seam from the hipline, and mark.
- Reshape the hemline from the center front to this new mark on the side seam.

Bustle for a train

For a foundation bustle that also supports the train of a gown, the back of the petticoat has to be extended away from the body and supported with boning.

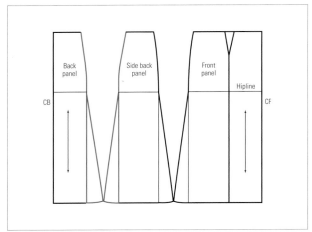

Step 2

- Divide the back into two panels from the end of the back waist dart nearest the side seam to the hem, but keeping the back dart shaping in the waistline. You now have a back panel and a side back panel.
- Depending on the fullness required at the hemline, extend the side of the back panel and side back panel out from the hipline to the hemline, following the instructions in Step 1.

Step 3

- Divide the length of the back panel into six equal sections and draw in five horizontal lines that will be used for the frill placement.

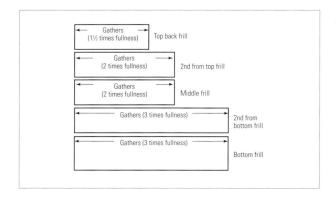

Step 4

- Depending on the size of the bustle and the length of the train, cut the frills so that each overlaps the previous one. Starting with the bottom frill, cut the frill the length of the bottom section on the bustle plus the length of the train (to the point at which it touches the floor) plus seam and hem allowances of ⅜in (1cm). For the width, multiply the width of the center back panel by 2½–3. Cut the next frill the same width as the bottom frill and long enough to overlap the bottom frill plus seam and hem allowances. The next two frills should be twice the width of the center back panel, and the final frill nearest the top should be 1½ times the width of the center back panel.
- If a fuller bustle is required, cut two top frills half the length of the lowest frill by the same width. These frills will be attached on the two top placement lines under the longer frills.
- On the three lower frill placement lines attach boning casing. This casing will sit over the frill seam allowances.

Designing a pannier

The pannier originated in the Spanish court. If you look at the paintings of Diego Velázquez you can see the women's skirts extending out at the sides, while remaining flat in both the front and back. The fashion was to spread throughout Europe; in France it was called a "robe à la française" and extended several feet either side of the wearer. Today the pannier is worn as a foundation for dramatic haute couture or costume skirts.

To make a pannier that sits at the side on the hemline of a hip yoke:

- Begin by making a hip yoke (see page 136).
- Trace the basic skirt sloper onto paper. Draw vertical lines from the darts near the center front and center back lines to divide the front and back skirt into panels.
- Retrace the center front and back panels onto paper.
- Depending on the amount of fullness wanted, extend the hemline by 2–3in (5–7.5cm) at the side and mark.
- Draw a line from the hipline to the mark on the hemline.
- Trace the side front panel of the skirt onto paper; divide the panel in half and draw a line down from this mark. Cut down this line and place a piece of paper under the two halves; spread the panels apart by 5½–8in (14–20cm) and tape to the paper. Redraw the hemline and waistline; at the side seam measure out at the hemline the same amount as added to the front panel and redraw the side seam. Round the top of the side seam into the waistline.
- Repeat for the side back panel.
- Measure down the center of the panels from waist to hemline. Measure this length down the side of each panel from the waistline and mark. Reshape the hemline following these marks.
- Add seam allowances, notch points, and label the panels. Mark the waistline of the side panels for gathering.

To make a wider pannier:

- Add gathered layers of strong net on either side of the petticoat over the gathers. The side panels can have boning added for extra strength if used as the foundation under a heavy, exaggerated skirt.
- On the side front panel measure down 2in (5cm) from the waistline on both seams and mark. Using a curved ruler connect the marks for the first boning placement.
- Measure down 2in (5cm) from the first boning placement line on both seams and mark. Again, draw a line joining these marks with a curved ruler. This creates the lower edge of the boning placement line.
- Measure down a further 3in (7.5cm) on both seams and mark. Again draw a line with a curved ruler.
- Again, draw in the lower edge of the boning placement line 2in (5cm) down from the last placement line.
- Draw another 4in (10cm) below that, with its corresponding line 2in (5cm) beneath.
- Draw in a final boning placement line 2–3in (5–7.5cm) down below the last placement line – it should be horizontal and under the extended curve of the side seams. Add the lower edge 2in (5cm) beneath.
- Repeat for the side back panel.

Left / Hip yoke pannier.
Right / Wider pannier.

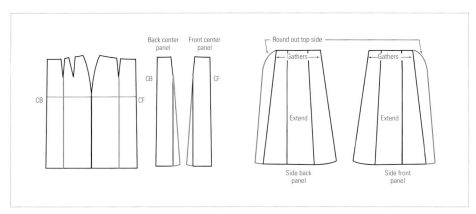

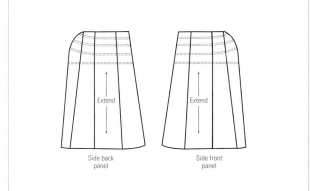

6 Construction Techniques
Foundations

A fashion garment, whether it is a glamorous gown or a sophisticated jacket, always looks better when worn over the correct foundation garment. The foundation can be layered inside so that it floats between the outer fashion garment and the lining, only becoming one with the garment around the neckline and maybe armhole. Alternatively it can be a separate garment that is attached by hand at the fashion garment's neckline, or it can be totally detached from any form of outerwear. While it is fun to draw attention to ourselves by wearing a tight-laced corset for that special day or historical occasion, it is not the way we dress in our everyday lives. However, today's foundation garments can still reshape the contours of the body and hold the silhouette of a garment, and they are not as inflexible, problematic, and demanding on the body as in past eras. New textile technology is constantly being introduced into foundation garments, making them more durable and comfortable to wear. Along with these new textiles come new construction methods, which means that trying out different construction techniques before applying them to your final garment is very important for achieving your desired finished look.

A stylist constructs a foundation shape on a dummy form.

A lightweight fashion foundation using polyester/rigilene boning

A lightweight foundation can be used to support the bodice of a gown or can be worn as a corset that will shape but not change the silhouette. It can also be worn as a support foundation floating between the outer fashion garment and the lining, or can be attached to the inside of the garment next to the body. If the foundation is going to be used to hold or balance the weight of a heavy embellishment on an accessory or garment, think of the right side of the foundation being made in the lining fabric or maybe even a contrasting color fabric that will shadow behind the finished embellishment, lace, or sheer fabric overlay.

This foundation will have no boning placement lines or stitching showing on either the inside or outside of the finished garment.

Rigilene

Rigilene can be set behind plastic-cased boning to give additional support, or added crosswise over vertical rigilene boning; an example would be to quickly flatten a bodice front across the bustline. Rigilene can also be added to large collars to make them stand up and away from the shoulders and head, to waistbands, bustles, and even sleeve heads and hemlines. Rigilene is also a good choice of boning to use in a muslin (toile) because it is inexpensive and quick to work with and can be shaped with the heat of an iron.

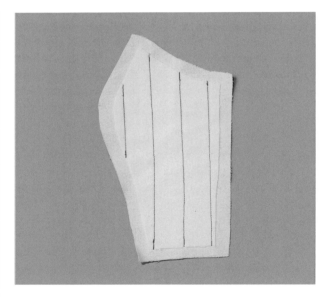

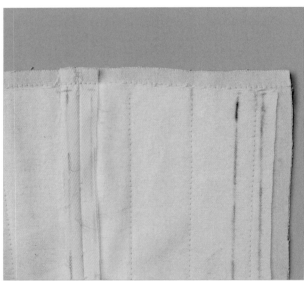

Step 1

- To create a lightweight foundation to be worn as a corset, first cut out one set of corset panels in cotton twill canvas. Cut out a second set in brushed cotton flannel but without the seam allowances.
- Place the cotton flannel panel pieces on the canvas panels and pin in place.
- Using a stitch length of 3mm, stitch the two layers together with parallel rows of stitching, working from the top of the cotton flannel to the bottom. Stitch the first row approximately ¼in (6mm) from the edge and subsequent rows approximately 1in (2.5cm) apart.

Step 2

- Mark the bone placement on the cotton flannel side of each panel (see page 146).
- Stitch the panels together, matching all the notch points and press the seam allowances open.
- Machine baste (tack) across both the neckline and hemline, or bottom edges, of the panels, stitching over all seam allowances to keep them open and flat.

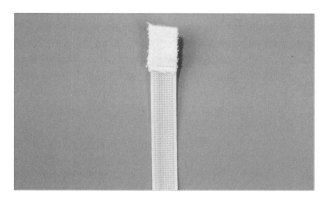

Step 3

- Cut the rigilene boning the length of the marked boning placement lines, measuring from the top basted stitching line down to the lower basted stitching line less ⅛in (3mm) at each end; this will allow you to stitch the lining or facing to the neckline and hemlines without catching the boning.
- Pad the ends of the cut rigilene with doubled cotton tape or a scrap of brushed cotton folded over and stitched. You can also use purchased end covers, or you can melt the cut ends over a flame to seal the sharp strands of polyester.

Step 4

- Holding the first piece of rigilene boning at the padded top, place it between the matching boning placement lines, ⅛in (3mm) down from the top stitching line.
- Using a sewing machine and a stitch length of 2.5–3mm, stitch each piece of rigilene in place. Start by back tack stitching up to the stitching line and then stitch down the edge of the rigilene boning to the lower stitching line, keeping the stitching in the border on the edge of the boning. Secure the stitching at the lower edge with back tacking.
- Repeat on the other side of the piece of rigilene and then attach the remainder of the rigilene boning between all the boning placement lines.

Marking the boning placement lines

Using a needle or tracing wheel, prick down the boning placement lines on the paper pattern. Place the paper pattern on the canvas panel piece and rub chalk over the prick marks. The chalk should go through the pricks in the paper and mark the boning placement lines on the canvas.

Next cut the boning to the required length by laying it along the placement markings. Draw across both the top and bottom of the boning, approximately ⅛in (3mm) in from the seam allowance. By working in this way you will not only have the correct length but also the correct shape for both the top and bottom of your boning.

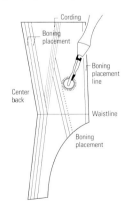

Cutting boning

Do not attempt to cut any kind of boning with your good scissors as this will blunt them.

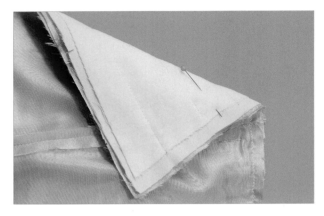

Step 5

- Cut out and sew together all the fashion fabric panels. Repeat with the lining panels. Press all the seam allowances open.
- Place the canvas side of the boned panels to the wrong side of the fashion fabric panels, matching all panels along the top and bottom edges, and pin in place.
- Stitch along the top neckline and bottom hemline edges with a stitch length of 3mm, securing both ends of the stitching. Be careful not to stitch over the ends of the rigilene boning.

Step 6

- Place the right side of the lining panels on the right side of the fashion fabric and pin in place. Turn the work over so that the wrong side (the cotton flannel side) of the boned canvas panels is facing upward.
- Place one edge of ¼in (6mm)-wide cotton tape or ribbon along the line of stitching right side up, across the top of all the panels so that the tape is facing away from the cotton flannel on the canvas panels or fashion fabric and is just covering the stitching.

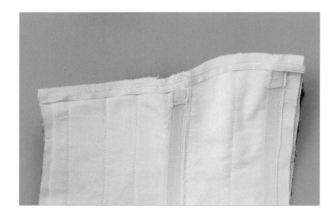

Step 7

- Stitch all the layers together, catching the top edge of the tape or ribbon in the stitching; secure both ends of the stitching.
- Repeat the taping and stitch across the lower edge, securing both ends of the stitching.
- Do not catch the ends of the rigilene boning in your stitching.

Step 8

- Turn your work to the right side through the closure opening and press. The tape will be sandwiched between the layers, sitting on top of the neckline and hemline seam allowances, rolling the lining toward the back of the garment and also preventing the edges from stretching out.
- The closure opening can now be finished with a separating zipper or the edges sewn together and eyelets added for lacing or your choice of closure.
- If you are placing this corset into a garment do not attach the lining to the top edge of the corset. Place the canvas panels on the inside of the garment bodice, matching up the seams across the neckline and closure opening. Then finish the neckline of the garment by taping the edge before stitching through all layers, including both garment and corset linings, securing both ends of the stitching.
- The boned canvas panels can also be sandwiched between the outer garment and lining. Tape the top edge and stitch all layers together from one side of the closure along to the other side, securing both ends of the stitching. Bind over the lower edge of the canvas panels so that they do not fray.

- If you want the boning placement stitching to show on the finished garment follow Steps 1 to 3; place the right side of the boned canvas panels on the wrong side of the fashion fabric foundation piece, making sure that all the seam lines are matching. Pin and hand baste down the seam line. Mark the boning placement lines on the cotton flannel panels and follow the directions for padding the ends of the boning in Step 3. Stitch the boning onto the foundation as in Step 4 and follow the remaining steps to finish the corset.

A double-layered canvas foundation with a front busk and back lacing

This corset, when constructed using plastic or steel boning, can be tight laced. The front can have a busk opening – but if the corset is to be attached into a gown you may not want to have a front closure, in which case you can finish the center front with one or two rows of boning. Rows of cording can also be used for added structure on the back, across the front neckline, and at the sides under the arm.

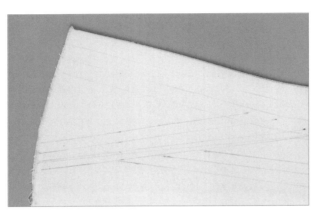

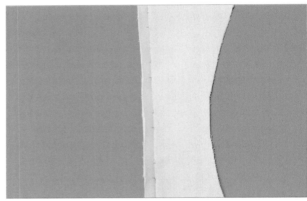

Step 1

- Cut two sets of pattern pieces from canvas, one for each layer of the corset. Transfer all of the boning and cording placements to one set of pieces.

Step 2

- Pin the two right-hand-side center front panel pieces right sides securely together, matching notch points.
- Lay the busk down the center front seam line and mark lines between the hooks with chalk or pencil.
- Stitch along each line, back tacking at beginning and end. This creates gaps in the center front seam to pull the busk hooks through. Use a strong polyester thread and a size 14 sewing machine needle. (See chart, Chapter 1, page 19.)
- Check the busk sits correctly; if not, make alterations.
- Press the seam open, turn the panels to the right side, and fold back at the center front so that the seam line is now the fold line; press in place.

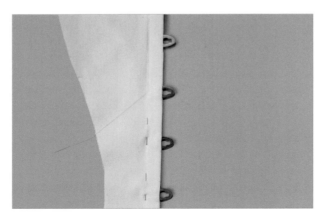

Step 3

- Place the busk into position, pulling the hooks through the gaps, and pin down behind to hold tightly in place.
- Being very careful not to hit the metal busk, stitch along the placement markings.

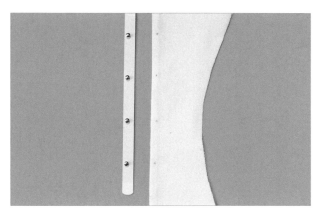

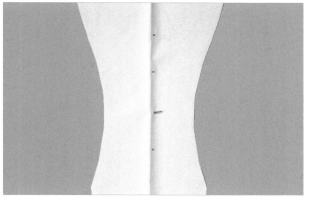

Step 4

- Place the two left-hand-side center front panel pieces right sides together and stitch down the seam allowance, securing both ends. Press seam allowances open, turn the panel pieces to the right side, and press the seam closed and flat down the center front.
- Place the busk with the studs or eyes between the two panels so it is sitting along the left front edge, right side facing up. Make sure the studs or eyes match with the hook side of the busk; mark the studs or eyes with chalk on the fabric and then remove the busk.

Step 5

- With a stiletto or awl gently make a set of holes in the top fabric panel only. If possible try to avoid breaking the fabric fibers by turning and twisting the stiletto or awl to enlarge each hole.

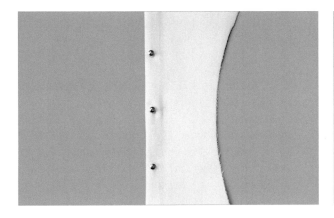

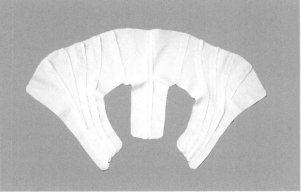

Step 6

- Place the busk back between the two panels so it is sitting up against the center front seam line and push the studs or eyes through the holes.
- Pin down the back edge of the busk through both layers and stitch along the placement marking.

Step 7

- Using a machine stitch length of 2.5–3mm, sew all the panels together on both layers, working around from the center front to the center back, matching notch points; secure both ends of the stitching on each seam.
- Press all the seam allowances open and flat.
- Place the two right-hand-side center back panels right sides together and stitch down the center back seam. Press the seam open; turn to the right side and press in place so that the seam line becomes the fold line. Repeat for the two left-hand-side center back panels.

Cording

- If you are adding cording, stitch down all cording placement lines through both panel layers, securing the ends of the stitching. Thread the cording into the cording channels.

- If you have cording channels passing over boning channels you will need a separate layer for the back of the cording channels.

- Cut an extra panel piece to match the panel to be corded; with right side facing, pin this new panel piece behind the top panel. Fold the back panel out of the way. Stitch down the cording placement lines, being sure to secure the ends. Thread the cording into the channels and cut away any extra panel not holding cording; fold the back panel back into place.

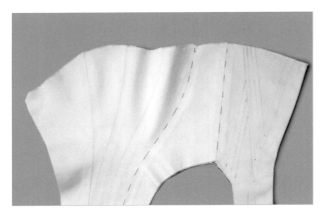

Step 8

- Place the corset body flat with seam lines matching.
- Hand baste all seam lines together and baste close to the fold line on both center back seams.

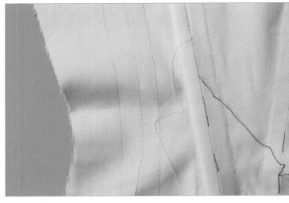

Step 9

- Make the boning channels by stitching down the seam lines then stitching parallel lines ³⁄₈in (1cm) on either side of the seam line using a 3mm stitch length; secure both ends of the stitching.
- Edge stitch down the center back panels close to the fold line, and again ³⁄₈in (6mm) over from the edge stitching, leaving a gap for eyelet placement.
- Stitch down any other marked boning placement lines.
- Cut your ¼in (6mm) boning the length of each boning channel less ⅛in (3mm) at each end. Shape the ends to match the shape of the top and bottom of the panel pieces. Thread the boning into the channels. With plastic boning the ends do not need padding, but file off any shape points with a nail file.
- Trim the top and bottom raw edges of the corset to remove any threads or rough edges, ready to bind the top and lower edges.

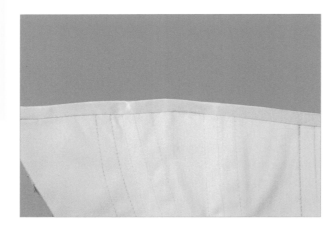

Step 10

- Cut two pieces of 1in (2.5cm)-wide binding plus seam allowances. This can be the same fabric as your corset or purchased separately.

- Lay the corset right side up and push the boning away from the end of the channel. Starting at the back top or bottom edge, pin binding along the raw edge, leaving 1in (2.5cm) extra at both ends. If using bought binding, unfold the edge before pinning.
- Stitch the binding to the raw edge of the corset along the seam allowance with a stitch length of 2.5mm.
- Fold the extra binding in at the ends and press. Fold the binding over the raw edge to the back and pin. Hand slip stitch in place, or turn the corset over to the right side and machine stitch along the edge of binding and fabric (stitch in the ditch). Hand slip stitch the ends for a neat finish.
- Mark the eyelet positions on the center back panels with chalk. To sew eyelets, see Chapter 9, page 268. Alternatively, set metal eyelets using an eyelet setter.
- Add flossing to the right side of the boning channels to secure the bones in place if desired (see page 273).

Adding waist and underbust stays to a foundation

Waist and underbust stays are added to a corset for support. The waist stay takes the strain off the closure at the waistline and the underbust stay holds the body of the corset to the torso under the bustline.

If you are adding both a waist and an underbust stay, they need to be set exactly parallel to each other all the way around the corset for balance. Stays are usually made from a strong grosgrain (Petersham ribbon).

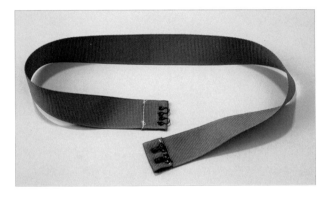

Step 1

- Cut a length of 1in (2.5cm) wide grosgrain the waist measurement plus ⅝in (1.5cm) at each end.
- Fold one end of the ribbon under by ¼inch (6mm) and again by ⅜in (1cm) and machine stitch across using a 2.5mm stitch length; secure both ends of the stitching.
- Repeat at the other end of the ribbon.
- Attach hooks and eyes to the ends of the ribbon, with the hooks attached to the top ribbon and the eyes to the lower. Alternatively, if the ribbon stay opens at the side, attach the eyes to the back ribbon and the hooks to the front.

Step 2

- Pin one end of the ribbon on the waistline inside the corset so it aligns perfectly with one edge of the closure; pin the ribbon to the boning around the waistline to the other side of the opening.
- Attach the ribbon with machine stitches on both sides of the boning – starting with the second bone in from the opening if you are using eyelets, or the first bone back from the opening if you are using a zipper, hooks and eyes, or loops and buttons.

Step 3

- Measure up from the waistline stay to the level of the underbust at the opening and mark.
- Mark all the boning around the corset at the same distance above the waistline stay.
- Measure around the corset through the marks and add ⅝in (2cm) at each end. Cut some ribbon to this length.
- Finish the ribbon ends as for the waist stay.
- Attach the underbust ribbon stay to the corset by placing it on the marks and stitching on each side of the boning; the two ribbon stays will be an equal distance from one another.

The boning casing

Boning needs to be inserted into a casing if you are constructing a single-layer or sheer foundation garment. Bone casing is used on every type of foundation, from corsets to hoops and panniers. Special bone casing tape can be purchased that is brushed on one side so it does not rub when next to the skin. On a sheer garment the boning is hidden behind or sandwiched between two layers of casing. Alternatively, the seam allowance can be made into a casing if no additional matching boning is required, or you can use ribbon or even a cotton tape to make the casing; velvet ribbon, for example, was once used as a boning casing.

Crossed casings
Because boning can be placed both vertically and horizontally on a foundation, be careful not to stitch one casing across another or you will stop the boning from sliding down both. Stitch up to the second casing, secure the end of the stitching, lift the machine foot, and move to the other side of the casing. Secure the stitching and then continue to attach the casing.

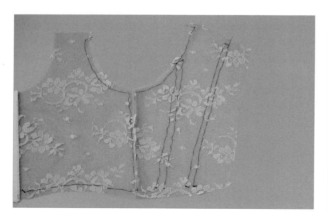

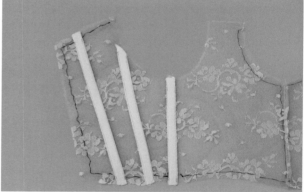

Step 1
- Place the boning casing on the placement lines marked on the foundation; the line should be centered under the casing.

Step 2
- Pin or baste in place before machine stitching down one side and then the other, keeping the stitching close to the edge of the casing and using a stitch length of 2.5mm. Secure both ends of the stitching.

Attaching a band around the neckline of a foundation garment

So the top edge of the foundation does not show around the neckline of a garment, a band of fabric can be placed around the foundation neckline, and can also take in or cover the bra cups. If the neckline stands away from the body, or is uneven, the foundation can be finished with a skin-tone or a fashion-fabric band and attached to the garment 2–3in (5–7.5cm) below the neckline edge, along the bottom of the facing.

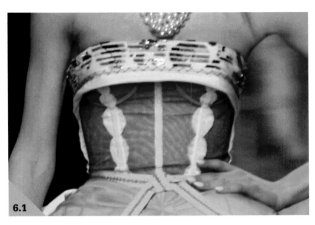

6.1

Step 1

- Construct the foundation but do not finish the top edge or neckline.

Step 2

- Fold a piece of paper in half and position the center front line on the center front panel down the fold line.
- Trace across the neckline and down the side of the pattern piece for approximately 3–4in (7.5–10cm), making sure the lower edge of the facing passes through the bustline.
- Place the side front pattern piece next to the side of the center front panel so the necklines connect; trace off the neckline and down the side of the pattern panel for approximately 3–4in (7.5–10cm).
- Continue with all the front pattern pieces so you have a continuous front neckline; connect the lines down the sides of the panels together so they form the lower edge of the facing.
- Repeat with the back panels, starting at the center back.
- Add seam allowances, markings, and notch points to all the pattern pieces.

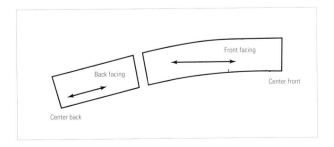

6.1 / A top band (Christian Dior, Spring/Summer 2009).

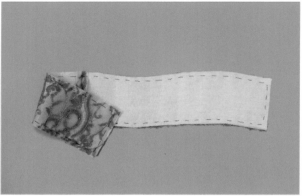

Step 3

- Cut a front and back facing from the fashion fabric. If you wish, cut a separate front facing from lace or other type of overlay; if the overlay fabric has a pattern, make sure it is centered and matches the neckline of the garment it will sit behind. Stitch the side seams together; press the seam allowances open. If using an overlay, set it over the front facing; join the front facing to the back facing along the seam line.

Step 4

- Place the right side of the facing to the wrong side of the foundation, matching all notch points, and attach by stitching around the top edge with a stitch length of 3mm; secure both ends.

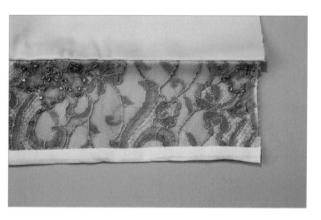

Step 5

- Cut a bias strip from the lining, or another lightweight fabric, and use it to bind the lower edge of the facing.
- Flip the facing to the right side of the foundation and baste along the top edge to hold in place.

Step 6

- Pin a ¼in (6mm) cotton tape to the top edge of the bias strip through all layers.
- Catch stitch across the tape so the stitches go into both edges; stitch along through all foundation layers.

Adding a guard behind the center back closure

Setting a guard behind the closure will protect the skin from abrasion. Careful design of the guard and closure details can make it into a feature.

- Draft two pieces for the guard, each slightly shorter than the garment opening and approximately 2in (5cm) wide.
- Add seam allowances and cut two pieces from fashion fabric and one from fusible interfacing.
- Apply the fusible interfacing to the wrong side of one fabric guard piece.
- Place the guard pieces right sides together and stitch across the top, down one side, and across the bottom. Press, turn right side out, and press flat.
- Stitch parallel rows of stitching the length of the guard, approximately ⅜in (1cm) apart, using a 3mm stitch length; secure both ends of the stitching.
- Edge stitch along the top, down the outer edge of the guard, and along the bottom edge.
- Place the guard behind the first row of boning and catch stitch to the foundation. For a neater finish, apply a strip of fusible interfacing as a binding over the raw edge of the guard before catch stitching.

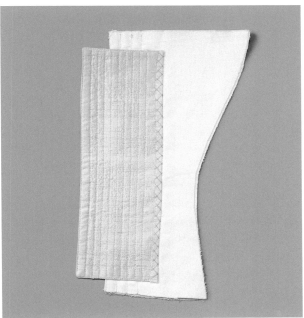

6.2 / A black guard sits behind the wide closure on this corset (Chantal Thomass, Spring/ Summer 2004).

Zippers

Zippers can be placed in a corset down any seam other than over the bustline. They can be either lapped or centered in the seam opening; an open-edged zipper works really well as a corset closure. Invisible zippers should only be used in a very lightweight foundation. You should not, however, use a zipper as the closure in a historic or reproduction corset. Zippers can be attached with pick stitching, or they can be machine sewn. It is wise to place a guard behind the zipper in a close-fitting garment so the wearer's skin will not get caught in the teeth.

Centered zipper

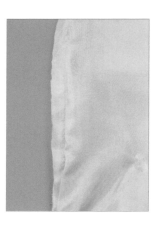

Step 1
- With right side facing, press the seam allowance toward the garment wrong side.
- Fold the seam allowance of the lining toward the wrong side of the garment and press. Machine stitch the zipper to the wrong side of the lining.

Step 2
- Place the zipper right side up, centered behind the center back seam. Pin, then baste the zipper tape on both sides of the seam allowance.
- Machine or pick stitch down each side of the zipper, ⅜in (1cm) from the seam line; remove the basting.

Lapped zipper

Step 1
- Fold the seam allowance toward the wrong side of the garment on the left side only.
- Fold back on the right side the width of the seam allowance less ⅛in (3mm).
- Fold back the seam allowance on the lining and press.

Step 2
- Open the zipper. Pin the right side down the right side of the garment opening so the folded edge just touches the zipper teeth.
- Machine or pick stitch down the zipper ⅛in (3mm) from the folded edge, being careful not to catch the lining.

Step 3
- Pin the left side of the zipper down the left side of the opening so the zipper teeth are ¼in (6mm) from the folded edge.

- Machine or pick stitch down the zipper ⅜–½in (1–1.3cm) from the folded edge, being careful not to catch the lining.

Step 4
- The lining can also be slip stitched onto the zipper.

A center back guard panel with hidden zipper

This works really well behind button and loop closures. It adds support to the closure by taking the strain away from the buttons and loops. The zippered guard can also enable a design detail such as an unlaced back closure.

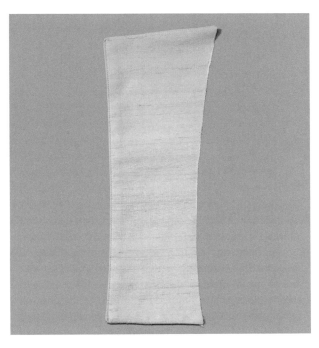

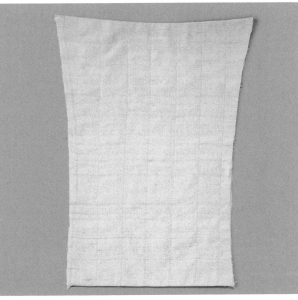

Step 1

- Trace the center back panel onto paper; fold the paper down the center back line so you are mirroring the pattern, and add seam allowances, markings, and notch points to both sides of the pattern piece. Label as hidden center back panel.

Step 2

- Cut one set of panels for the corset from fashion fabric and a second set from lining. Cut a further set from fusible interfacing. Fuse the interfacing onto the back of the fashion fabric panels.
- Construct the foundation, leaving the left-hand side back fashion fabric, center back fashion fabric, and lining panels unattached.
- Place the lining of the left-hand center back panel on the fashion fabric with right sides facing and machine stitch across the top, down one side, and across the bottom edge; press and turn to the right side. You can also choose to edge stitch down the center back.

Step 3

- Cut one hidden center back panel from fashion fabric, one from lining, and one from fusible interfacing. Fuse the interfacing onto the back of the fashion fabric hidden center back panel.
- Working from the center of the hidden back panel out to the sides, stitch rows of channel stitching approximately 1in (2.5cm) apart.
- Attach the lining to the hidden center back panel by stitching across the top and bottom edges; press and turn to the right side.

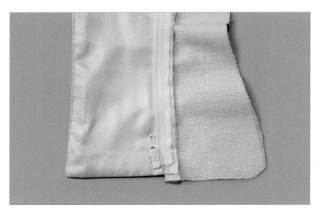

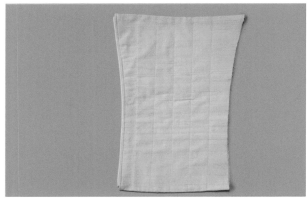

Step 4

- Stitch the side and center back panels together, securing the stitching at both ends; press the seam allowances toward the side back panel and turn so that the wrong side is facing up.
- Place one side of the separating zipper tape upside down on the seam allowance on the wrong side of the left center back panel, so the teeth are facing toward the center back. Leave a ¼in (6mm) gap at the bottom edge of the center back panel and the zipper, pin in place, and machine stitch using a 2.5mm stitch length and securing both ends.

Step 5

- Pin the other side of the separating zipper tape onto the seam allowance of the fashion fabric side of the hidden center back panel, on the left-hand side. The zipper should be upside down with the teeth facing toward the center back. Before attaching the zipper, check it matches perfectly with its other side.
- Taking care not to catch the lining, stitch down the zipper tape using a 2.5mm stitch length and securing both ends.
- Turn the zipper to the wrong side and press. Edge stitch the fashion fabric along the side of the zipper to hold it in place.

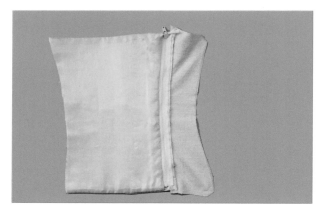

Step 6

- Turn to the wrong side and press under the seam allowance of the lining for the hidden center back panel. Slip stitch it to the zipper tape.

Step 7

- Turn to the right side and press. Zip the hidden back panel to the center back and side back panels.

Step 8

- Now join the side back panel to the rest of the corset. Press open the seam allowances and then press in the seam allowance of the lining of the side back panel before slip stitching to the other side of the zipper tape.
- Attach the right side of the hidden center back panel to the right center back panel and stitch together.

Working with tulle or net

Tulle is a lightweight net named after the city of Tulle in France, famed in the eighteenth century for its lace and silk production. Today's tulle is made on a bobbinet machine, invented by John Heathcoat in England in the early nineteenth century. It can be made from cotton, silk, or synthetic fibers. Soft tulle is used behind lace to provide some modesty in a nude look design, while layered stiffer tulle is used for petticoats.

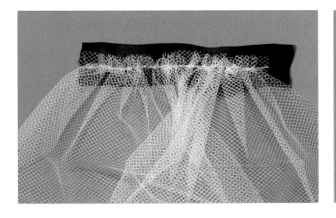

- The choice of needle and thread are both important to help prevent the tulle snagging. A Microtex needle is a slim, sharp needle recommended for sewing tulle, but any thin sharp needle will work. Cotton-covered polyester thread is ideal because both cotton and polyester threads tend to break.
- The edges of cut tulle do not fray so they can be left unfinished.
- When stitching tulle use a stabilizer, such as clear tape or tissue paper, and then tear it away.
- While tulle does not have a grainline there can be stretch in the width.
- Never iron directly onto tulle as it can melt; protect it under a pressing cloth.
- When gathering tulle, gather two to three layers together before stitching to the edge of 1in (2.5cm)-wide grosgrain, or other firm ribbon with no stretch, cut to the correct length. Layer the gathered tulle onto the ribbon in parallel rows.

- Place a second piece of ribbon cut to the correct length on top of the rows of gathered tulle, so the tulle is sandwiched between the ribbons, and stitch across the top and bottom edges of the ribbon. You can also sew through the center to flatten the tulle further, removing bulk.
- Use your left hand to flatten the tulle as you sew.
- Stitch slowly to help prevent puckering and gathers when joining tulle together. Do not pull the tulle as you sew as this will cause the needle to break or the machine foot to get caught in the tulle.

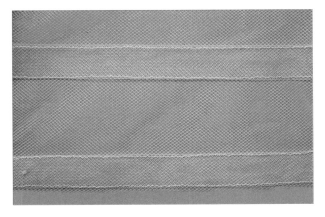

- Bands of horsehair braid or boning can be added to stiffen or shape tulle further. The hemline can also be wired.

7 Designing and Pattern Drafting
The bra

There are depictions of women athletes wearing something like a brassiere that date back to the fourteenth century BC, while wall paintings that survived the destruction of Pompeii in AD 79 also show women wearing an early form of the bra. In Ming Dynasty China (1368–1644) a foundation cloth with cups and straps over the shoulders was worn by rich women, and throughout modern social history, the status of women and the history of the brassiere have been intertwined with the changing image of the body. Madeleine Vionnet, Lucile, and Paul Poiret all claimed credit for popularizing the brassiere in the early twentieth century, as corsets that molded the body into exaggerated shapes fell out of fashion and were replaced by styles that ended just beneath the breasts. This necessitated the wearing of a bust bodice to support the breasts.

In the 1920s it was fashionable for women to flatten their breasts, but styles changed as women followed the lead of starlets and pin-up girls, and the emphasis returned to the breasts. By the 1930s brassieres were made with separating cups; these bras were made in different cup sizes out of newly introduced elastic fabrics.

Women's breasts are rarely symmetrical and every breast is a different shape. Relative to the chest the breast can change shape and has its own center of gravity; it can be moved up, down, or from side to side. Over the decades designers have created incredible effects by padding and manipulating the breasts into positions and shapes into which they were never intended to go. To design a bra you have to have an understanding of the anatomy of the breast and chest, and of the mechanics of the bra – the cut and fit. Textile technology is responsible for the bra evolving from a purely functional undergarment to today's fashion statement.

The burlesque dancer Dita Von Teese wears a push-up bra by Von Follies at the 2012 Melbourne Fashion Festival.

Anatomy of the bra

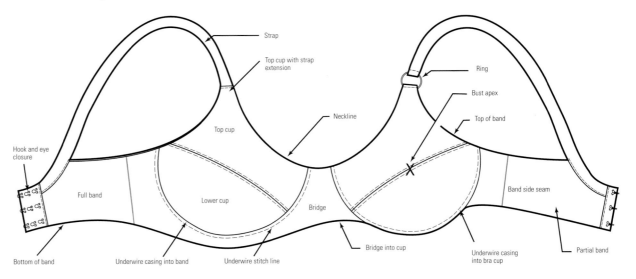

The cup

It is the bra cup that holds the breast. The cup can have one or more seams, which can be horizontal, vertical, or a mixture of both, so long as they intersect the bust apex. The cup can also be made from a one-piece mold, which will limit the designer to the manufacturer's cup specifications. The top cup is the area of the bra where you will find embellishment; it can be made from a sheer fabric or have a contrasting overlay. The cups can be made with or without underwires, depending on the design. Padding, power bars, collars, and spiral stitching can all be added to the bra cup.

The band

The band, or bra frame, sits around the rib cage of the body and can be made from one or multiple pieces of fabric. It can have a front or back closure; some sports bras have no closure at all, you just step in or pull it on over your head. The bra cups are usually attached to the band, but in some sports bras band and cups are integrated.

The side seam can have boning for added bust support, especially for larger cup sizes and sometimes in strapless bras. The band can be made from a different fabric than the cups, or can be side seamed with the back band made in powernet while the front band and cups of the bra are made from the same fabric.

The bridge or connecter

The bridge is the center front of the bra between the cups. It can be incorporated into the band or cut as a separate piece. It can be made and decorated in an alternate fabric, but must be stabilized to keep it from stretching out of shape. It can be extended under the cup to the side seam, creating the front band.

The straps

The straps can be stretchy and made from elastic or from the same fabric as the cups. Straps can be narrow or wide, and made adjustable or not. The strap should not be the support for the bra cup because this is the job of the band and bridge. The strap can be padded for extra comfort.

Bra findings

All extras other than the fabric are known as findings. These include the strap slides and rings, hook and eye tape, front clasps, underwire, continuous or uni wires, and separators.

Measuring for the correct bra size

Seven out of ten women are wearing the wrong bra size. Most women will have had one bra fitting that resulted in a comfortable proper-fitting bra. This could have been their very first bra and from that time on they have continued to buy off-the-peg bras in that size. Life happens, and the breasts will change, as will the rest of the body; a bra size will, therefore, change over time. Like shoes that pinch, an uncomfortable bra makes women feel miserable so they would need to be regularly refitted. To find the correct band and cup size you need to take three measurements: under the bustline, the bustline, and the high bustline.

You can take these measurements over your clothing or over an unpadded bra. Larger ladies will get a more accurate measurement if they are braless.

Band size (US and UK)

To find the band size, measure under the bustline at the top of the rib cage, keeping the tape measure tight and breathing out. Make sure the tape measure is kept level around the body.

Band sizes are always given in even numbers. To add ease and to get an even number for the band size, if your measurement is:

- An even number, add 4in
  E.g., if you measure 28in, add 4in = a band size of 32
- An odd number, add 5in
  E.g., if you measure 29in, add 5in = a band size of 34
- An odd number plus ½in, add 5in then round down to the nearest inch
  E.g., if you measure 31½in, add 5in = 36½in, then round down to a band size of 36
- An even number plus ½in, add 4in then round down to the nearest inch
  E.g., if you measure 30½in, add 4in = 34½in, then round down to a band size of 34.

Band size (European/metric)

In the metric system, sizes are given in increments of 5cm, so round up or down to the nearest 5cm:

- If your measurement is 71cm, round down to 70cm
- If your measurement is 73.5cm, round up to 75cm.

Rib cage measurement		Band size	
27–28½in	(68.5–72.5cm)	32	(70)
29–30½in	(73.5–77.5cm)	34	(75)
31–32½in	(78.5–82.5cm)	36	(80)
33–34½in	(84–87.5cm)	38	(85)
35–36½in	(89–92.5cm)	40	(90)
37–38½in	(94–98cm)	42	(95)
39–40½in	(99–103cm)	44	(100)
41–42½in	(104–108cm)	46	(105)
43–44½in	(109–113cm)	48	(110)
45–46½in	(114.5–118cm)	50	(115)

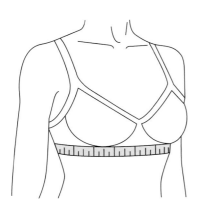

Cup size (US and UK)

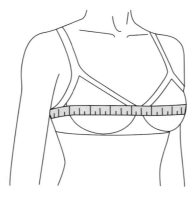 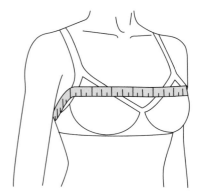

Now measure the bustline at the fullest point. With arms at the side and standing straight, exhale and make sure the tape measure is not twisted and passes over the nipples. Once again this measurement can be taken over your clothing or over an unpadded bra. Larger ladies will find that going braless will give a more accurate measurement.

Measure the high bustline, above the bust and just below the underarm. Exhale and hold the tape measure tight.

Subtract the high bust measurement from the bustline measurement. You can use the resulting measurement to find the cup size in the chart below. Each additional 1in (2.5cm) increases the cup size:

- 1in = A cup, 2in = B cup

If the measurement is between cup sizes, always choose the larger size.

Cup size chart

Difference between band and bustline measurements		Cup size
The same or less		AAA
Less than 1in	(2.5cm)	AA
1in	(2.5cm)	A
2in	(5cm)	B
3in	(7.5cm)	C
4in	(10cm)	D
5in	(12.5cm)	E or DD
6in	(15cm)	F or DDD
7in	(17.5cm)	G or FF
8in	(20cm)	H or GG or FFF
9in	(23cm)	I or HH
10in	(25.5cm)	J or II
11in	(28cm)	K or JJ
12in	(30.5cm)	L or KK

Band size conversion chart

US/UK	Europe/International	France	Italy	Australia
28				
30	65	80	0	8
32	70	85	1	10
34	75	90	2	12
36	80	95	3	14
38	85	100	4	16
40	90	105	5	18
42	95	110	6	20
44	100	115		
46	105	120		
48	110	125		
50	105	130		

Underwire

The underwire holds the cup in a fixed diameter, giving both maximum shaping and support. On the cup size chart, a B cup has a 2in difference between the high bustline and bustline measurement.

Each diameter of wire is interchangeable between some sizes. For example a 36B bra size will take a 36 wire, but so does a 32D, 34C, and 38A. As the band size increases, the cup size that will hold the wire decreases. A 40 wire will fit 40B, 38C, 36D, 34DD, and 32F.

Each increase in cup size causes the wire to go up by 2, so that a 36 wire is only one size up from a 34, the size difference of the wire being 3.8in diameter, or ¼in per size.

Use the underwire conversion chart below to find your correct underwire. Find the band size down the side and the cup size across the top to find the wire size.

Note that underwire size can change from supplier to supplier. For Europe/international, French, Italian, and Australian sizing, follow the band size conversion chart on page 182.

Underwire conversion chart (US and UK)

	A	B	C	D	E	F	G	H	I	J	K
32	30	32	34	36	38	40	42	44	46	48	50
34	32	34	36	38	40	42	44	46	48	50	52
36	34	36	38	40	42	44	46	48	50	52	54
38	36	38	40	42	44	46	48	50	52	54	56
40	38	40	42	44	46	48	50	52	54	56	58
42	40	42	44	46	48	50	52	54	56	58	60
44	42	44	46	48	50	52	54	56	58	60	
46	44	46	48	50	52	54	56	58	60		
48	46	48	50	52	54	56	58	60			
50	48	50	52	54	56	58	60				
52	50	52	54	56	58	60					

Different bra styles

Soft cup bra

The soft cup bra is another name for a bra with no underwire; a triangle cup bra is also a soft bra. Some soft bras will have an underwire channeling with no wire for added support. This style comes in a variety of different cup and band designs. The soft bra is for smaller cup sizes, A–C, that really do not need much support.

Triangle cup bra

The triangle-shaped cup bra will give good support for A and B cup sizes. The triangular cup can be shaped by a vertical center seam that passes over the bust point, or the lower cup can be shaped by darts or gathers. Triangle cup bras usually do not have underwires. The straps are usually thin and can be constructed as a halter neck. Push-up pads can also be added to the cups.

Underwire bra

The underwire supports and shapes the cups. A well-fitted underwire bra will be comfortable to wear, with no pinching and digging into the rib cage. The underwire bra is suitable for all cup sizes.

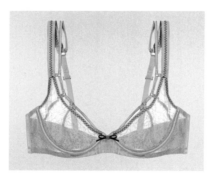

Demi bra

A demi cup is also known as a half cup or semi cup. This bra has about three-quarter cup coverage and dips low in the front. It is usually designed for smaller cup sizes and may have a front opening. The underwire for a demi cup is approximately 1½in (3.8cm) shorter than a regular wire.

Molded or padded cup bra

The molded bra has a cup that is molded and shaped by a manufacturer. It is also known as a T-shirt bra because it has no seam lines to show under close-fitting clothing and its complete coverage also means that nipples will not show. It can be made with full or demi cups.

Cone bra

The bullet or cone bra was a favorite of the pin-up girls from the 1940s and 50s. The breasts are shaped into a conical shape rather than being lifted upward and inward.

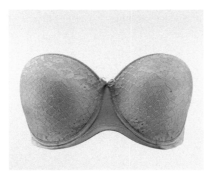

Balconette bra

Also known as a shelf bra, the balconette is a more revealing version of the demi bra. While it offers little coverage, it gives dramatic cleavage and uplift.

Strapless bra

All the support for this bra comes from the band. The band is usually longer and may have boning added. Gripper elastic can be added to the band and neckline to hold the bra to the body. These bras sometimes come with convertible straps that attach with a G-hook to the neckline and the top of the band at the back of the bra. This gives the wearer more options: strapless, halter, or crisscrossed.

Sports bra

A specialty bra that gives the wearer added support while exercising. These bras may be made from wicking or moisture-control fabrics and have anti-chafe seaming. Many are made with no findings and are pulled on over the head or stepped into; some will have a front zipper closure. The back can be one piece or a racer back so the straps cannot fall off the shoulders during exercise.

Mastectomy bra

Soft cotton pockets are added to the inside of this bra to hold a prosthesis, or the cups can be filled with tiny lightweight plastic beads that are permanently sewn in. Some of these bras are made with both front and back closures, giving more choice to the wearer.

Nursing bra

This bra has two cup layers with a fastener. The inner cup has a hole cut to expose the nipple and supports the breast while the baby feeds. The outer cup is dropped away then pulls up and fastens after the baby feeds. These bras are usually made of cotton for easy laundering.

Boned bra

Boning can be added to both the top and lower cups. Adding boning to the cups will give more support, especially in a strapless bra cup. The boning can also give you more design options.

The fit

The considerations when designing, making, or choosing a bra are that it will give support, coverage, and comfort. The style and fabric are additional aesthetic choices of the designer and wearer. When putting on a bra, the wearer should bend over and allow the breasts to naturally fill the cups. The bra can then be adjusted by raising up each breast so that the nipple is sitting in the center of the cup.

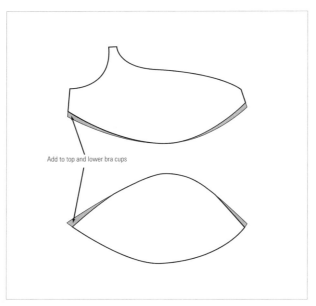

Add to top and lower bra cups

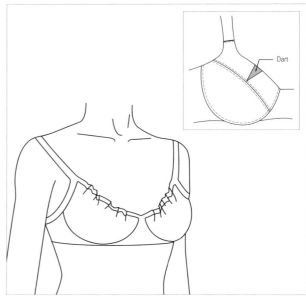

Dart

Step 1

- The bridge should sit flat against the breastbone; if you can put more than two fingers between the bridge and breastbone, the bra is not fitting.
- The cups should be smooth, with no wrinkles. If the band fits, go up or down a cup size.
- If there are pull lines at the center front and underarm of the cup on the bustline, then the outer circumference of the cup is too small; add an allowance of fabric to both the top and lower cups at the armhole and center front edges at the bustline.
- Remember to make an equivalent adjustment to the band at the same point.

Step 2

- If the cup is molded, the breast should fill it with no gapping. If there is gapping, go down a cup size.
- If the cup is puckering along the cup neckline, shorten the length of the neckline in the top cup, removing the excess fabric by making a small dart at the center of the neckline.

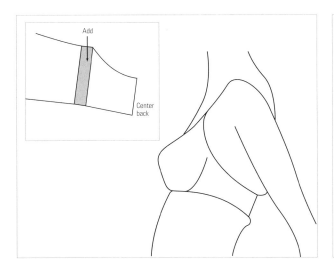

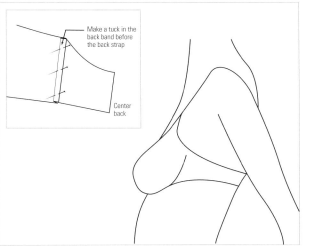

Step 3

- If wearing a soft bra or bra without underwires, the breasts should be separated. A badly fitting bridge will give the appearance of a "mono" breast.
- If the band is too tight it will make the underwires dig into the ribs and hurt. If the band rolls it is also too tight. Add an allowance of fabric to the length of the back bra panel just before the strap position.

Step 4

- If the bra back is too long it can also cause poor fit. Shorten the bra back before the strap position to resolve the problem.

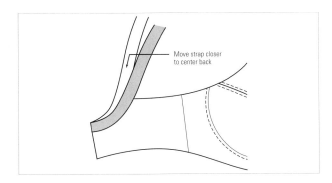

Step 5

- If the wearer is pulling their bra straps up at the front or down at the back the band is too loose. If it is too loose it will cause the breasts to sag. Again, shorten the back band to resolve the problem.
- The band should not ride up at the back and should be level around the rib cage. If it is too loose it will let the bra lift when the arms are raised. First check if the

band can be tightened at the closure; if not, the band size is too big, so go down a size. You should be able to put two fingers under a well-fitting band.

- Not cutting pattern pieces with the greatest stretch or using a knit fabric with four-way stretch can also be contributing factors to poor fit.
- Another common problem is straps falling off the shoulder, which happens when the strap setting is too wide. The strap position should run in a straight line from the bust point up to the midpoint of the shoulder. Also check that the straps are not set too far apart at the back. The strap should sit at the midpoint between the spine and shoulder.
- If the underwire pokes into the breast tissue when you move, it is too small; if it is poking into flesh at the underarm it is too long. Change the underwire for the next size up, or remove some of its length at the underarm edge by using a different shaped/sized underwire.

Customizing underwires

To customize underwires, mark the wire at the length you want and cut through this mark with wirecutters. Dip the cut end of the wire into a liquid rubber like Plasti Dip, Household Goop, or some form of liquid rubber coating and hang with the dipped end pointing down until dry.

Fabric

Bras can be made from either woven or knit fabrics, or a mixture of the two. Some women prefer very little movement in their bra so will like a fabric with little or no stretch. If the fabric you want to use has a lot of stretch, then consider bonding to another fabric with less or no stretch.

The most important consideration in bra making is the direction of the greatest stretch in a fabric, rather than the grainline. Knit fabrics can have one- or two-way stretch, while wovens will have more stretch if cut on the bias or cross grain. By learning the direction of the greatest stretch you can use this to your advantage in bra making. Get this wrong and your bra can be a disaster. The best thing about choosing your fabric is that it actually takes very little fabric to make a bra.

How to use the direction of the greatest stretch

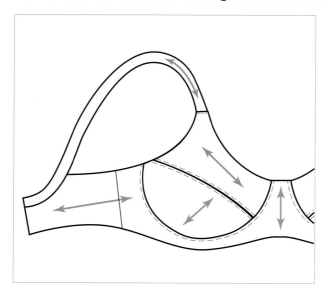

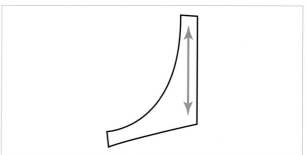

You do not want any cross stretch in the bridge and, because this area is always stabilized, remove any stretch by placing the direction of the greatest stretch parallel to the center front line.

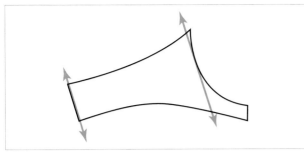

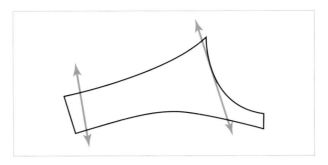

The band runs around the body, supporting the bra, so needs little stretch. Lay the pattern piece on the fabric so the greatest stretch is parallel at the center back and underwire line. You can make the stretch work for you by changing the direction of the greatest stretch in the top and lower cups, without altering the direction of stretch in the band and the bridge.

It is more important, however, that the underwire line is parallel to the greatest stretch, rather than the center back, because it helps support the cup.

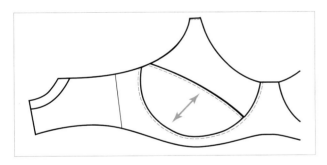

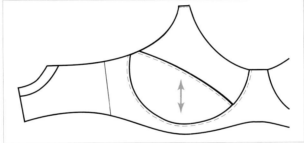

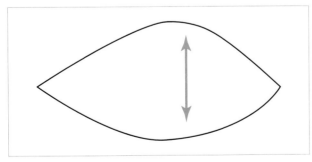

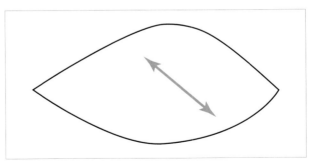

The lower cup holds the weight of the breast and you can get different effects by changing the greatest stretch. If the greatest stretch is placed straight up and down or vertical you will push the breast up, because it will pull diagonally on the body, as in a push-up or padded bra.

Most ready-to-wear lower cups are cut with the greatest stretch diagonal to the center front, which will put the pull in a vertical position on the body. Having the greatest stretch in this position will give you the most bounce.

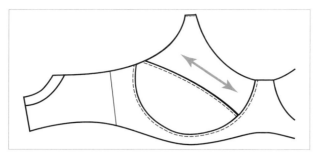

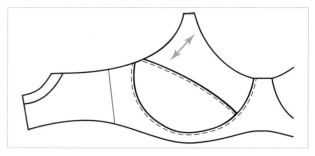

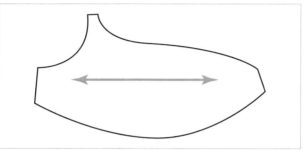

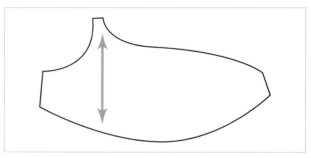

About 90 percent of ready-to-wear bras are cut with the greatest stretch in the top cup running horizontally so that it is parallel to the neckline.

If you have the greatest stretch running vertically to the neckline you will get too much stretch in the strap, but you can counteract this by adding a power bar – see power bars and collars, pages 208–10.

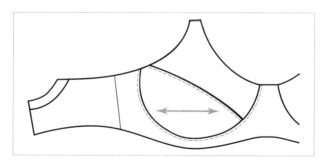

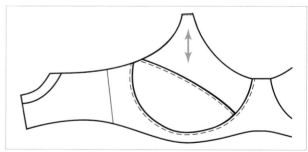

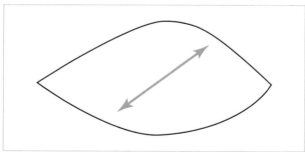

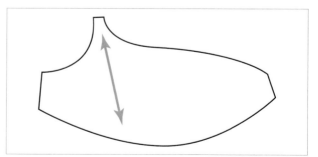

Putting the greatest stretch in a diagonal position – away from the center front – will put the pull in a horizontal position on the body. This will push the breast into the chest wall and eliminate bounce, which is what you look for in a sports bra.

Cutting the greatest stretch on the diagonal will also give too much stretch to the straps, thereby giving no support to the breast.

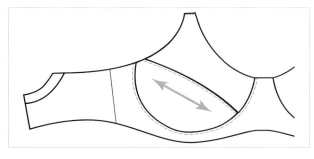

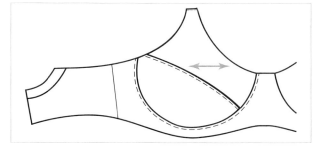

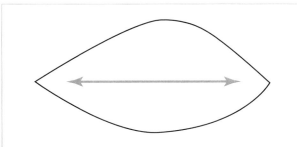

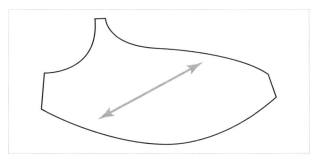

To push the breast mass out toward the sides and center front, change the greatest stretch to a horizontal position so that it pulls at a right angle to the center front line on the body. This works well for someone with a very full lower cup because it redistributes the mass.

Placing the greatest stretch on the diagonal from center front up to the underarm, so that the neckline is on the bias, will flatten the breast area because it will pull horizontally on the body.

Draping the bra

This method of draping the bra cup dates all the way back to the ancient Greeks and Romans. Greek women wore an "apodesmos" to accentuate their breasts. This breast band, made from wool or linen, was draped around the rib cage, just under the breasts, and tied at the back. The "strophium" was a form of strapless bra worn by Roman women when they were exercising or taking part in athletic competitions.

The wooden breast forms that were created by draping the breast in plaster or gummed fabric have been used by French corsetieres far longer than the padded dress forms we know today, which were first introduced at the end of the nineteenth century.

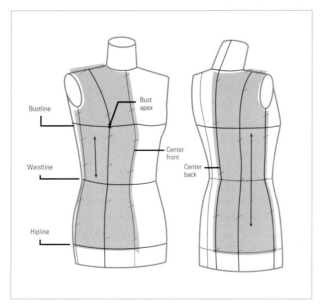

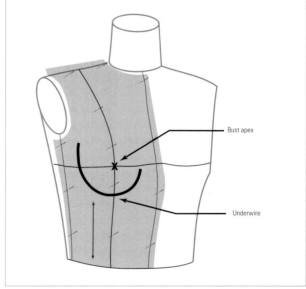

Step 1

- Drape a princess line bodice sloper (block) or muslin in medium-weight fabric on the dress form. Do not include any ease.

Step 2

- Tape the correct sized underwire to the under-breast crease of your drape on the dress form, making sure that the center of the underwire is sitting approximately ¼in (6mm) lower than the crease to allow for the tape. Draw around the wire onto the muslin.

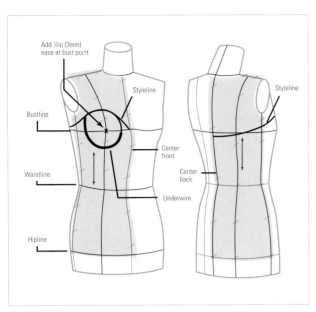

Step 3

- Mark in the bust point if you have not done so already, and add ⅛in (3mm) on the side panel at the bust apex. Adding this little bit of ease will stop the bustline from flattening out.

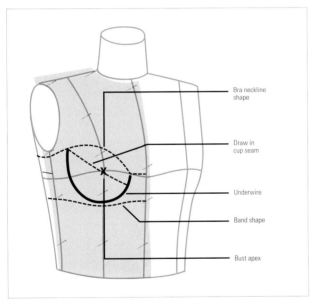

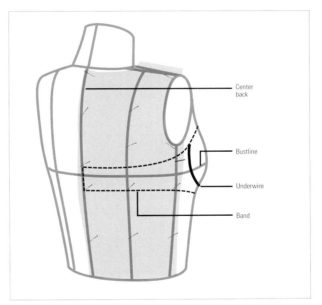

Step 4

- Mark in the stylelines of your design. Usually the measurement from the bust apex to the neckline is approximately 3in (7.5cm).

- Add notch points to both front and back. Carefully remove the drape from the dress stand and cut along the stylelines so that your drape becomes flat. The stylelines can really be any shape as long as they can be flattened when cut apart so that you can transfer them to paper.

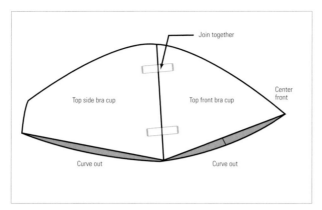

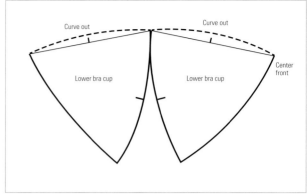

Step 5

- Transfer the draped muslin to pattern paper. The easiest way of doing this is to fold your paper in half, and place the draped muslin pieces between the two paper layers. Place weights on top of the paper so nothing can move, and trace around the outline of the drape.
- Cut out your paper pattern pieces – do not forget to include the notch points and grainlines. Join the top bra cups together to create one pattern piece.

- Curve the line from bust apex out to center front and again from bust apex out to the underarm. Repeat on the lower bra cups.

Adapting the dress form

To change the size or shape of the breast on the dress form, use shoulder pads to form the lower breast and follow this with batting (wadding) until you have the breast shape and size you want.

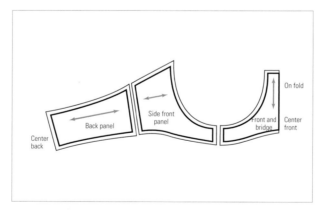

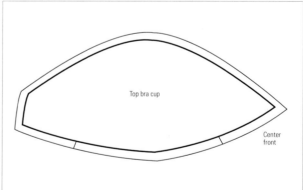

Step 6

- Add seam allowances to all the pattern pieces.

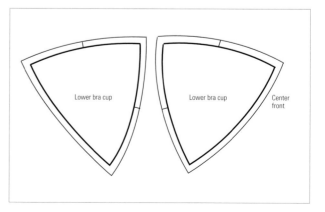

Making a bra cup from the underwire

The lower cup

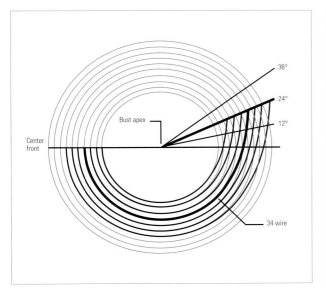

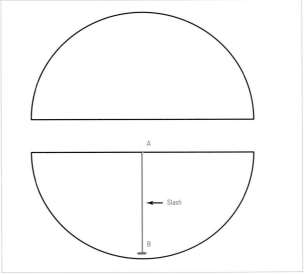

Step 1

- Measure your wire and use this measurement to draw a circle. Draw lines horizontally and vertically across the diameter of the circle. The horizontal line is the bustline.
- Position the underwire on the bustline at the center front. The tail of the wire on the opposite side will extend above and out from the bustline, but do not allow it to extend more than 36° above or the wires will dig into the body and hurt.

Step 2

- Redraw the circle in two halves without the wire tail so you now have a top cup and lower cup; cut out the lower cup.
- Cut down the center line of the lower cup to approximately ⅛in (3mm) from the bottom. Label the top of the slashed line as A and the bottom of the line as B.

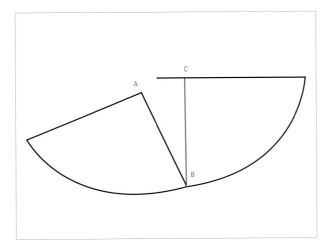

Step 3

- Spread the left side of the cup until the top edge measures the diameter of the breast. To find this measurement, divide the bustline measurement by 4 and the underbust by 4. Subtract the second from the first to give the width increase needed; usually it is between 1½–2in (3.8–5cm).
- Spread the left side of the cup the length of the width increase and mark as C.

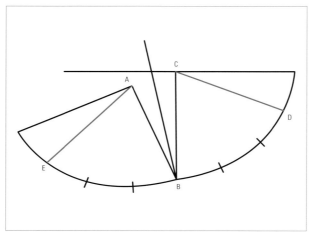

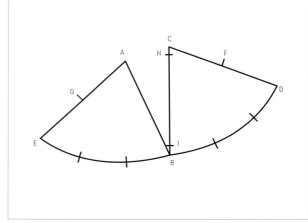

Step 4

- Divide the circumference on each side of the cup into four equal parts working from the center (B). Label the first mark from the top of the right-hand side as D and the first from the top of the left-hand side as E.
- Draw a line from A to E and C to D. Cut down both lines, removing these two segments of the circle.

Step 5

- Measure down ½in (1.3cm) from C and mark as H. Measure down ½in (1.3cm) from B and mark as I. Find the halfway point along the line from A to E and mark as G. Repeat along the line from C to D and mark as F.
- Draw lines ⅛in (3mm) long out from F and G.

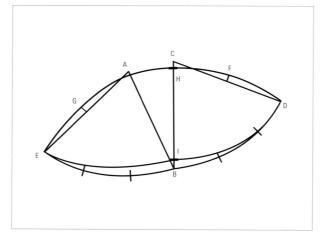

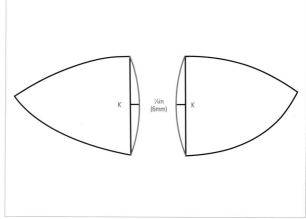

Step 6

- Using a curved ruler, draw a line from E through the point above G, through H and round to the point above F and along to D. Again using a curved ruler and starting at E, draw a line to D that passes through I.

Step 7

- Cut out the two lower cup pattern pieces along the curved lines. Measure down the cut line on both pattern pieces (from H to I and along the same line on the opposite piece) and mark the center. Draw out ¼in (6mm) from these marks and mark as K. Using a curved ruler, draw lines from the top to bottom of each line through point K.
- Add ¼in (6mm) seam allowances to all sides of the cup.

The top cup

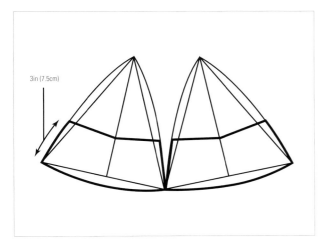

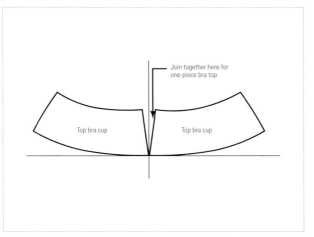

Step 1
- Make a copy of the pattern of your lower bra cups and turn it upside down. Draw a line down the center of each cup.
- Measure approximately 3in (7.5cm) up from the bottom of this line and at both sides of each triangle. Draw a line joining all three points on each triangle.

Step 2
- Cut through the line to create two top bra cups.

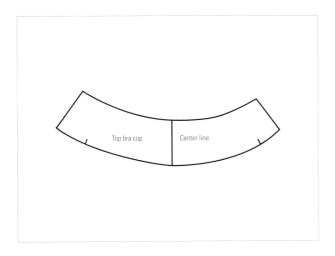

Step 3
- Join the two top cups together at the center line to create a single pattern piece.

Step 4
- Add ¼in (6mm) seam allowances to all sides of the cup.

Creating the top cup from a half circle

You can also create the pattern for the top cups by using the top half of the circle you created in Step 2 when creating the lower cup, and the calculations you made in Step 3 (see page 195).

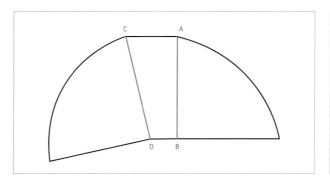

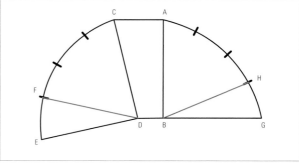

Step 1

- Divide the top half of the circle into two halves by cutting down the center line.
- Taking the right-hand segment first, label the top of the center line A and the bottom as B. Draw out 2½in (6.5cm) from A and mark as C. This is equivalent to the cup width increase plus the underbust difference.
- Draw out 1½in (3.8cm) from B and mark as D. This is the cup width increase. Draw a line connecting C to D.
- Attach the left-hand segment to this line, matching C and D to the top and bottom of the center line.

Step 2

- Divide the circumference on each segment into four equal parts, working from A and C respectively. Label the first mark from the bottom on the right-hand side as H and the first from the bottom on the left-hand side as F.
- Draw a line from B to H and from D to F. Cut down both lines, removing these two segments of the circle.

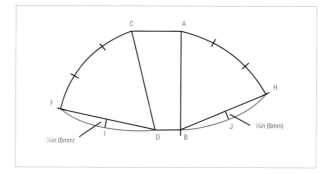

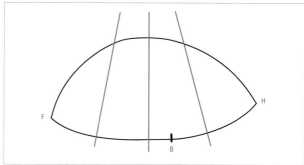

Step 3

- Find the halfway point along F–D and measure out ¼in (6mm); make a mark and label it I and repeat along the line from B to H, labeling the point J.
- Using a curved ruler, draw a line connecting points F, I, and D, and B, J, and H. Make a notch point at B which is the bust apex and will match the seam line joining the two lower cups together.

Step 4

- To find the strap position, fold the cup in half, matching the front and side points H to F. Fold in half again, keeping the lower edges aligned. Draw down these three fold lines.

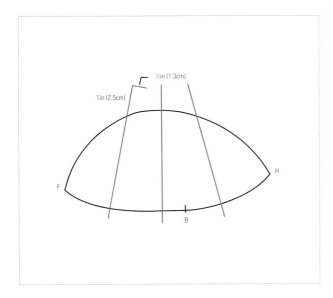

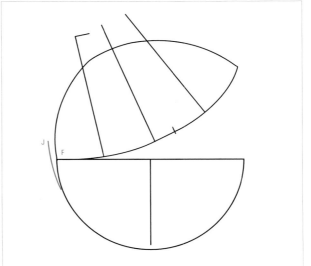

Step 5

- Measure 1in (2.5cm) up the line closest to F from the top of the cup and square across ½in (1.3cm) or the width of the strap toward the middle of the cup.

Step 6

- Return to the circle with the underarm wire extension in Step 2 (page 195). Lay the underarm side of the top cup pattern, F, onto the center line where it meets the edge of the circle. Draw in the wire extension line from Step 1 at the side of the cup and mark the tail end as J.

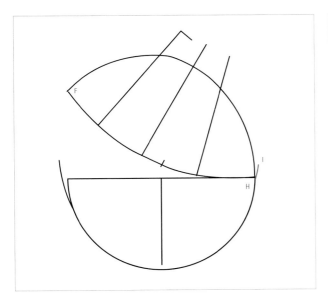

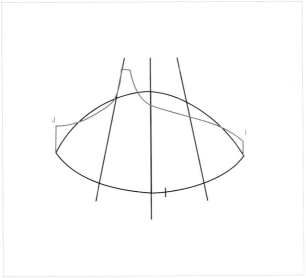

Step 7

- Lay the front of the cup H on the center front line on the circle. Measure up the circle from the center front ½in (1.3cm) and mark.
- Measure out ⅛in (3mm) from this and mark as I. Using a curved ruler draw a line from I to H.

Step 8

- Now, using the new points at I and J, draw in the armhole shape at the side of the top cup.
- Draw in the neckline from the top of the strap to the center front.

Step 9

- Add a ¼in (6mm) seam allowance to all sides of the cup.

Strapless top cup

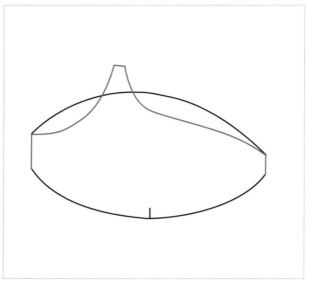

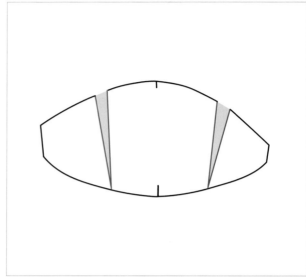

Step 1
- Round the neckline of the top cup, taking out the strap and underarm shaping. Cut out the cup.

Step 2
- Fold the cup in half and in half again, keeping the top edges aligned, so the last fold lines are angled outward at the top. Draw a line down the angled fold lines.
- Make a dart that is ¼in (6mm) wide at the top edge; tape together and reshape the neckline. This may have to be altered again if you have a fitting.

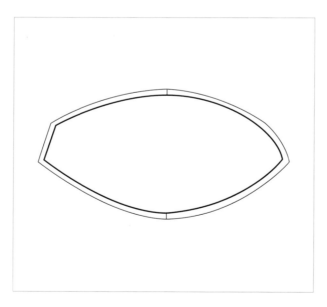

Step 3
- Add ¼in (6mm) seam allowances to all sides of the cup.

Triangle cup

The triangle-shaped cup bra will give good support for A and B cup sizes.

The triangle cup can have a vertical center seam that passes over the bust point, or the lower cup can be shaped by darts or gathers. Triangle cup bras usually do not have underwires; the straps are usually thin and can be constructed as a halter neck. Push-up pads can also be added to the inside of the cups. The width of the triangle needs to hold the fullness of the breast. Begin with the bust radius or bustline measurement and multiply it by 2.

Example: bust radius of 3½in x 2 = 7in (9cm x 2 = 18cm).

If you are gathering the bottom edge of the cup, multiply this measurement by 1.5 to create fullness. This fullness can then be gathered or darted to give the cup shape. Add 3in (7.5cm) that will not be gathered, and is positioned at the underarm.

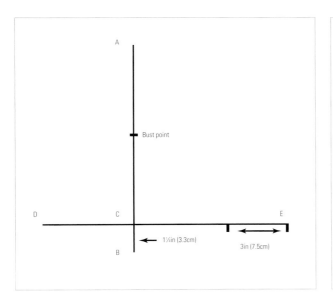

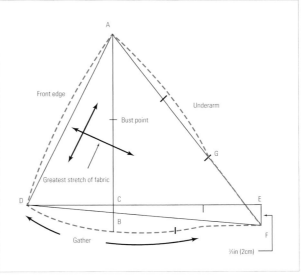

Step 1
- Draw a line that is twice the bust radius measurement and label it A to B. Measure up 1¼in (3.3cm) from B; mark as C. Draw a line at this level, D to E, which is the measurement you found above for the bottom edge of the cup. Divide A–B in half and mark as the bust apex or point.

Step 2
- Measure down ¾in (2cm) from E and mark as F. Draw a line connecting D to F. Then draw another line, starting with a convex curve from D to B and on to a point midway between B and F, where you can reverse the curve slightly to meet the original line just before F. Draw a slightly convex curve from A to D. Divide A to F into three equal parts, marking the lowest point as G. Draw a slightly convex line from A to G.

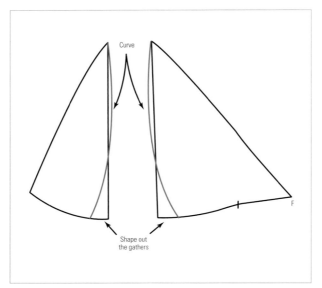

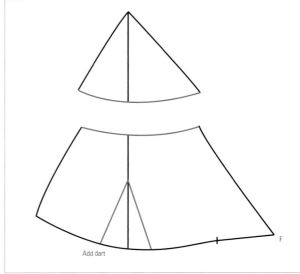

Step 3

- Make design changes to the cup now, remembering that if you want to include a dart it should finish 1in (2.5cm) below the bust point. Cut through the center line for two pattern pieces or cut a horizontal line through the bust point to make a top and lower cup. Make a notch 3in (7.5cm) in from F along the lower edge.

Adding styling details to the bra

There are many cup shapes. As long as the seams intersect the bust apex, you can be as creative in your styling as you like. Unless you are looking at a molded bra cup with no seams, most cups will have at least one cross seam. When designing, it is important to consider the fabric: a print fabric, for example, may require multiple seams to make the best use of the print, whereas too many seams will spoil a lace fabric.

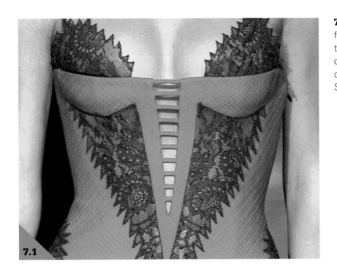

7.1

7.1 / By cleverly combining fabrics and contrasting colors, the house of Versace has created very interesting bra cups for this dress. (Spring/ Summer 2002).

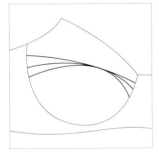 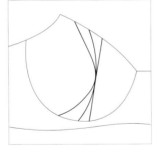 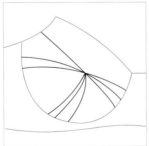 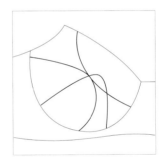 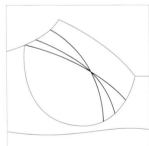

Horizontal seams

You can add curve to this seam line but it should always start and finish inside the wire. This works well for larger cup sizes because it will reduce the projection of the breast. A horizontal seam line like this shaped virtually all bra cups before the 1970s.

Vertical seams

This seam starts in the neckline and runs under the breast, giving great support. Curve can be added to both the inner and outer cups.

Adding more seams

Add extra seams for aesthetic appeal, extra support, or more room in your cup, so long as one seam runs over the bust apex. This is a great way to add a front neckline band, contrasting fabrics, or color blocking.

Curved seams

These seams can start and end under the breast, changing direction at the bust apex. This seam stabilizes the breast area while giving uplift.

Diagonal seams

These seams can start anywhere in the underarm curve and end anywhere, so long as the seam intercepts the bust apex.

The bullet bra

This retro bra is from the 1950s; worn under tight-fitting sweaters it gave the breast a pointed cone shape. It hit the headlines when Madonna wore a range of lingerie items featuring cone-shaped bra cups designed by Jean Paul Gaultier for her Blonde Ambition tour in 1990.

The fabric has to be rigid, with any stretch removed, for this bra to work; you do not want the points to collapse or flatten. Add padding to the back of the fabric and channel stitch all the layers together.

7.2

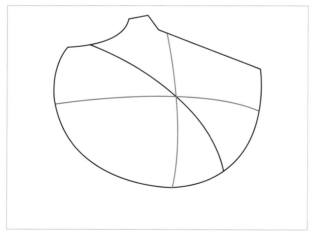

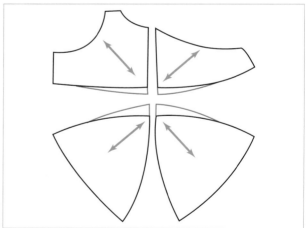

Step 1
- Working with the full cup, mark the bust apex. Making sure you pass through the apex, divide the cup into four equal parts and mark. Cut the cup apart down these lines.

Step 2
- Straighten out the line from the underarm to the bust point on all four cup pieces; add a slight curve to the line. The straighter the line, the sharper the points on the cone-shaped cups will be.

7.2 / Madonna on stage in 1990 wearing Jean Paul Gaultier's corset featuring cone-shaped bra cups.

The soft bra cup

The soft cup bra is reminiscent of the beautiful silk bra cups from the 1920s and 30s.
This bra cup has no underwire, so all the support has to come from the band.

A soft bra cup can been made up of two or three panel pieces. The cups can extend to the center front, taking in the bridge. The back panel extends into the cup at the underarm, giving a softer edge to the cup where it transitions into the band. The cup can also be framed all around, giving a softer edge. Darts can be added to the lower cup for shaping and the band can be longer for more support.

Tape together

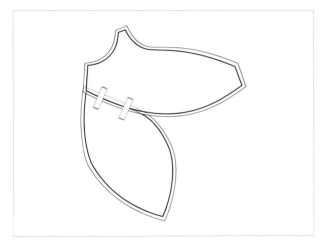

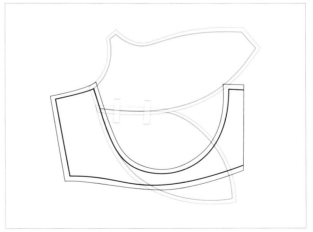

Step 1
- Tape the front band pattern pieces together, overlapping the seam allowances.
- Align the pattern piece for the lower bra cup with the top cup, overlapping the seam allowances, and tape together starting at the side seam line.

Step 2
- Line the side of the cup up with the band, overlapping the seam allowances.

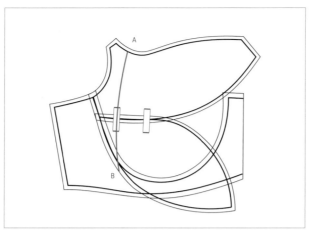

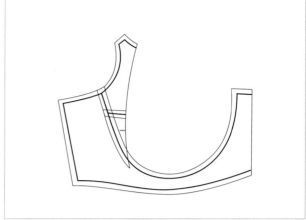

Step 3

- Draw a curved line from a point on the top cup just over from the strap point A, down to where the lower cup is touching the bottom of the band B.

Step 4

- You will have to slash the lower cup where the seams start to move apart so that the seam line on the cup follows that on the band. This should form a small dart or overlap in the cup. The cup should also be lying flat.

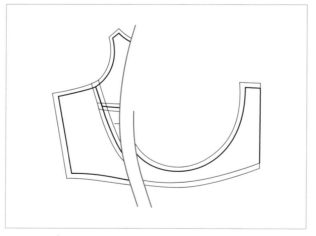

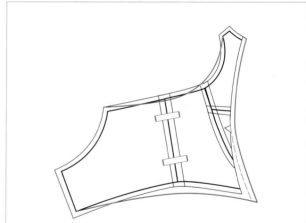

Step 5

- Cut down the line separating the cups from the band, cutting the band apart.

Step 6

- Join the back band to the front band at the side seam and tape together.
- Straighten out the bottom of the lower band to give more support and blend all the curves. Add seam allowances.

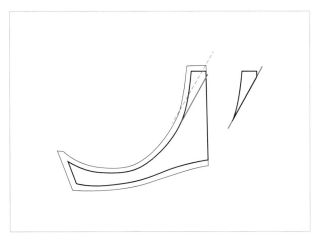

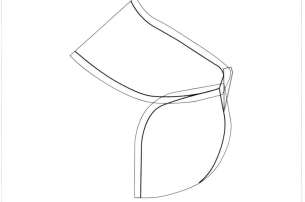

Step 7

- Straighten out the bottom of the bridge at the center front. Draw a straight line from the bottom of the band at the bust point up to the center front. Recurve the band, adding seam allowances.

Step 8

- Align the pattern piece for the lower bra cup with the top cup, overlapping the seam allowances, and tape together, starting at the front edge. Add the piece that you have just removed from the bridge to the cups.

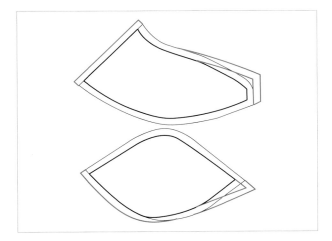

Step 9

- Reshape the front neckline on both the top and lower cups. Add seam allowances.

Power bars and collars

The power bar (also called a "sling" or "frame") is made as a separate piece of the cup, directly underneath the strap. Usually it is made from a different, non-stretch fabric, with the stretch direction running perpendicular to the strap extension, giving maximum resistance to strap pull. It can be made as part of the inner cup and so be invisible, or be part of the seaming showing on the outside. The power bar is essentially what makes the push-up bra work.

7.3

Adding a power bar that sits inside the cup

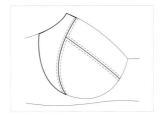

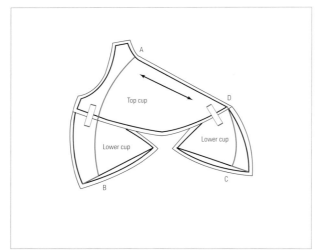

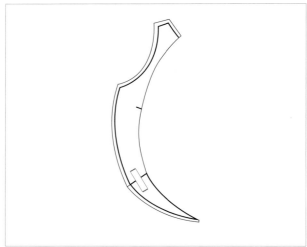

Step 1

- Trace a three-piece cup pattern with the lower cup divided into two (see page 194). Align the lower cup pieces with the top cup at center front and armhole edges and tape together.
- Redraw the straight seam line on both lower cups to give additional lift. Draw a curved line from A to B and C to D the width of the power bar.

Step 2

- Trace the power bar onto paper, joining the underbust line, creating one paper piece. Make a notch point where the top and lower cups meet at the armhole edge.
- Add a seam allowance to the outside edge only. The inner edge is left unfinished or serged (overlocked).

7.3 / This bra has a power bar inside the cup. You can just make out its outline.

Adding a power bar to the bra cup

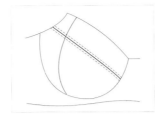

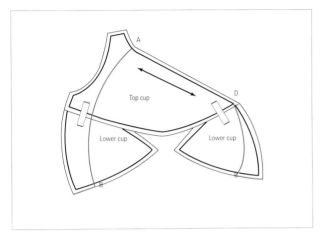

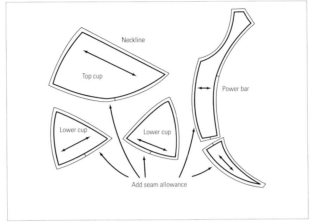

Step 1

- Trace off a three-piece cup pattern with the lower cup divided into two (see page 194). Align the lower cup pattern pieces to the top cup at center front and armhole edges and tape together.
- Draw a curved line from A to B and C to D the width of the power bar.

Step 2

- Cut through the curved lines, making two new pattern pieces. Trace off the new shapes for top and lower cup.
- Add seam allowances to all pattern edges and make a notch point on the power bar where the top and lower cups meet at the armhole edge.

Which type of power bar?

The classic push-up bras of the 1960s were cut with the power bar as a separate pattern piece, with the collar circling the cups. They were often made from a contrasting fabric to the cups and added interesting detail to the bra. Today they are mostly hidden away inside the cup. An interior power bar will push the breast forward and can also give lift. This type is often used if there is a lace cup, in order to absorb the strap pull on such a delicate fabric.

Collar

A collar is a circle of fabric on the inside of the cup to support a heavy breast, made from a fabric with little or no stretch. The collar can be part of the outer cup and made from powernet or another contrasting fabric. The collar can also be worn alone as a provocative bedroom bra.

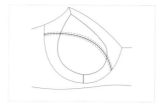

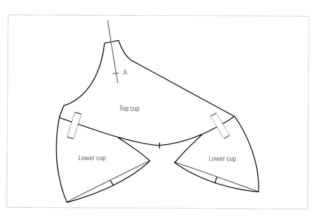

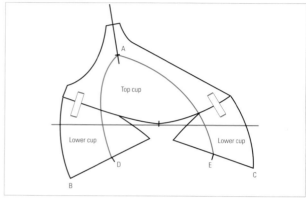

Step 1

- Trace off the pattern pieces of a top bra cup and two lower bra cups (see page 194). Align the pattern piece for the front lower bra cup to the top cup and tape together, starting at the front edge.
- Align the back lower cup at the armhole edge and tape in place. Only tape the cups until they start to shape so that you keep them flat.
- Draw a line down through the center of the strap. Measure the length you want the collar at this point and mark as A. Redraw the straight seam line on both the lower cups.

Step 2

- From B, measure up the height of the collar on the back lower cup seam line and mark as D. Repeat from C on the front lower cup and mark as E.
- Starting at A draw a line that curves down to D. Again, starting from A and curving around the front of the cup, draw a line down to E.
- Draw a horizontal line across the bust apex, which is marked with a notch point on the top cup; this will be the grainline.

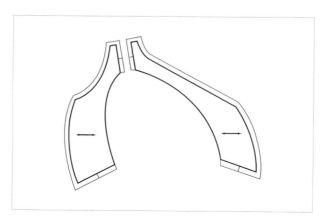

- Trace off the two collar pattern pieces, dividing them at the line marked A.
- Add seam allowances to the outside edges and add notches at the strap seam and on the lower cup seam. Mark the grainline.

Designing the bridge

This is the area of the bra that gets the most pull and strain because it carries the weight of the breasts. This is an important factor to remember when thinking of lowering the bridge, or adding a closure at the center front that must sit on the point of most strain. The breasts will swing out to the sides if the closure is too high or fall out of the cups if it is too low.

7.4

Bridge types

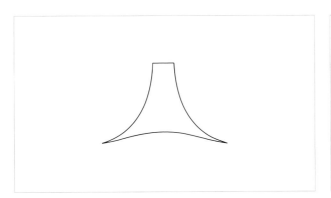

Bridge for a partial bra band.

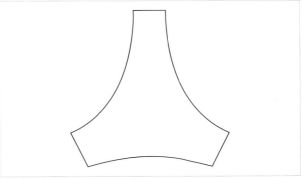

Bridge that is cut to match up with the cup seaming.

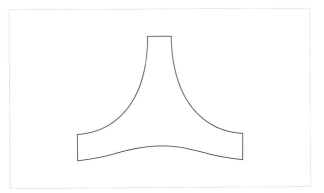

Bridge that finishes under the bust apex.

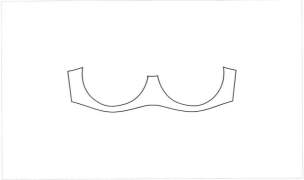

Bridge that frames the front of the bra to the side seams.

7.4 / Full cup bra with a good height bridge.

Changing the bridge

Changing the bridge by lowering the top edge and creating
a partial band still enables you to have a full cup. The
underwire and bra cup will extend above the bridge, with
no change to the neckline.

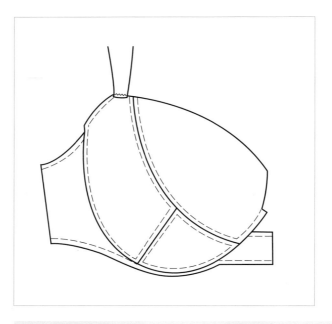

Styles of bridge

The bridge can be a crisscross of ribbon, a piece of
cord or be part of the underwiring when a continuous
underwire is used. The width of the bridge can
decrease as the cup size increases. The length of the
bridge will increase with the increase in cup size. For
the fit of the bra it is important that the bridge is sitting
on the rib cage with no gapping. If the bridge is rising
up so that it appears to be sitting on top of the breasts,
the bra is not the correct fit and it could be that the cup
size is too small. Sports and bandeau-style bras can be
knitted on a circular knitting machine with the tension
being tightened in the bridge area.

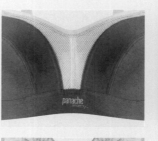

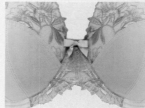

Designing the band

A full-band bra can carry a design detail from the bridge to the center back. You can split the band at the side underarm, under the bust apex, or match a cup seam line. The band can cover the upper torso, finishing at the waist, as in a bustier that is either worn as underwear or outerwear. A partial band can begin at the side of the cup extending around to the back. The band can be made in powernet, or from fashion fabric that matches the cups, or a mixture of both.

7.5

Making a full band from a wire

If you are using powernet or other stretch fabric you will need to deduct the amount of stretch from your pattern pieces. Please refer to the stretch deduction chart in Chapter 1, page 17.

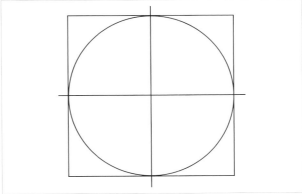

Step 1

- Measure the diameter of your wire and draw a square with this width and height.
- Draw lines dividing the square in half both lengthwise and widthwise to form a cross.
- Draw a circle inside the square, touching each side at the halfway point.

7.5 / A very deep and ornate band (Victoria's Secret, 2013).

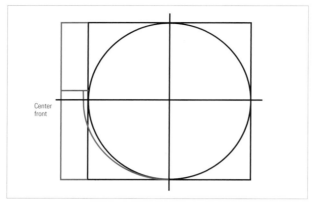

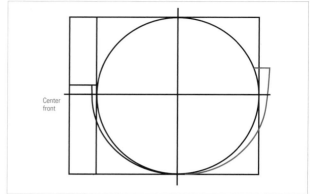

Step 2

- Decide which side of the circle is going to be the front of the bra and which is the back. Extend the top, middle, and bottom lines of the square out ¾in (2cm).
- Draw a line parallel to the vertical line on the side you decided is the front and label it as the center front.
- From the horizontal line, measure up ½in (1.3cm) along the vertical line at the side of the circle, parallel to the new center front line, and out ⅛in (3mm), and make a mark. From this point, draw a curved line, blending back into the lower half of the circle.
- Draw a line out to the center front line from the top of the new blended line. This is the top of the bridge.

Step 3

- From the horizontal line on the opposite side of the circle, measure up ¾in (2cm) and out ¼in (6mm) and make a mark.
- From this point draw a curved line, blending it back into the lower half of the circle. Draw a horizontal line to the edge of the circle.

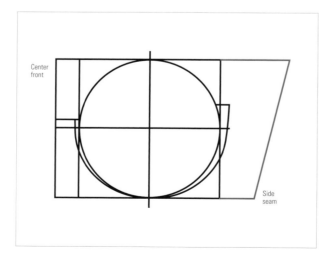

Step 4

- Find a quarter of both the bustline and underbust measurements. Subtract the measurement of the diameter of the wire from the quarter of the bustline measurement.
- Using this new measurement, draw a line extending out from the top of the square at the side of the cup. Subtract the diameter of the wire from the quarter of the underbust measurement.
- Using this new measurement, draw a line extending out from the bottom of the square at the side of the cup. Draw a line connecting these two lines and label as the side seam.

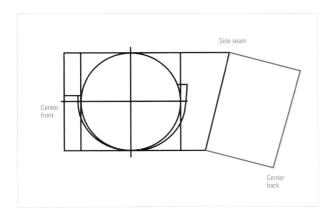

Step 5

- Draw a line measuring a quarter of the bustline measurement at right angles to the top of the side seam. Draw a parallel line measuring a quarter of the underbust measurement at right angles to the bottom of the side seam. Connect these two lines and label it as the center back.

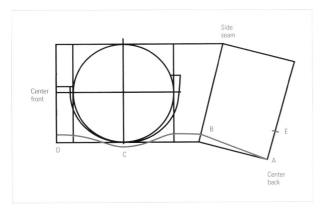

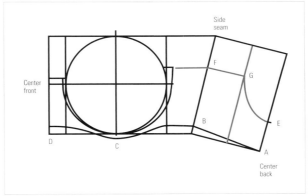

Step 6

- Now shape the lower edge. Decide how many rows of hooks and eyes you want for the back closure and measure up the center back from A the length of the hook and eye tape; make a mark, labeling it as E.
- Measure from the bottom up the side seam between ⅛in (3mm) and ¾in (2cm), depending on your design, and mark as B.
- Measure down from the center of the circle ⅜in (1cm), once again depending on your design, and mark as C.
- Finally measure up the center front line between ¼in (6mm) and ¾in (2cm), and mark as D. Using a curved ruler, draw a line, connecting A and B with a straight line, curve down to C, and curve back up to D.

Step 7

- Shape the top edge. Measuring up from B on the side seam, make a mark level with the top of the cup and label as F.
- Draw a line from here across to the side of the cup. Divide the section in half between the side seam and the center back and draw in a line.
- Make a mark on this line that is level with F and label it as G. Draw a line from F to G. Then draw a line that curves down from G toward E on the center back, forming the back strap curve.
- Curving the back of the band down so it is lower on the pattern than the bottom of the cup will give you the most support. You will get less support if you keep the curve level with the bottom of the cup. A band that is not curved will offer no support and is most likely to ride up.

The partial-band bra

The partial band starts at the side of the bra cup; there is no band under the cup. This kind of band can be used when the cup has been lowered into a demi cup, which also lowers the back band. The support for this bra comes from the underwires. The center back length is still determined by the number of hook and eye closures. Follow the steps for the full band down to the end of Step 5. Vertically halve the section between the side seam and center back.

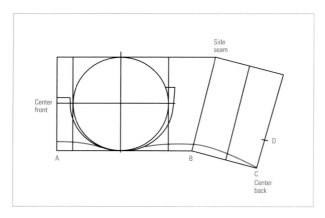

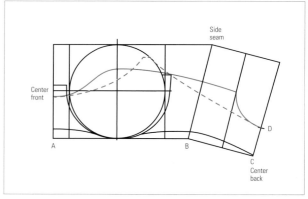

Step 1

- Shape the lower edge of the band, removing it from under the cup. Starting at A, measure up the center front line ½in (1.3cm) to ¾in (2cm) – this is a design decision – and draw in the bottom edge of the bridge, curving it down to the bottom of the lower front cup.
- Measure between ⅛in (3mm) and ¾in (2cm) up the side seam and mark as B. From the bottom of the side lower cup draw in the bottom of the band, curving up at B and down to C.
- Measure up the center back the length of your hook and eye closure and mark as D.

Step 2

- The shape of the top edge of the band will change with the design of the neckline of your cups. Begin by drawing the neckline of the cup and continue this line over to the center front line.
- The bridge can also be lower than your cup neckline – the choice is yours. Now draw in the back of the partial band. This is also your choice of design.
- Shown here are two different stylelines; one shows the partial band with a strap extension and the other with a back strap curve.

The long-line bra

Another name for the long-line bra is a bustier. In the 1970s, Frederick's of Hollywood made a whole range of different bustiers when underwear as outerwear first became fashionable. The band of a long-line bra is lengthened, and can go all the way down to the waist, which distributes the support over the whole of the lower torso. Boning can be added to the band front and back panels, and to side seams, to flatten and smooth out the abdomen. Because the support is in the longer band and not from the shoulders, the bra is perfect strapless.

7.6

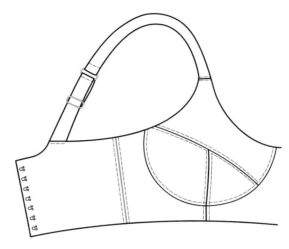

Band for a strapless bra

Follow the steps for making a band from the underwire for a short band or even a partial band. The following steps show how to extend the band down to the waistline, covering the upper torso.

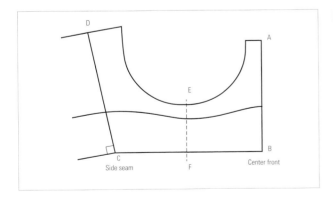

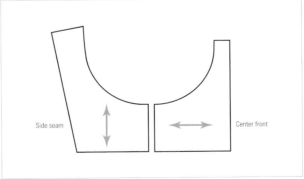

Step 1

- Draw a line from the top of the bridge at the center front A to the waist at B and label it as the center front.
- Square across at the waist from B one quarter of the waist measurement; mark as C.
- Draw a line up from this point to the top of the side seam; mark as D. Draw a line down to the waistline from under the cup apex point E; mark as F.

Step 2

- Divide the front into two pattern pieces or leave as one piece. By cutting the front band you are able to change the direction of the greatest stretch in the fabric.

7.6 / Long-line bra with lacy band.

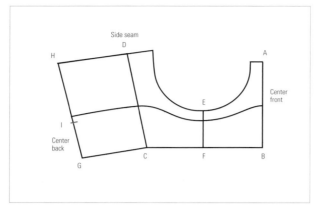

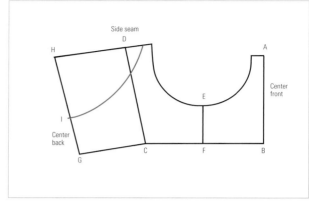

Step 3
- Square over for the back from C one quarter of the waist measurement. If you are using a stretch fabric the amount of stretch will have to be subtracted from the waistline measurement. Also subtract ⅞in (2.2cm) for the hook and eye closure. Make a mark and label it G.
- Draw a line up to the top of the center back; mark as H. Decide the amount of hook and eye closures for the center back and, measuring up from G, mark as I.

Step 4
- Drop the back the depth you want for a backless style, finishing at the center back hook and eye mark at I.

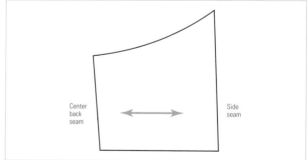

Step 5
- Curve the waistline for a better fit on the body.

Step 6
- Cut the front and back apart through the side seam. Mark in the greatest stretch on the back pattern piece.

Straps

The strap can be an extension of the top cup or it can be attached to the cup either with stitching or through a slider or ring. If the strap is an extension of the cup, include it on your pattern. The strap can also be shaped and padded at the shoulder point. This will stop it from indenting the shoulder and can help relieve both the back and shoulder pain that is often associated with heavier breasts.

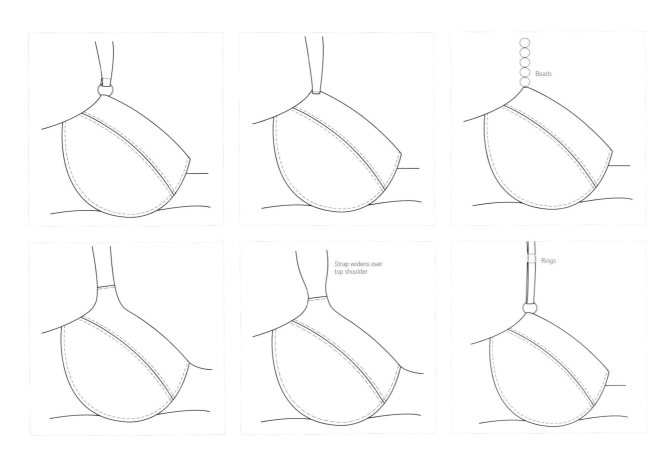

The straps can be made from the same fabric as the bra – giving a uniform look – or a mix of elastic and tape. The adjusters can either be at the front or back of the strap. Straps can also be removable or interchangeable, spaghetti, or even made from beads, all of which can be attached to the cup using a loop of fabric, tape, or ribbon and a G-hook.

The back elastic strap can be integrated with the top of the band, finishing at the end of the hook and eye closure, sewn to the top of the band, or attached to the back band via a ring and elastic extension.

Changing the neckline

The neckline can be raised for a full-cup bra, especially for larger sizes, or lowered as for a demi or balconette bra. When you lower the neckline the front strap position will become wider. The neckline can be finished with lace appliqué, embroidered and beaded, or finished with a band or binding.

7.7

Making a demi cup from a regular cup

Drop the neckline to 1in (2.5cm) above the bust apex. The underwire will be shorter and the cup will be tilted and pushed toward the center. The top edge of the bridge will also drop to give you a continuous neckline. The red line shows a continuous line from the center front up to a strap extension. The dotted line shows a slightly shaped neckline with no strap extension and a dropped front bridge.

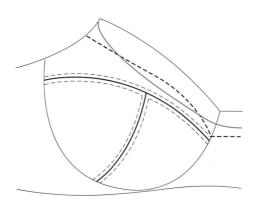

7.8

7.7 / A variety of neckline types.
7.8 / Demi cup.

Faux demi cup

The faux demi cup is molded today from silicone. It is held together with a continuous underwire over both molded cups, which forms the bridge at the front of the bra. As the cup is molded with a strap extension the strap is then made with a front slider. The channeling for the wire can be attached to the right side of the cup and, as it is also continuous, can be made in a contrasting color or fabric.

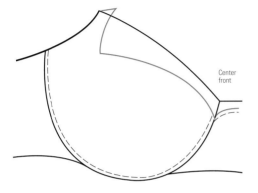

Center front

7.9

Full cup

This cup works well for the larger-busted woman and can also be known as the full-support bra. Raise the top of the bridge and adjust the top cup at the front, so that the neckline finishes at the strap.

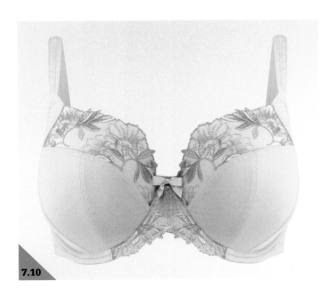

7.10

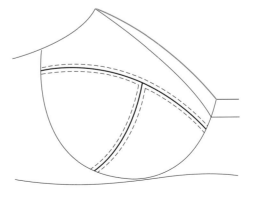

7.9 / Faux demi cup.
7.10 / Full cup.

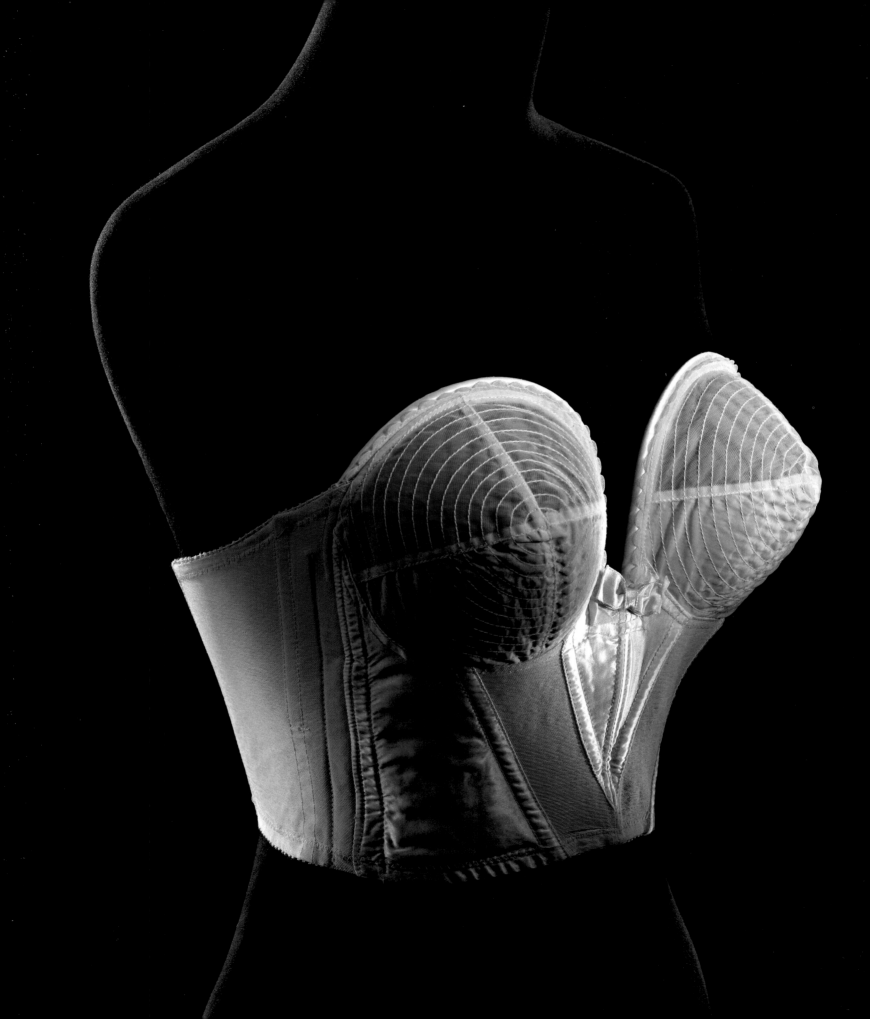

8 Construction Techniques
The bra

To construct a bra, first make the cups and then join together all the pieces that make up the band. The cups are then set into the band and the straps attached to the top of the neckline on the top cup. The elastic is then attached to the bottom of the band, followed by the underarm elastic and neckline trim, and finally the closure. The seam allowance is ¼in (6mm) and a straight stitch with a stitch length of 2.5mm is used for all construction. A zigzag stitch with a width of 2.5mm and stitch length of 2mm is used to attach the elastic, followed by a 3 step zigzag set at 4.5mm wide with a stitch length of 1.5mm–2mm to finish attaching the elastic to the band. A machinist is given just 12½ minutes in the industry to make a bra.

Bra construction materials

- Fabric for the cups, bridge, and band
- Lining for the cups (optional)
- Sewing thread
- Lace and trims
- Seam cover tape (optional)
- Padding (optional)
- Interfacing (optional)
- Plush hem elastic and picot-edged elastic
- Strap elastic and tape
- Underwire channeling and underwires
- Findings, sliders, rings
- Hook and eye tape
- Embellishments (optional)

Bra bustier from France, 1950, featuring a low bridge and spiral stitched cups.

Bra cup construction

Bra cups can be made from a sheer fabric, all-over lace, tricot, or your choice of fashion fabric. The lower cup can be lightly padded and channel stitched for both strength and additional decorative detail, while the top cup can be made from all-over lace and embroidered sheer fabric, or from the same fabric as the lower cup. The cup can be made from two or more pattern pieces; the whole cup can be divided into four pattern pieces to create a cone shape, for example, or the lower cup can be divided into two or three pattern pieces, with the top cup cut in one piece.

Seam cover tape
A bias-cut tape is usually made from lightweight nylon. Narrow satin, organza, plush, or velvet ribbon can also be used as a seam cover. Do not confuse this seam cover with boning casing, which is heavier and stronger. A seam cover can be used to cover any seam allowances where you do not want to add any bulk such as in bra cups. When working with lace or other sheer fabrics, the lightweight nylon or soft organza ribbon or tape will hide the seam allowances on the back and not show through to the front of the garment.

Two-piece cup

This is the simplest cup construction, with all the shape created by one central dividing seam that can be drafted vertically, horizontally, or angled across the bustline.

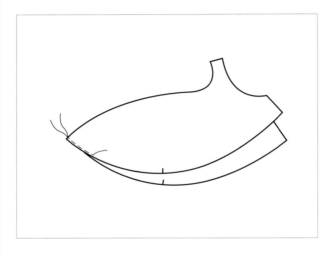

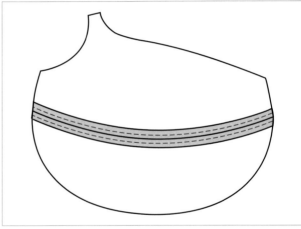

Step 1
- Using a straight stitch with a stitch length of 2–2.5mm, attach the lower cup to the top cup.

Step 2
- Press the seam open and cover it with seam cover tape. Topstitch along both sides of the seam through the seam allowances, keeping the stitching very close to the seam. Cut the seam cover tape back so that it matches up with the seam allowance.

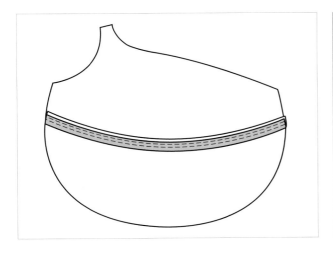

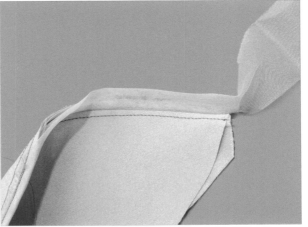

Step 3

- Alternatively, you can press the seam allowance up, cover the seam with seam cover tape, and stitch two rows of topstitching along the seam allowance.

Step 4

- If you are making a delicate sheer or lace cup you can bind the seam with a piece of bias-cut fabric or stretch knit and then topstitch it in place.
- If the cup is all sheer or lace fabric, press the seam allowances together and up toward the top cup; if the top cup only is sheer or lace, press the seam allowance together and down toward the lower cup.
- Place your binding along the back or under side of the seam allowances and stitch in place, being careful not to stretch the binding as you stitch.

Step 5

- Fold the binding over the seam allowances and stitch along the line of stitching, joining the binding to the back of the seam allowance.
- Turn the cup to the right side and finish with either one or two rows of topstitching close to the seam line.

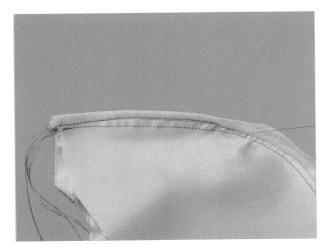

Adding darts to the lower cup

Darts can be added to the lower cup for shaping. A dart can be placed on either side of the center on the lower cup, with the top of the dart pointing away from the bustline or apex. Adding two darts in this way will give more support than adding one centered dart if you are making the cup in a soft silk.

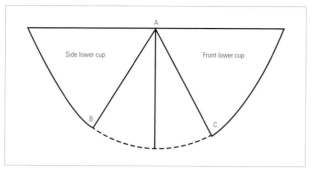

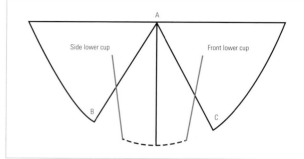

Step 1

- Draw a horizontal line and mark the center point on the line as A. Place the top edge of both the side lower cup piece and the front lower cup piece along the line, joining the two together at A.
- Mark the center bottom of the side lower cup as B and the center bottom of the front lower cup as C. Draw a smooth curved line from B to C. At 90° to A draw a straight line to meet this curved line.

Step 2

- Measure from B to the center line and C to the center line; these two measurements give you the width of the front and underarm darts.
- Measure approximately 1in (2.5cm) from C toward B for the front dart placement line. Draw a line up from this point, pointing toward the front edge of the neckline, ending approximately 1in (2.5cm) from the top edge. Repeat from B for the underarm dart placement line, pointing the line toward the underarm or strap point.

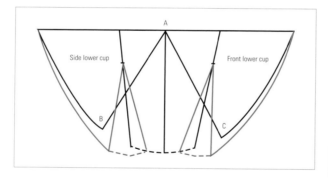

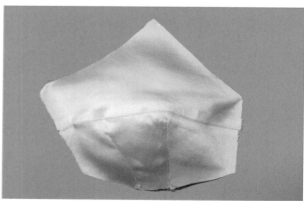

Step 3

- Divide the front dart width measurement (see Step 2) in two. Measure that distance to either side of the front dart placement line.
- From the new points, draw both dart legs to the top of the dart placement line. Repeat for the underarm dart.
- Draw a new curved line from the front edge of the lower cup to the outer dart leg. Repeat from the underarm point.
- Fold the darts and redraw the bottom edge of the cup as a smooth, curved line. Open up the new pattern.

Step 4

- Make the darts in your fabric, securing both the top and bottom of the darts; press the darts so that they are facing in toward the center.
- Finish with topstitching or appliqué lace over the darts on the right side.

Three-piece cup

This cup has a one-piece top cup and a lower cup that has been cut in two pieces. The lower cup can be padded, channel stitched, and lined, while the top cup can be made in the same or contrasting fabric, lace, or sheer fabric.

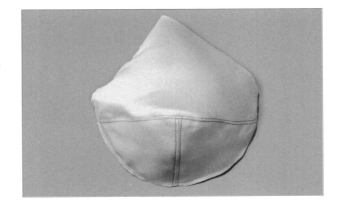

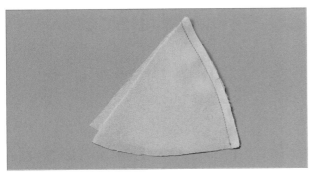

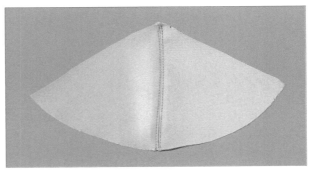

Step 1

- If the lower cup is divided into more than one pattern piece, join them together before attaching them to the top cup. Use a straight stitch with a stitch length of 2–2.5mm.

Step 2

- Press the seam open, cover the seam with seam cover tape, and topstitch through the seam allowances, stitching close to the seam line. If you are not padding the lower cup, move to Step 4.

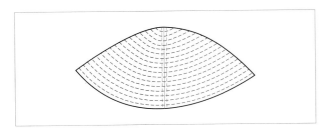

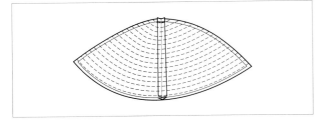

Step 3

- The lower cup can be padded and channel stitched for added support or as an embellishment. Again, this has to be done before joining to the top cup. Cut the padding out minus seam allowances because you do not want to add extra bulk to the seams.
- Following the shape of the bottom of the cup, and with a stitch length of 2.5–3mm, work parallel rows of stitching approximately ¼in (6mm) apart.

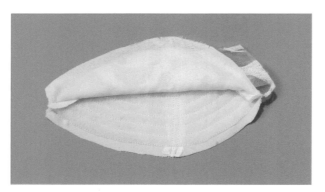

Step 4

- Attach the lower cup to the top cup (see the two-piece cup, Step 2, page 224). Press the seam open and topstitch along both sides of the seam through the seam allowances, keeping the stitching close to the seam line.
- You can now add a lining to cover the padding, making the bra more comfortable to wear against the skin. Cut the lining to fit inside the lower cup. Press the seam allowance at the top of the lining down and edge stitch close to the seam line at the top of the lower cup.

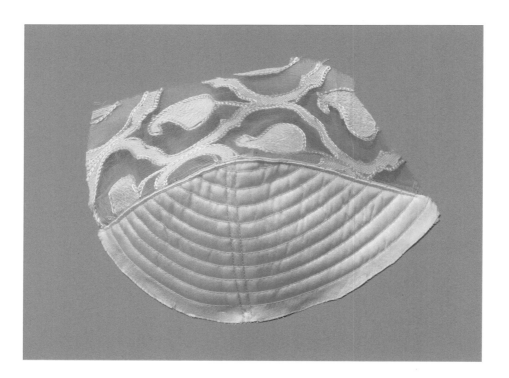

The soft bra cup

All the support for the soft bra has to come from the band. To create this support the band can entirely encircle the cup, as in a sports bra, or extend up the underarm to the strap. Consider using a contrasting fabric such as lace or a mesh to make these band extensions.

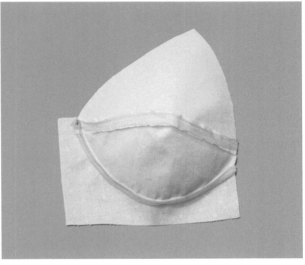

Step 1

- Stitch the top and lower cups together. Cover the seam with seam cover tape and topstitch through the seam allowances along both sides of the seam.

Step 2

- Attach the front band to the cups. Press the seam allowance toward the band and cover with seam cover tape, channeling or seam binding before finishing with two rows of topstitching sewn through the seam allowance, close to the seam.

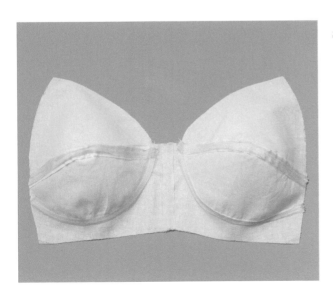

Step 3

- Sew the center front seam of the band together. Press open the seam and cover with seam cover tape; topstitch along both sides of the seam through the seam allowances, keeping the stitching close to the seam.

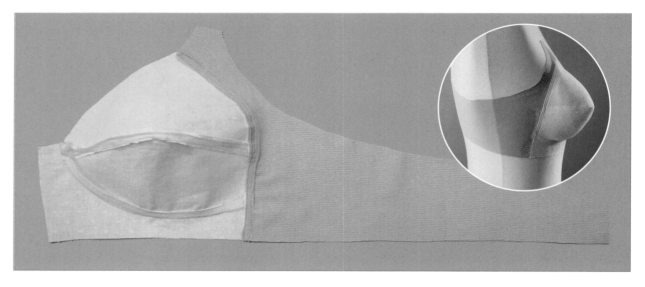

Step 4

- Sew the extended band to the underarm cup, matching the notch points. Press the seam allowance onto the cup.

- Cover the seam with channeling or a seam binding; finish with two rows of topstitching through the seam allowance, keeping the stitching close to the seam.

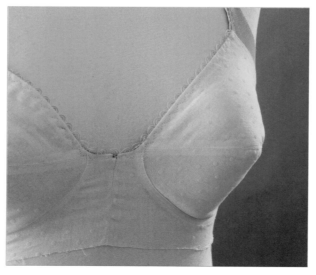

Step 5

- Finish the neckline with elastic trim. Lay the elastic trim on the right side of the cup with the wrong side up and the flat edge of the elastic along the neckline. Zigzag in place with a stitch width of 2mm–5mm and length of 2mm close to the picot edge.

- Fold the edge to the wrong side of the neckline so that only the picot edge is showing on the right side and stitch in place with either a zigzag stitch or three-step zigzag stitch with a stitch width of 2mm–5mm and length of 2mm.

Triangle cup

The bottom of the triangle cup is usually attached to a
narrow fabric band, through which a piece of elastic is
threaded. The sides of the cup are usually finished with
elastic trim.

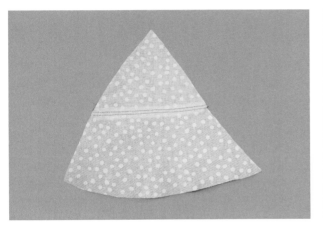

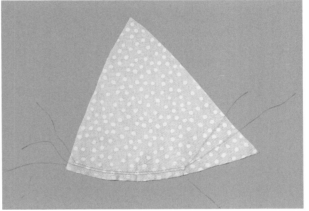

Step 1

- If the cup has been divided into two pattern pieces,
  sew them together. Cover the seam allowance with
  seam cover tape and topstitch through the seam
  allowance along both sides of the seam.

Step 2

- With the stitch length set to 4mm, stitch two rows
  of gathering stitches along the bottom of the cup
  between the notch points indicating the gathering.

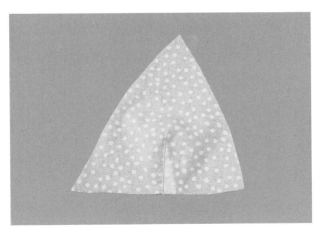

Step 3

- If the cup has a dart, sew the dart together, press the
  dart toward the neckline edge, and topstitch through it
  with a stitch length of 2.5–3mm, close to the seam.

Step 4

- Lay the elastic trim on the right side with the wrong side up, and the flat edge of the elastic along the neckline. Zigzag in place with a stitch width of 2mm–5mm and length of 2mm close to the picot edge.
- Fold the edge to the wrong side of the neckline so only the picot edge is showing on the right side and stitch in place with either a zigzag stitch or three-step zigzag stitch with a stitch width of 2mm–5mm and length of 2mm. Repeat on the underarm side of the cup.
- Pull the gathering stitches up so that you are taking out the added fullness only.

Step 5

- To construct the band, cut a piece of fabric twice the width of your elastic plus seam allowance. The length of the fabric needs to be the under bust measurement plus 10 percent. For example, if your underbust measurement is 34½in (88cm) + 10% = 38in (97cm). Cut a piece of elastic the length of the underbust measurement.
- Find and mark the center of the fabric band. You will sew the cups either side of this mark.
- Turn in a seam allowance of ¼in (6mm) along one edge. Along the other edge, place the cups with the right side of the band to the wrong side of the cups. Press the seam allowance down into the band.

Step 6

- Fold the band in half and turn up so that the stitching attaching the band and the cup is covered. Press.

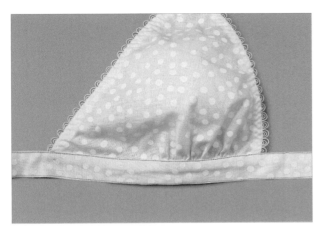

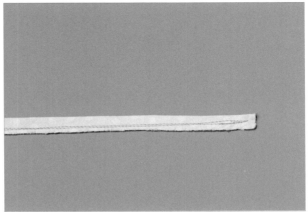

Step 7

- With a stitch length of 2.5mm topstitch along the top of the band and then again along the bottom folded edge, keeping the stitching close to the edges.
- Attach a large safety pin or loop turner to one end of the elastic and thread the elastic through the band.
- Stitch across both ends of the band to secure the elastic in place. The band can be finished with hook and eye tape (see page 253).

Step 8

- To make the rouleau straps, cut two bias strips of fabric, 1in (2.5cm) wide. The length will depend on your design but add 1in (2.5cm) to this length. Fold the fabric in half with the right sides together.
- Being careful not to stretch the fabric as you sew, stitch down the strap, starting farther away from the folded edge than the finished width and then over the first 1in (2.5cm), bringing your stitching closer to the folded edge and the desired strap width. The width of the strap will change with your fabric choice.
- Always make a sample first and make sure you can turn your strap to the right side. Stitch along the strap again close to the first row of stitching to add strength.

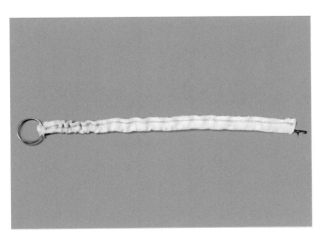

Step 9

- To turn the strap to the right side push a loop/rouleau turner through the tube from the narrow end, bringing it out at the wider end. Hook the loop turner to one side of the fabric at the end and slowly pull it back, bringing the end of the strap through the tube so it is right side out.

Step 10

- Place the first 1in (2.5cm) of the strap under the top of the cup and securely stitch in place with a straight stitch or zigzag stitch. Trim any extra strap back to the stitching on the wrong side of the cup. The stitching on the front of the cup can be hidden under a bow.

Adding lace or embellishment to the top cup

Adding lace appliqué to the neck edge of the top cup is an easy way of changing the appearance of a bra. Make sure that the lace placement is balanced by ensuring the pattern begins and ends in the same place on both cups. If you are using an all-over lace overlay on the top bra cup, attach it before the cup is attached to the lower cup.

Embroidery and beading can also be added to the top cup at this stage, especially if you are going to add a facing by making a double-layered top cup.

The cone cup or bullet bra cup

The bullet bra cup is not padded; instead it has rows of channel or spiral stitching that help hold the extreme shape of the cup.

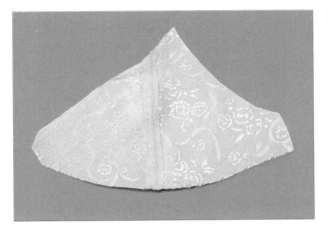

Step 1

- Sew the two top cup pieces together using a straight stitch set at a stitch length of 2.5mm. Press the seam open. Cover the seam allowance with seam cover tape and topstitch down both sides of the seam through the seam allowances.

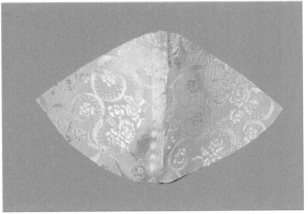

Step 2

- Sew the two lower cup pieces together; press the seam open. Cover the seam allowance with seam cover tape and again topstitch down both sides of the seam line through the seam allowances.

Step 3

- Attach the top cups to the lower cups and topstitch as before.

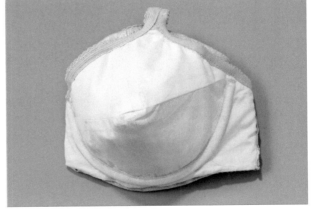

Step 4

- If you are adding a lining, make a cup in lining fabric following the directions above (but without topstitching) and place inside the finished cup. Baste around the outer edge to hold the lining in place.
- To make the cup stiff, like the original bullet bra, cut the lining with the fabric grain running in the opposite direction to the grain of the outer fashion cup.

Stitching patterns for a cone bra

To spiral stitch the cup, after sewing all the cup pieces together and topstitching all the seams, open along the seam allowances and baste (tack) the lining into the fashion fabric cup. Begin the spiral stitching from the bustline/apex and work out to the edge of the cup using a stitch length of 2mm. Spiral stitch to the left on one cup and to the right on the other.

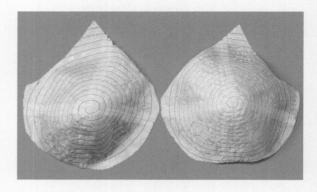

To stitch with contrasting thread on the top and lower cups, add the stitching before joining the two top cups to the two lower cups. Starting at the bustline, stitch a half-circle from one side of the top or lower cup to the other, with a stitch length of 2–2.5mm. Continue to stitch concentric rows approximately ¼in (6mm) apart, following the shape of the first row of stitching. Join the top and lower cups together (see Step 3 on page 235).

Alternatively, before you join the top cups to the lower cups you can create a pattern of spokes radiating out 1–1½in (2.5–3.8cm) from the bustline. At the end of the stitched spokes, stitch concentric rows of stitching around the cup, approximately ¼in (6mm) apart, with a stitch length of 2.5mm. You can work as many rows and spokes as you wish. Join the top and lower cups together.

The strapless bra cup with boning

A strapless bra cup can be padded or have boning added to hold the shape. The addition of boning to larger cup sizes helps to support and hold the shape of the breast. A boned long-line band attached to the cup also gives better support to a strapless bra.

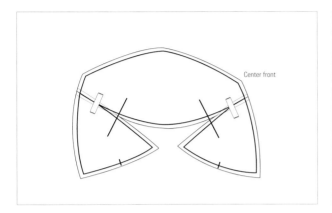

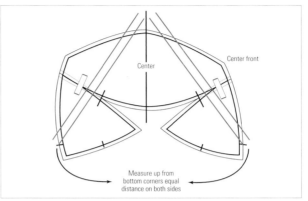

Step 1

- Working with the three-piece bra cup pattern, align the pattern piece for the underarm side of the lower cup to the outer side of the top bra cup and tape together, starting at the outside edge and overlapping the seam allowances. Repeat on the other side, taping the front of the lower cup to the top cup at the front edge.
- Divide the two lower cups in half at the top edge by folding the pattern pieces in half and mark this point on both the lower and top cups.

Step 2

- Fold the top cup in half and draw a line down this fold line, labeling it as the center line. At the top of the cup measure out on either side of this line to where you feel the boning should finish and mark on the top edge. There is no specific measurement for this but it looks more balanced if the boning finishes an equal distance from the middle of the cup on both sides.
- Measure up from the center bottom of both lower cups along what will be the bottom edge and mark. Draw a line for the boning from these marks on the lower cups to the marks on the top edge of the top cup. Draw a second line parallel to this first line. These are now the bone placement lines.

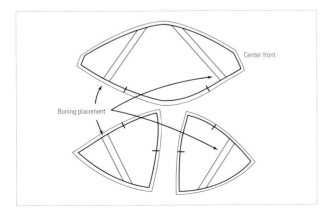

Step 3

- Sew the two lower cup pieces together, then sew to the top cup, topstitching all the seams. Sew a casing to the cup for the boning, stitching it inside the cup between the two placement lines.

Step 4

- Calculate the boning length by measuring the casing less the seam allowances plus ¼in (6mm). However, only insert the boning after the cup has been attached to the band and the underwire casing is also attached, but before the neckline edge has been finished.

Adding padding to the lower one- or two-piece cup

Bras are usually padded with specially manufactured bra cup foam that is available in sheet form. It can be used in the lower cup pieces only, or made into a complete cup. A cup lining has to be added behind the foam to protect and provide comfort for the wearer.

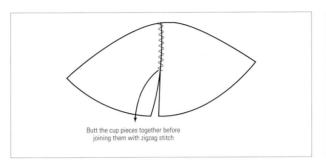

Butt the cup pieces together before joining them with zigzag stitch

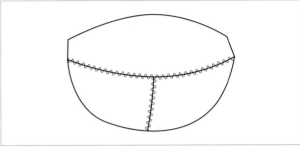

Step 1

- Cut the cup pattern pieces from the foam minus the seam allowances. Butt the cup pieces together and, using a 4mm-wide zigzag stitch, sew them together, being careful not to tear the foam.

Step 2

- The cup can be quilted or channel stitched to the foam cup. Consider using metallic or contrasting colored thread for this stitching.

Nursing cup

The nursing cup has an under cup that frames and supports the breast, leaving the nipple exposed so the baby can feed. The outer cup pulls up over the under cup, attaching at the strap point. Use the two-piece bra cup pattern to make this nursing bra.

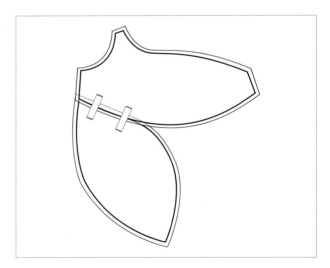

Step 1

- First make the pattern for the under cup. Align the top cup pattern piece to the lower cup pattern piece and tape together, starting at the underarm edge and working up to the bustline.

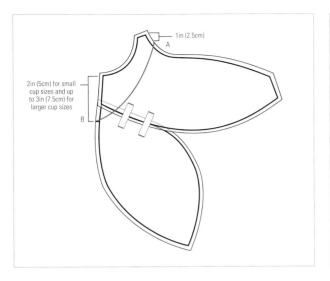

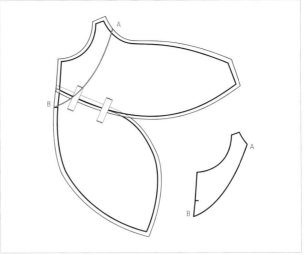

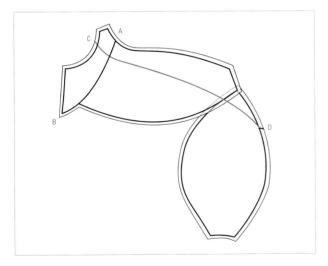

Step 2

- Measure down 1in (2.5cm) from the neckline strap toward the center front and mark as A. Measure down 2in (5cm) at the underarm for smaller cup sizes – up to 3in (7.5cm) for larger cup sizes – and mark as B.
- Draw a curved line to connect the two marks. Make a notch on the lower cup at B.

Step 3

- Trace off this new pattern piece.

Step 4

- Remove the tape at the underarm side of the cups and join the cups at the center front, taping them in place.
- Measure down 1in (2.5cm) at the underarm and mark as C. At the center front curve measure down 2–3in (5–7.5cm) depending on cup size, and mark as D. Draw a curved line to connect C to D, following the curves of the original design. Make a notch at D.
- Trace off this pattern piece along the line to D so that it joins with the pattern piece traced off in Step 3. This is now the under cup.

The bra

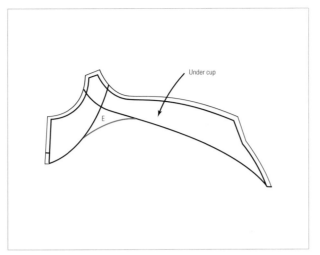

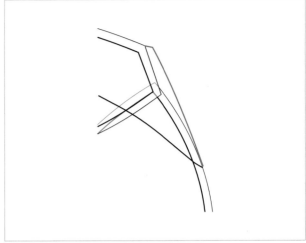

Step 5

- Round out the point at E on the under cup.

Step 6

- Where the cups overlap at the center front edge, draw a line to straighten out this edge.

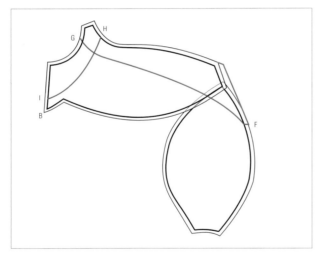

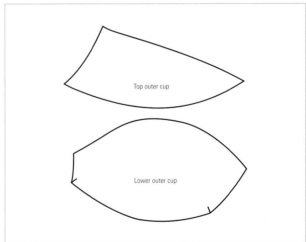

Step 7

- To adjust the pattern for the outer cup, tape the top and lower cup pattern pieces together at the center front. Measure ½in (1.3cm) down the inner edge of the strap over toward the center front and mark as H.
- Measure down 1in (2.5cm) at the underarm and mark as I. Draw a curved line connecting H to I.
- At the outer edge of the strap measure down ½in (1.3cm) and mark as G. Measure down 1in (2.5cm) at the center front and mark as F. Draw a curved line connecting G to F to lower the neckline at the outer edge. Cut along the lines from H to I and from G to F.
- Where the cups overlap at the center front edge, draw a line to straighten out this edge.

Step 8

- Separate the cups and label them as the top and lower outer cups. The lower outer cup will have two notch points (which you marked as B and D in Steps 2 and 4).

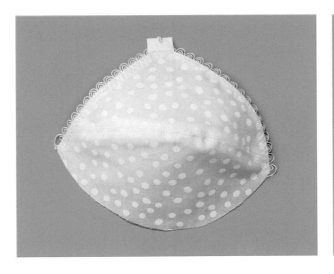

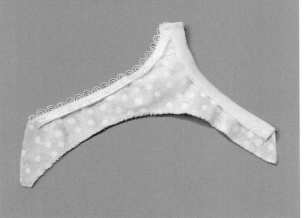

Step 9

- Sew the top outer cup to the lower outer cup and topstitch along the seam line.
- Finish the neckline and underarm edge with trim.
- Attach one hook from the hook side of some single hook and eye tape at the strap placement point, with the hook facing up and out. Stitch to secure, and finish with a bar tack.

Step 10

- Finish the neckline of the under cup with trim and serge (overlock) or bind the lower curved cup edge.
- Finish the underarm edge with elastic. With the fabric right side up, place the elastic on the underarm edge with the picot edge up and the flat edge along the cut edge. Zigzag in place with a stitch width of 2.5mm and length of 2mm. Flip the elastic to the wrong side, so the picot edge shows below the fold line. Sew in place with a three-step zigzag with a stitch width of 4.5mm and length of 1–1.5mm, keeping an even tension.

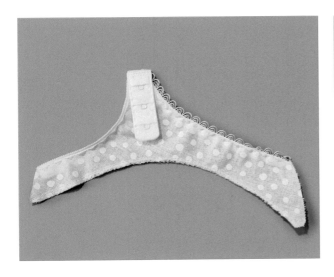

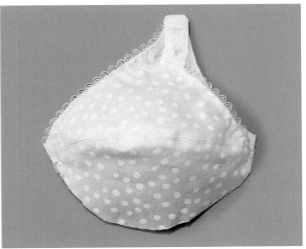

Step 11

- Attach three eyes, placing the eye side of the hook and eye tape at the strap placement point, with the eyes facing out and down into the cup. Place the strap on the eye tape and stitch in place to secure, before finishing with a bar tack.

Step 12

- Place the finished under cup behind the outer cup, lining it up with the notches on the lower outer cup. Stitch in place from the notches to the top edge of the outer cup. For more support, use a four-column hook and eye tape at the center back.

Adding a pocket to the inside of the cup

Pockets can be attached to the inside of the top or lower bra cup to hold a prosthesis. These pockets can also hold a "cookie" that can add one or two cup sizes to the breast, or be worn to even out the breasts if one side is bigger than the other. You can also position a pocket if you want the look of a more rounded breast from the underarm area. Pockets can be added to the finished bra by hand, too, stitching them into position. They are usually made from a soft jersey or brushed cotton fabric.

Making a top-cup bra pocket

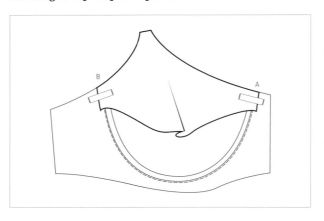

Step 1

- Start by creating the under pocket piece. Working on a flat surface, attach the top cup pattern piece seam to the under band pattern piece at A and B.

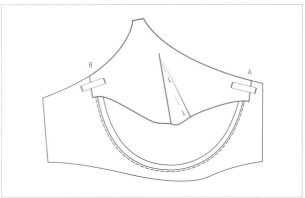

Step 2

- Using the flat of your hand, brush the excess paper over from A to the center; repeat from B. The excess paper will form a dart that will be removed when you trace the new paper pattern to create the under pocket pattern.

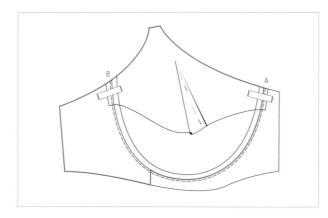

Step 3

- Next, make a pattern for the overlapping pocket. Make a second tracing around the cup, without removing the under pocket, from the strap down the neckline to the end of the cup at the center front; around the bottom of the cup and up to the seam at the end of the bridge piece; continuing over to the side seam; and back up the armhole to the strap.

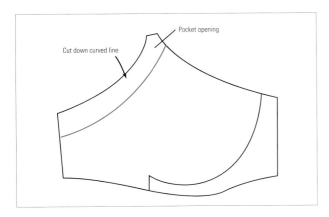

Step 4
- Measure down approximately 1in (2.5cm) from the inside edge of the strap and along the neckline, and draw a curved line that drops down to the side seam. This is the opening for a prosthetic. Trace the final pattern piece for the overlapping pocket.

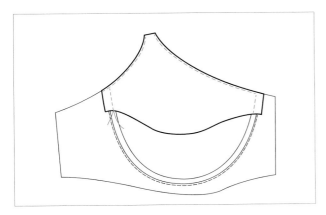

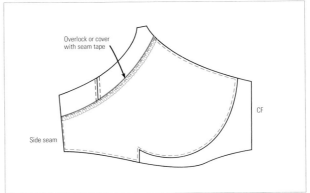

Step 5
- Construct the cup from the fashion fabric and attach it to the band. Cut the under pocket from a soft jersey or brushed cotton fabric, place it in the cup, and stitch along the underarm edge, neckline, and down into the sides of the top pocket.

Step 6
- Serge the opening edge of the overlapping pocket, or finish it with covering tape. Place it on top of the under pocket on the bra cup and stitch from the center front around the cup until the pocket drops down to the band. Stitch along the band to the side seam and up the side seam.
- Stitch down the neckline and finish the neckline edge with trim.

Adjusting fit for a prosthetic

If you are making a pocket to fit a prosthetic, you may have to change the neckline of the bra cup and reshape the lower edge of the pocket to accommodate the shape of the prosthetic.

Making a lower-cup bra pocket

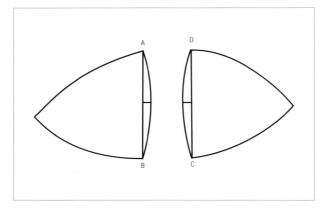

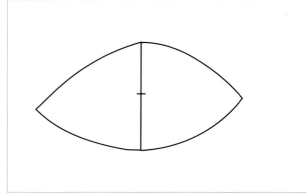

Step 1

- To create the pattern for the pocket, use the two-piece lower cup pattern pieces on page 196. Draw straight lines from A to B and from C to D.

- Trace the new shapes onto paper, joining the two cup pieces together.

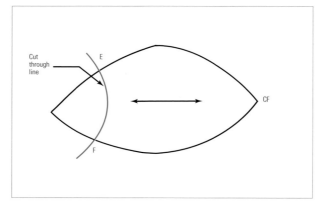

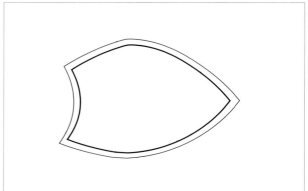

Step 2

- On the armhole edge of the cup, draw a curved line across the corner. This is the pocket opening where a cookie can be inserted.

Step 3

- Trace off the pocket pattern and add seam allowances to all edges.

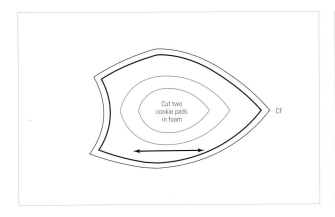

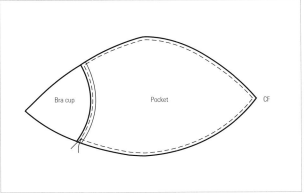

Step 4

- Make the cookie from the pocket pattern. Following the inside shape of the pocket, draw a small egg-shaped pad. If more padding is required, you can draw a second, smaller shape.

Step 5

- To construct the pocket, fold under the seam allowance on the pocket opening and stitch close to the fold line. Place the pocket inside the lower bra cup and stitch along the edges to hold it in place.

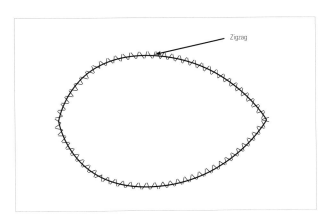

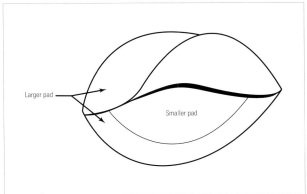

Step 6

- Cut out two of the larger cookie shapes. Put one pad on top of the other pad and zigzag stitch around the edge.
- If you are adding a smaller pad, sandwich it between the two larger pads before zigzag stitching around the edge.

Power bars and collars

Also known as slings and frames, power bars can be hidden inside the cup or be cut into the cup. A collar that circles the cup on the inside can be used to provide additional support, or to make a softer transition from the cup shape to the band.

Adding a power bar to the bra cup

This power bar will frame the cup. It can be made from a contrasting fabric or color.

- Sew the three pattern pieces of the cup together (see pages 208–9), taping and topstitching along the seam lines. Join the two sections of the power bar together.
- Stitch the power bar along the outer edge of the cup, matching the notch and underbust seams. Press the seam open and cover the seam allowance with seam cover tape before finishing with topstitching.

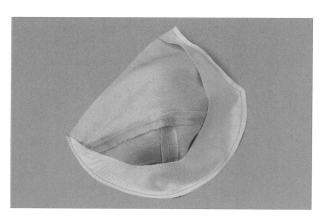

Adding a power bar that sits inside the cup

This power bar will be smaller than the cup, giving less room for the breast and thus pushing it up.

- Sew the three pattern pieces of the cup together. Place the power bar on the wrong side of the cup, matching notch points.
- Stitch around the outer edge, attaching the power bar to the cup.

Adding a collar to the bra cup

Today the collar is hidden inside the cup, but you could consider using a powernet collar to frame the cup. The collar gives maximum support and lift by keeping the breast in the forward position. It gives the best support for a heavier breast.

- Make the bra cup, taping seams and topstitching. Cut the collar pattern pieces (see page 210) with the grainline following the direction of the least stretch.
- Stitch the two collar pieces together at the strap and underbust line points. Serge the inner edge of the collar.
- Place the collar in the cup and stitch around the outer edge to hold in place.

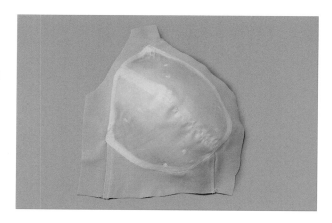

Band construction

The construction of the back of the band will change, depending on the design and whether you have a full band or partial band. A full band, for example, can be made from two or three pattern pieces from the bridge to the center back. Some bands will also have an underarm seam.

The partial band

The bridge of a partial-band bra can be shaped at the lower edge, have a keyhole, be lowered, or simply be embellished with a bow or flower. The band can be made from a mix of fabrics, with the front and bridge matching the cups or lower cups, and the back cut from powernet. The partial-band bra has the wire channeling running around the inside of the cup. It is important to add notch points to the cup, marking where the bridge starts and stops, so that the cups are stitched to either side of the bridge in the same position.

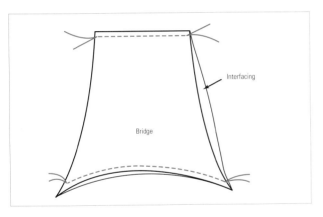

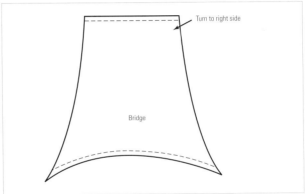

Step 1
- For a more finished look to the back of the bridge sew fusible interfacing to the fabric, right sides together, along the lower and upper edges.

Step 2
- Turn to the right side and finger press. Topstitch both edges before fusing and go to Step 3.

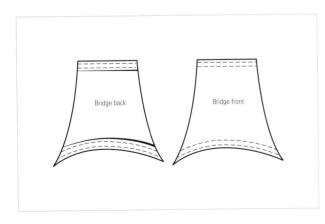

- Alternatively, you can turn under the seam allowance on the lower bridge, cover with seam cover tape and straight stitch in place. If you have lowered the bridge, finish the top edge in the same way.

Check the stretch of the elastic

Always make a test sample to check the stretch of the elastic with your fashion fabric. While it is not usual, you may find that you have to stretch the elastic onto the band. If this is the case, make sure that the stretch in the elastic is kept at an even tension.

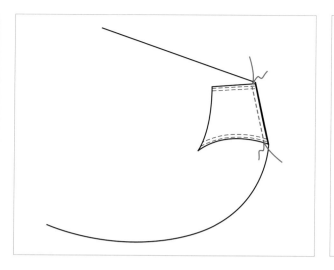

Step 3

- Attach the bridge to the cups, making sure that it is aligned with your markings.
- If the bridge is cut from powernet and you are attaching this to a fashion fabric, to avoid puckering, place the powernet under the fashion fabric with least stretch; the feed dogs on your machine will help to control the ease.

Step 4

- Sew all the seams on the band together. With the fabric right side up, place the elastic on the lower edge of the band with the picot edge up and the flat edge of the elastic along the cut edge of the band. Zigzag in place with a stitch width of 2–5mm and length of 2mm.

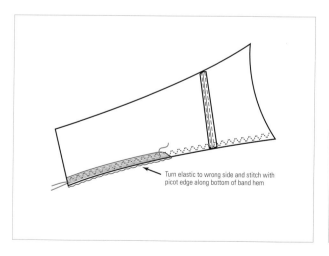

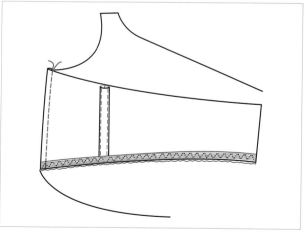

Step 5

- Flip the elastic to the wrong side, or back of the band, so that the decorative or picot edge of the elastic is showing below the fold line.
- Use a three-stitch zigzag with a stitch width of 4.5mm and length of 1–1.5mm and sew along the lower band, keeping an even tension. The lower edge of the band should be sitting flat and be slightly gathered.

Step 6

- Attach the band to the cup using a straight stitch with a stitch length of 2–2.5mm. When working around the curve of the lower cup you will get a neater line of stitching with a shorter stitch length.

The full band

A full-banded bra covers the torso below the cups. The length of the band can extend down to the waistline, thus turning the bra into a bustier. The bra can be wired, with the channeling running around the cup, or soft cupped.

The band gives the bra added support and can be made from the same fabric as the cups, or elasticized for an easy, flexible fit.

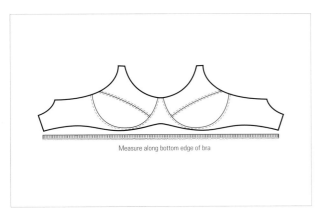

Measure along bottom edge of bra

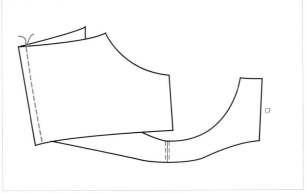

CF

Step 1

- With the fabric right side up, lay the elastic along the lower edge with the plush side up and flat edge of the elastic along the cut edge of the band. To find the length of the elastic needed, measure the length of the band and deduct 1in (2.5cm).

Step 2

- Sew all the seams together on the full band, beginning at the bridge and working around to the back.
- In areas where you are attaching powernet to a fashion fabric, place the powernet under the fashion or fabric with least stretch; the feed dogs on your machine will help to control the ease.

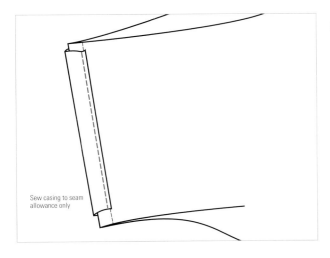

Sew casing to seam allowance only

Step 3

- If there is boning down the side seam, cover the seam allowance with a casing that finishes ¼in (6mm) in from both the top and lower band edges. Stitch the casing along the edge of the seam allowance.

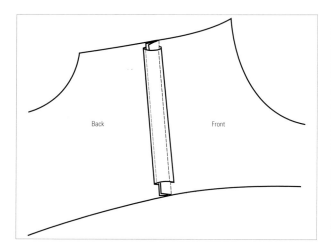

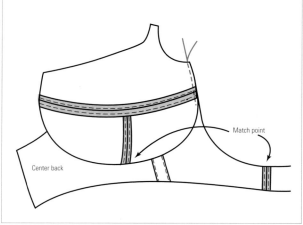

Step 4

- Press the seam allowance toward the back panel and stitch the casing onto the back panel along its edge.
- Insert the boning into the casing only after you have attached the elastic to the top and bottom edges of the band.
- This casing can also be used as a seam finish if you are not adding boning.

Step 5

- Attach the cups to the curve of the band. Match up the center or under cup points on both the cup and band to avoid any puckers or extra fabric, and sew using a straight stitch.

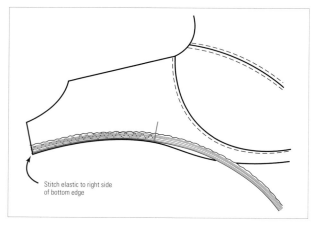

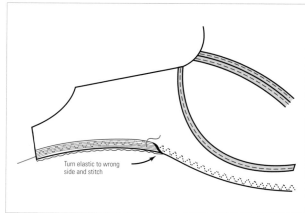

Step 6

- Attach the elastic to the lower edge of the band following Steps 5 to 6 of the partial band (page 248).

Adding elastic panels

When the band is made in a fabric with little or no stretch, elastic panels can be added to help with fit as well as comfort. The bridge can be replaced with elastic, as can part of the front band, or a triangle of elastic can be added into the back panel at the side seam. Remember to deduct ⅜–⅝in (1–1.5cm) from the elastic, depending on its stretch.

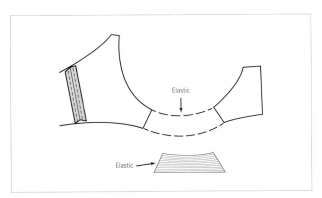

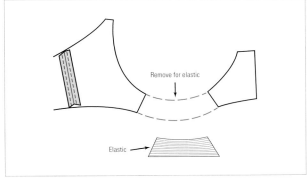

Step 1

- Mark on the pattern piece where the elastic is going to be placed, which can be under the bra cup and at the side seam. Trace off the elastic placement.

- Add seam allowances to the pattern for the band and remove the area where the elastic will be placed.

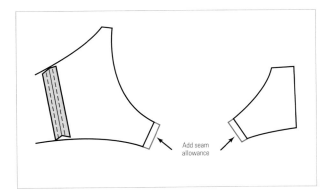

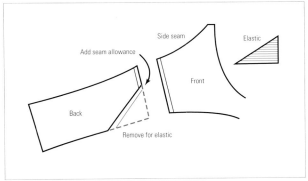

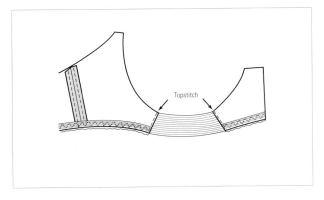

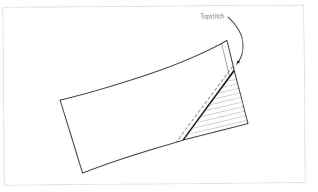

Step 2

- Stitch the elastic panel to the band. Press the seam allowance toward the band and topstitch the seam.

Making a gate on the back of the band

You can finish the back band with a triangular-shaped loop of strap elastic that is attached to one row of hook and eye tape. This is also known as a "gate" and makes a nice finish to a powernet or all-lace band.

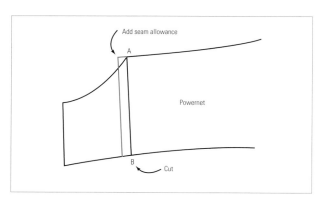

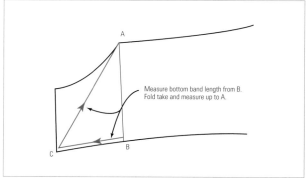

Step 1

- Begin by making the changes to the back band pattern. If the back band is being made using powernet, draw a straight line down from the back curve and mark the top as A and the bottom as B. Add a seam allowance to this line.

Step 2

- Measure over from B to the center back at C. Measure down from A to C and add the two measurements together. This is the length to cut the strap elastic that is going to form the triangular-shaped gate – do not add a seam allowance to the elastic. Fold the elastic into shape and stitch through the fold using a straight stitch.

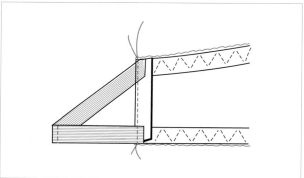

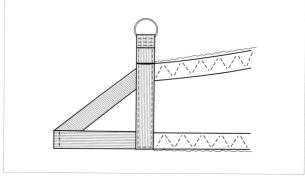

Step 3

- Cut away the rest of the back band beyond the seam allowance.
- Attach plush elastic to the lower edge of the band and picot-edged elastic to the underarm top edge of the band following Steps 5–6 of the partial band (see page 248). Attach the elastic triangle to the seam allowance.

Step 4

- Using strap elastic cut two lengths of 4in (10cm). Thread one end of the strap elastic through a strap ring, fold down, and securely sew in place.
- Place the strap elastic over the seam allowance with the strap ring protruding above the top of the band. Fold up the bottom of the elastic so it forms a casing with the opening level with the top of the band. Stitch down one side of the elastic strap, across the bottom, and up the other side to the top of the band, forming a casing for a piece of boning.

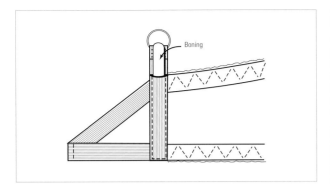

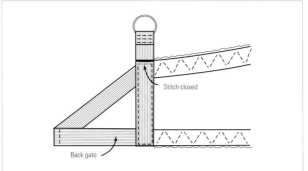

Step 5
- Cut a piece of ⅜in (1cm) plastic boning, ¼in (6mm) shorter than the casing, and push into the casing.

Step 6
- Stitch the casing closed across the top end. The boning is put here to stop the band from stretching out, and to hold the elastic gate in place so that it does not wrinkle up.
- Attach a single row of hook and eye tape to the end of the strap elastic gate on both sides of the bra band.

Hook and eye tape

Hook and eye tape is used as a fastening on a bra. This comes as a single column or can be made in up to three columns so that the bra band can be adjusted for fit. Four columns are also used for bras that require extra support, such as nursing bras. The hooks and eyes are placed on the tape approximately every ¾in (2cm).

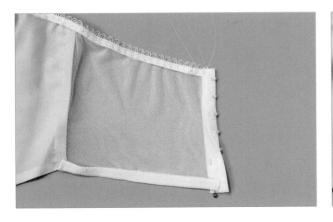

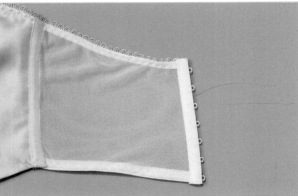

Step 1
- Encase the left side of the center back with hook tape. Keep the hooks facing up and stitch in place.

Step 2
- Encase the right side of the center back with the eye tape and stitch in place.
- You can also finish the edges of the tape using satin stitch.

Attaching the underwire channeling

Measure the length of the seam line that attaches the cup to the band. Cut two lengths of channeling to this length plus 2in (5cm) each.

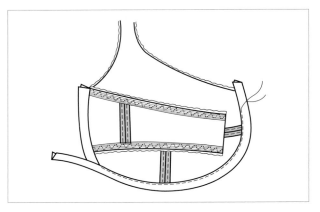

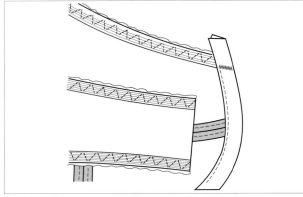

Step 1

- Lay the bra on a flat surface, wrong side facing up. Fold the bra so the bridge, band, and other cup are under the remaining cup, exposing the seam allowance. Position the edge of the channeling on the seam allowance, leaving a 1in (2.5cm) extension at each end.
- Beginning ½in (1.3cm) down from the center front, straight-stitch along the edge of the channeling, finishing approximately 1in (2.5cm) down from the underarm. Keep your stitching on the seam allowance only, so it will not show through on the right side.
- Finish the neckline with elastic (see opposite).

Step 2

- Close the channeling at the center front with a bar tack made only through the channeling and seam allowance, about ½in (1.3cm) down from the top edge of the bra. You do not want the bar tack showing on the right side of your bra. Make it using zigzag stitch with a width of 2mm and a length of 1mm or less.
- Now attach the straps and underarm elastic edging (see opposite).

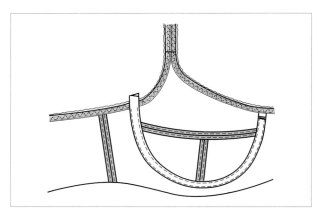

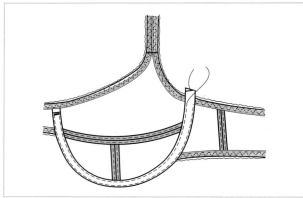

Step 3

- For a full-band bra press the channeling down onto the band and topstitch on the right side around the cup, beginning ½in (1.3cm) down from the center front and finishing 1in (2.5cm) down from the underarm. Do not sew into the underarm elastic.

- For a partial-band bra press the channeling up into the cup and topstitch in place, beginning and ending ½in (1.3cm) down from the edge.
- Trim back the excess channeling to just below the neckline edge and at the underarm.

Finishing the neckline edge

The neckline edge should be finished before attaching the straps. The usual finish is a delicate picot-edged trim. If the top cup has a scalloped neckline, attach a clear elastic to the back of the neckline, below the scalloped edge.

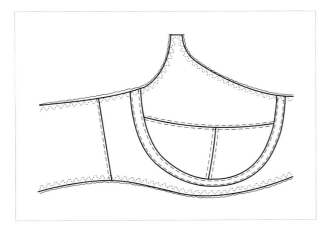

- Place the trim around the bra neckline with right sides together and the picot edge facing in toward the bra cup as you did with the band elastic (see Steps 5 and 6, page 248).
- Using a three-step zigzag stitch, attach the trim to the neckline, keeping the stitching close to the picot edge of the elastic.
- Turn the trim to the wrong side of the bra and use a three-step zigzag stitch or regular zigzag to sew it in place, making sure to cover the ends of the front underwire channeling. Trim back the channeling if necessary.

The underarm elastic for both the partial and full band

Attach the elastic to the underarm edge of the band as described for attaching the elastic to the lower edge of the partial band (see Steps 5 and 6, page 248). Leave a 2in (5cm) extension of elastic at the center back of the band.

If you are adding boning into the side seam, thread it into the channeling before you flip the elastic to the back of the band and finish with a three-step zigzag stitch. Work slowly over the boning so that you do not break your sewing machine needle.

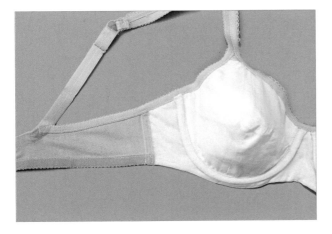

The straps

Straps can be made from strap elastic, ribbon or rouleau, clear plastic, or a strand of beads, all of which can be further embellished. Rings and adjusters, called findings, are added to the straps either at the front or the back. The strap can be attached to the back band with a bar tack; strap elastic can be folded back on itself, forming a triangle-shaped loop, or it can be shaped around the curve on the back band, finishing at the center back. The front strap can be attached to the bra cup with a ring and loop, or stitched securely to the strap position or strap extension point.

If the top cup has a strap extension, attach the strap to this and finish with two rows of topstitching before attaching the underarm elastic.

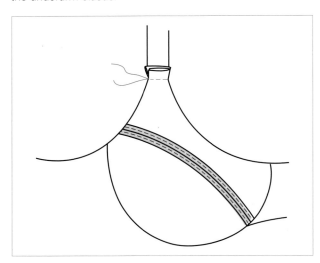
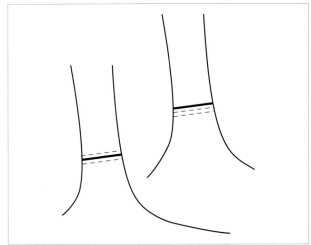

Removeable straps
For removeable bra straps, attach a detachable G hook to both ends of the strap. Attach a small loop of strap elastic at the strap placement point at the top of the bra cup, big enough for the G hook to fit through. On the back of the strap place the G hook instead of the ring before threading on the adjuster. Make a small loop from strap elastic on the back band for the G hook to fit through.

The strap elastic and adjusters

If you have attached the front straps to the bra cups, it is now time to add the adjusters to the back strap elastic.

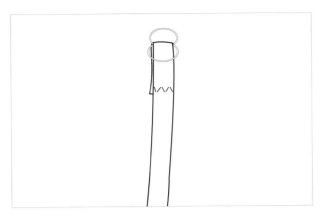

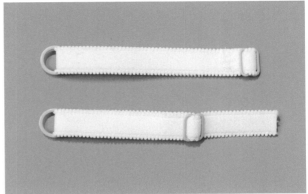

Step 1

- Push the strap elastic up through and over the center bar of the slider. Fold it back on itself and securely stitch in place with a narrow zigzag stitch.

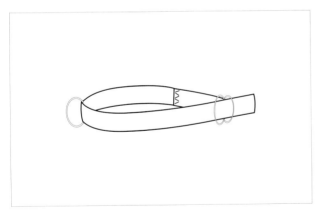

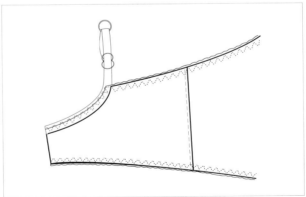

Step 2

- Feed the other end of the elastic through the ring and then back up through the slider again.

Step 3

- Lay the strap flat along the curve starting at the center back. Using a straight stitch or extended three-step zigzag stitch and working from the center back, stitch the inside edge of the elastic, stitching along the curve to the top. Turn and stitch down the center of the elastic to the center back. Trim away any excess fabric.

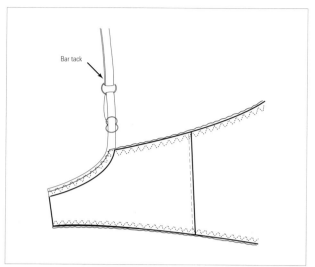

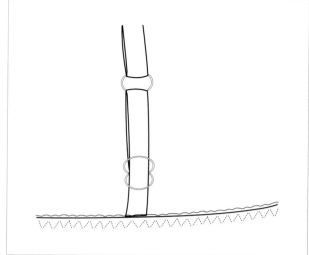

Step 4

- Bring the end of the front strap through the ring, fold back and securely stitch in place with a bar tack.

Step 5

- If the back band has no curve, attach the back strap to the band at the back strap placement point; first secure with stitching and then finish with a bar tack.

Ribbon or rouleau straps

Finish the bra neckline and underarm before attaching these straps.

- Thread the ribbon or rouleau strap through the ring.
- Push the end of ribbon or rouleau at the back up through and over the center bar of the slider.
- Fold it back on itself and securely stitch in place.
- Thread the end of the ribbon or rouleau at the front through the slider and secure to the back band strap position.

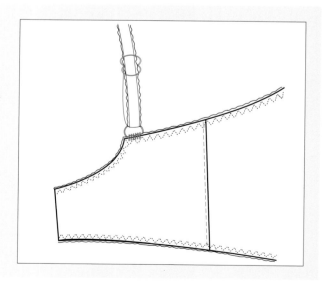

The wires

The underwires are now placed into the channeling from the underarm and the
channeling finished with a bar tack.

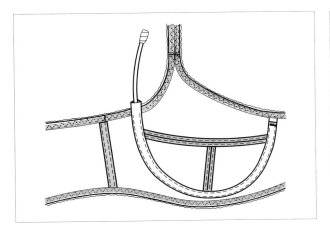

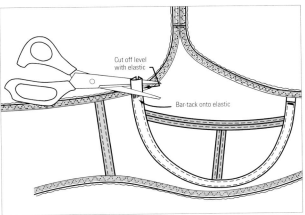

Step 1

- At the underarm end of the channeling, thread the
  colored or shorter end of the wire into the channeling
  around the bra cup. Make sure that the wire is in the
  channeling and not between the channeling and bra.

Step 2

- Finish off the underarm channeling in the same way as
  you finished the center front, Step 2, page 254, but this
  time stitch the channeling on top of the elastic. Do not
  fold the channeling.

9 Embellishments and Embroidery

Embellishments and embroidery can be used to exaggerate details and add interesting ornaments to personalize and beautify your designs. A bride once worked for months on a trousseau that included alluring hand-embroidered and embellished underwear, and looking back at the embellishments worked onto such vintage lingerie and sleepwear will provide you with plenty of inspiration.

A silk crepe-de-chîne nightdress with appliqué work and embellished with marabou feathers. Probably from France, circa 1935.

Detached chain stitch

Detached chain stitch is an easy and versatile way to embellish a garment, used on its own, scattered as a filling, or mixed with other embroidery stitches. Stitches can be grouped in a circle to form daisy-like flowers.

Using color to add detail
The securing stitches can be in a contrasting color to give more detail to the flower petals.

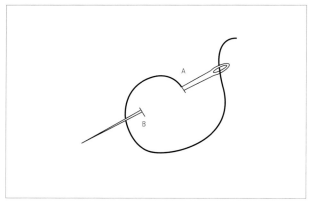

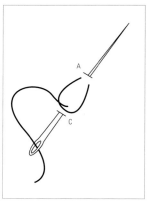

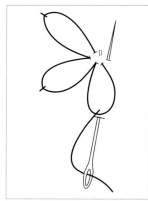

Step 1
- Bring your needle to the front of the fabric at A and reinsert just to one side. Do not pull the thread all the way to the back of the fabric – leave a loop on the front. Holding the loop down with your thumb, bring the needle back to the front of the work at B, inside the loop.

Step 2
- Make a small stitch over the loop to hold it in place at C, to complete a single chain stitch.

Step 3
- If you are making a circle of stitches to create a flower, bring the needle back to the front of the fabric at D, to the side of A, and repeat Steps 1 and 2.

French knots

French knots can be used to mark a spot, such as a flower center, to give textured shading to a design, or they can be scattered as evenly spaced or packed dots.

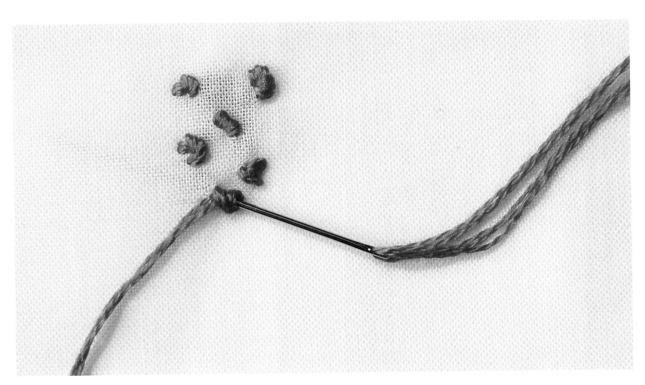

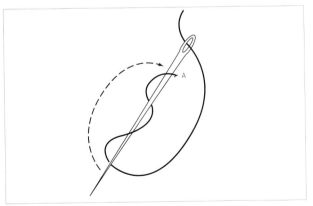

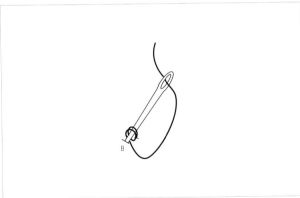

Working knots

Keep your thumb over the threads wrapped around the needle as you draw the needle through them. Also, don't pull on the thread too hard or your knot will follow the needle to the back of your fabric.

Step 1
- Bring the needle to the front of your work at A. Keeping the thread taut and holding it about 1½in (3.8cm) from where it emerged, encircle the tip of the needle with the thread twice.

Step 2
- While still holding the thread firmly, twist the needle back to the starting point and reinsert close to where it first emerged, at B. Slide the thread wraps down the needle onto the fabric as the needle returns to the back of the fabric, leaving a small knot on the surface.

Bullion stitch / bullion knot stitch

Bullion knots can be used scattered in groups, or arranged into flowers – particularly roses – or leaves.

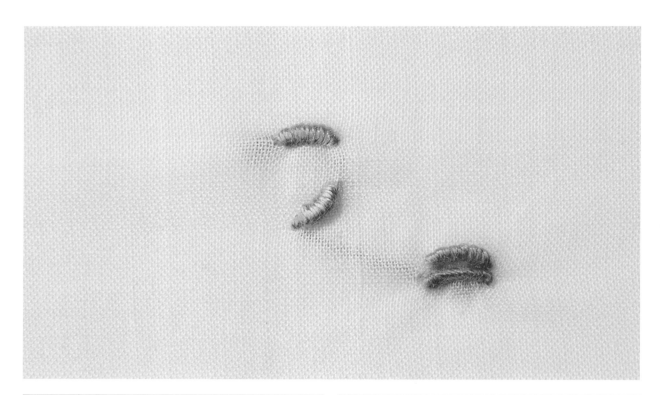

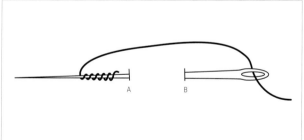

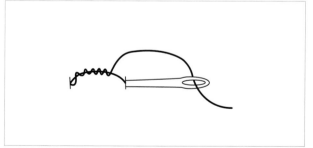

Step 1

- Bring your needle to the front of your fabric at A and back down at B, the required length of the knot. Bring the point of the needle back up again at A. Do not pull the needle all the way through the fabric.
- Make the bullion twist by wrapping the thread around the needle 5–10 times or more. The number of twists will depend on the length of the knot.

Step 2

- Hold the threads in place as you pull the needle and thread through the twists. Insert the needle at B, pulling through to the wrong side of the fabric.

Bullion knot roses and buds

Bullion stitch or bullion knot stitch is a very versatile hand embroidery stitch. You can use it to make dainty little roses and rosebuds using a single strand of thread, or add strands for larger, chunkier roses. You can also group stitches together to form stems of lavender, or use one bullion knot as a leaf.

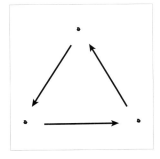

Step 1

- To make a rose, first form a triangle of bullion knots in the directions shown in the diagram.

Step 2

- Now form a second triangle on top of the first triangle, adding more twists than needed for the length of the knot so that it will curl to make the petals until a rose is formed.

- For a bud, make one bullion stitch with the twists wrapped around the needle to the left or right, then make a second stitch parallel to the first but with the twists wrapped around the needle in the opposite direction. You can finish with a small detached chain stitch on either side of these two stitches in a different colored thread to form leaves or a base for the bud.

Creating shading effects

Use a variegated thread or work the roses in two or more colors to create a shaded effect.

Picots

The ornamental picot has been worked along hemlines and garment edges as a design detail on all the finest lingerie. Picot stitch can be worked by hand, or you can buy a picot edge trim. The picots can be small and delicate and sit close to the edge, or they can be larger to make more of a statement.

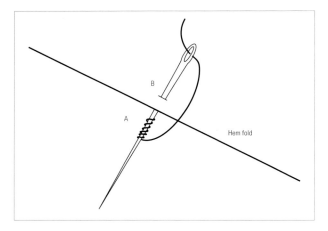

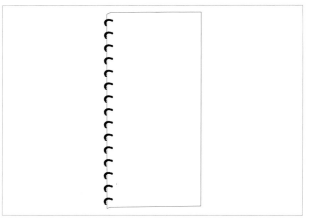

Making picots with different stitches
Here, bullion stitch has been used, but picots can also be made using a chain or buttonhole stitch (see opposite).

Step 1

- Bring your needle out through the fold at the finished edge of your garment at A, and wrap the thread around the needle, following the directions for the bullion knot. Twist the bullion so that it curls into a semicircle and re-insert the needle back into the edge of the fold at B, securing with a small knot at the back of your work. Return your needle to the inside of the folded edge for approximately ¼in (6mm) and repeat as from A, continuing to make a row of loops along the edge of your garment or hem.

Cutwork

Cutwork is a surface embroidery technique in which designs are embroidered onto fabric, after which some fabric is cut away. Buttonhole and running stitch are the two main stitches used, but Richelieu embroidery, a type of cutwork, uses a combination of techniques, such as eyelet, ladder, and picot stitches, and often resembles lace.

Buttonhole stitch

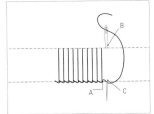

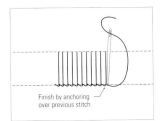

Finish by anchoring over previous stitch

Step 1

- Begin by bringing the needle out at the base of the work at A. Reinsert the needle through to the back of the work at B and bring the needle out beneath C, keeping the working thread under the point of the needle. Pull up the stitch to form a loop and repeat.

Step 2

- To finish, anchor the thread by taking your needle down over the loop you formed when you came up in front of the needle at C, into the fabric right next to C, and secure your working thread.

Eyelets

From the Middle Ages to the eighteenth century, before metal eyelets or grommets were available, hand-worked eyelets were used to lace up clothing. While you can make stitched eyelets by machine they are still neater worked by hand. The edge of the finished eyelet should be no closer to the fabric edge than ¼in (6mm), otherwise the strain on the eyelet from the lacing may cause the fabric to fray or the eyelet to unravel or become detached from the fabric. The eyelet should only be big enough to thread the cord or ribbon through. Small eyelets can also be worked down a hem for a decorative finish.

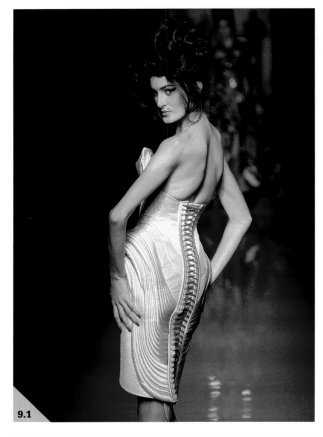

9.1

Increasing the strength of eyelets
For added strength, buttonhole-stitch eyelets can be worked over a small steel ring or washer available in any hardware store.

9.1 / Eyelets are holding the lacing on the back of this dress (Jean Paul Gaultier, Spring/ Summer 2012).

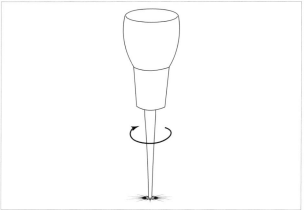

Step 1

- To create an eyelet, begin by pushing an awl or stiletto through all the layers of fabric to make a small hole. If possible try not to break any fibers; try to spread them so there is no fraying. To do this, place the awl or stiletto on the fabric and twist it until you feel the tip come through the cloth; continue to twist to enlarge the hole, making it slightly bigger than needed because the stitches will reduce its size.

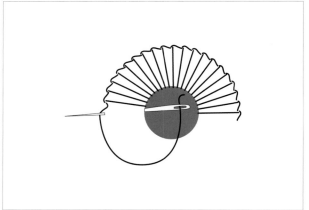

Step 2

- Work evenly spaced buttonhole stitches neatly all around the hole.

Ladder stitch

Ladder stitch looks like its namesake, and you can thread a ribbon through the bars for added interest or color. It can be made by hand on a fashion fabric, or brought as an insertion trim and set into your work.

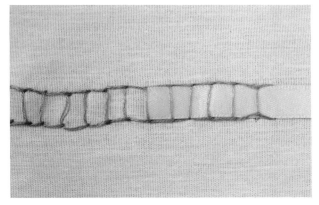

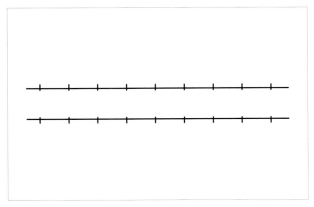

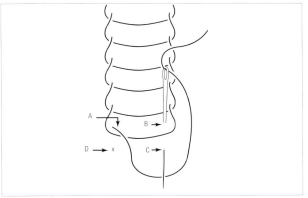

Step 1

- Begin by drawing two parallel lines on your fabric; the distance between them can be determined by the ribbon that is going to be threaded through the bars. Mark the positions of the bars between the lines.

Step 2

- Bring your needle up from the back of your work on the first bar at A and make a stitch into the opposite bar mark at B. Bring the needle under the thread loop at the position of the next bar mark, C, and make a small stitch on the bar, then come up on the first side again at D, with the needle coming back up inside the loop. You will have formed a wide chain stitch.

Stepped ladder stitch

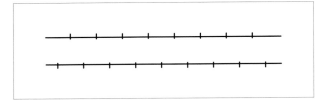

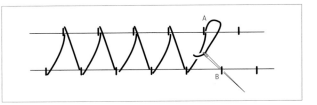

Step 1
- Mark your fabric as in Step 1 of ladder stitch (see page 269), but this time mark the position of the bars so that they will be made diagonally across the ribbon.

Step 2
- Bring your needle from the back of your work and make a small stitch into the first bar mark at A, then make a stitch into the bar mark on the opposite side at B. Work back and forward, making a small stitch into each bar mark along your work.

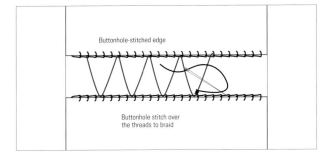

Buttonhole-stitched edge

Buttonhole stitch over
the threads to braid

Step 3
- Carefully cut the fabric under the bars down the center and fold back the edges before finishing them with buttonhole stitch. You can also work buttonhole stitch along each bar to give the ladder a braided effect.

Using paper
Rather than marking your fabric, draw the parallel and spacing lines onto paper. Cut the fabric down the center and turn under the raw edges and press. Place the folded edges onto the parallel line on the paper and baste stitch approximately ¼in (6mm) back from the edge. Work the ladder stitching over the paper using the marked spacing lines. Remove the paper and finish the edges with buttonhole stitches.

Fagoting

Fagoting is a decorative insertion stitch that is used to join two pieces of fabric together. This can be done using lace or ribbon. It is also used as an insertion stitch in corsetry, usually down the center front of a corset or girdle. It can be worked by hand, or by using the fagoting stitch available on some sewing machines – or you can buy insertion tape trim.

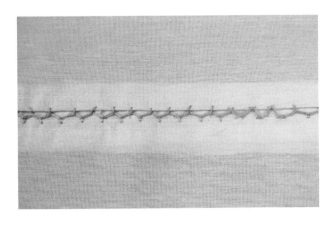

Step 1

- Turn under both raw edges in a small hem, and slip stitch or machine stitch in place. Baste (tack) the hemmed edges onto firm paper, parallel to each other and approximately ⅛in (3mm) apart; if being worked by hand the distance can be wider but it must be regular, with the same tension throughout. For machine sewing use heat-away or water-soluble stabilizer and iron the two edges parallel to each other. If the stabilizer is fusible follow the manufacturer's instructions or baste in place.

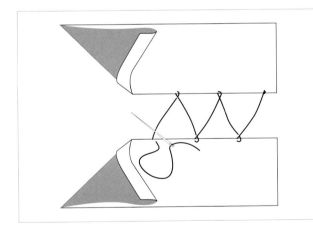

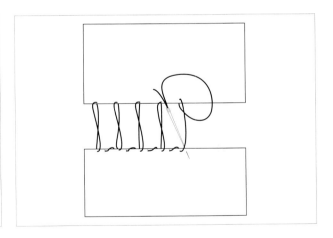

Step 2

- Join the thread to the top edge at the right-hand side. Picking up about ⅛in (3mm) of the hem each time, insert the needle into the bottom edge a little to the left and from the back of the work. Bring the thread to the front and twist it behind the bar before reinserting it at the back of the hem above and a little to the left.

- There are many variations of the technique. You can create bars at right angles to the hem and twist the needle around the straight thread, bringing it out a little way along the bottom edge. Then make a tiny oversewing stitch over the bottom edge to reach the position of the next stitch.

Fur

Fur can be used as an embellishment – particularly on negligees, where rosettes of fur can be scattered across the surface, inset into lace or other sheer fabrics, or used on the collar and cuffs.

There are many interesting techniques that you can use when working with fur. It is sold by the pelt or plate; pelts can be sewn together, and are available new or recycled. The nap of fur changes from the shoulder to the rump. It is available in every color of the rainbow and the pelts can be sewn and sculpted. It is not hard to work with if you follow a few basic rules:

- Always work with the fur of each pelt, the nap, running in the same direction. The hair can then be brushed to smooth and conceal the seam.

- Seaming is usually done on a pelting machine but you can use a serger (overlocker) or basic zigzag stitch.
- For a really flat seam dampen along the ridge of the seam on the wrong side and smooth out with your fingers or the flat of your hand on a board, before leaving to dry.
- Always use a knife to cut on the wrong side so as not to cut the hair.
- Apply fusible tape to the raw edge of the fur before finishing to both give support and to stop the edge from stretching out.

To create a simple flower from fur, cut a small circle or rectangle of fur. Fold a piece of ribbon in a contrasting color into the shape of a bow, slightly smaller in size, and place on top. Place another smaller ribbon bow on top of that and stitch them all together onto the garment.

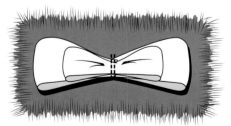

Flossing

Flossing is used to hold steel and cane boning in place, but can also be applied to the top and bottom of boning as a decorative finish. Flossing can be tonal or worked in a contrasting color. Once worked using silk or cotton embroidery floss (thread), you can now also add shine by using a rayon or even metallic thread. Flossing can be added to a finished garment.

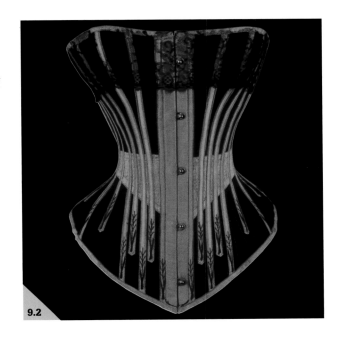

9.2

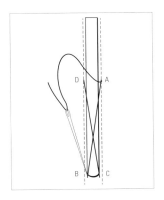

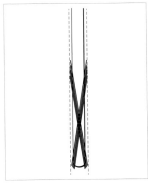

Step 1
- Working with a knotted thread, bring the needle from the back to the front, about 1in (2.5cm) from the end of the bone at A. Reinsert the needle at the end of the bone, slightly off center on the opposite side, at B. Take a small stitch and bring the needle back up at C. Then take it up and over to the opposite side of the bone at D, and pull the needle through to the back.

Step 2
- Pass the needle under the bone and bring it back up under the first stitch at A. Insert the needle again beside B, bring it out again beside C, and insert it again beside D. Repeat this sequence 3–5 times before securing the thread at the back of your work.

Variations
Flossing can become very decorative when you add embroidery down the center of the bone. Star bursts and flower sprigs can also be worked over the bone.

9.2 / The black decorative flossing is in strong contrast to the red material used for the boning on this basque.

Cording

Cording can be used in corsets instead of boning. On earlier corsets the narrow channels were created on the cut panel pieces – parallel lines were hand stitched using back stitching or saddle stitching, between which a cord or string was then threaded. Later, machine-stitched channels were made on the fabric before it was cut out, with an added layer of canvas for extra strength. The result was finer, less expensive, and created a very pliable, supportive fabric that could then be cut into the corset panels. Trapunto is a more intricate form of cording.

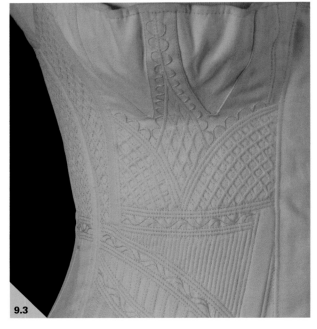

9.3

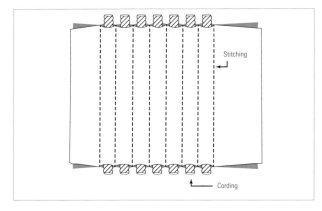

Stitching

Cording

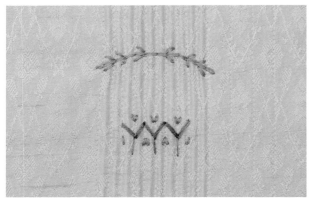

Step 1

- Working over two or three layers of fabric, sew narrow rows of channeling, wide enough for the cord to thread through. Cut the pattern pieces out and then thread the cording through the channels.

Step 2

- Finish the cording with flossing worked between the rows of cording if desired.

9.3 / Cotton corset with silk thread quilting, or trapunto work, and cording, circa 1830.

Honeycomb or direct smocking

This is a one-step process worked on a grid of dots, with stitches drawing the fabric up into regular pleats or folds. It has the suppleness of English smocking but it is not as elastic.

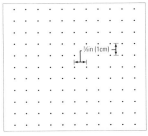

Step 1

- Begin by marking a grid of dots on the wrong side of your fabric. The dots are usually evenly spaced, ⅜in (1cm) apart. You can also use a ready-made iron-on dot transfer sheet.

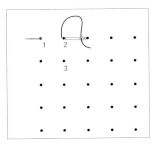

Step 2

- Using embroidery floss, make a small back stitch into dot 2, and bring the needle out at the next adjacent dot, 1.

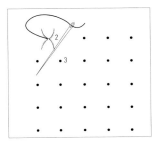

Step 3

- Pull the thread so that the dots come together.

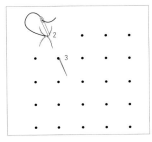

Step 4

- Insert the needle back into dot 2, and bring the needle back out at dot 3 on the lower row.

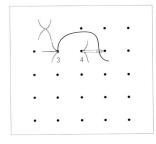

Step 5

- Make a small stitch into dot 4 and back into dot 3, pulling the dots together. Continue alternating up and down between the rows of dots.

Experimenting with smocking for different effects

You can work on a grid of unevenly spaced dots to change the appearance of the smocking. You can also work without a grid, allowing the stitching to wander across the fabric. You may find that you have a grid pattern already in the weave or print of your fabric that you can use.

Ribbon work (see page 278) and bullion roses can be scattered on or included in your smocking.

Ostrich feathers

In the years leading up to World War I the demand for ostrich feathers by fashionable ladies led to the feathers becoming worth more than their weight in gold, which made ostrich farmers and feather merchants very wealthy. A legacy of this is the "feather palaces" – huge homes in the town of Oudtshoorn, South Africa – built on the profits obtained from the export of ostrich feathers.

At the peak of their popularity these luxurious feathers were available in wonderful shapes and sizes, as indeed they are today. Ostrich molt twice a year, and skilled handlers gather the feathers by walking through groups of birds and gently removing loose feathers without panicking the birds. A drab is the name given to the body feathers – with the smallest feathers coming from the belly; the tail feathers are longer; the longest – plumes – come from the wings. The natural gray drabs from the female bird and black from the male can be stripped, bleached, and dyed any color. Feathers can also be mixed successfully with fur.

Ostrich feathers can be attached to a cord and sold as a fringe – this is the quickest and easiest way to attach them to a garment. Mark the placement of the trim and hand sew in place.

If the cord feels hard or ridged, however, you will have to remove it. The feathers are attached to the cord in one direction and this is the way that they will come off. Begin sewing with the machine in this direction just under the cord, removing the cord as you go. A zipper or clear embroidery foot makes it easier.

If using individual feathers, each feather will have to be attached by stitching over the spine or quill a couple of times, or using a hot needle to pierce the spine or quill and stitching through it to attach it to the garment.

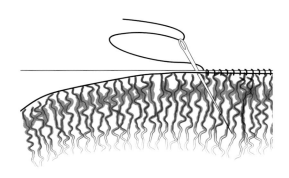

Marabou feathers

True marabou feathers are the fluffy white feathers found under the wings and tail of the large marabou stork. The feathers are short in length, very fine, dense, downy, extremely fluffy, and soft, with no gaps along the shaft. In the nineteenth century marabou was sometimes used as a fur substitute. A native of North Africa, today the marabou stork is a protected species, so the soft, downy feathers of young turkeys and chickens are now sold as marabou. They are inexpensive and easily dyed.

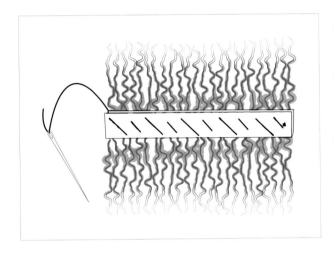

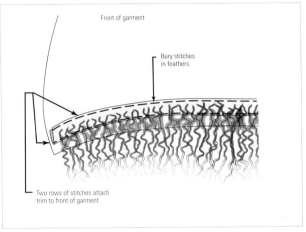

Front of garment

Bury stitches
in feathers

Two rows of stitches attach
trim to front of garment

Step 1

- If purchased as loose feathers, marabou must be attached to a double layer of soft, thin fabric, such as China silk or cotton lawn, color matched to the feathers. Cut a 1in (2.5cm)-wide strip of fabric and fold it in half lengthwise. Lay the marabou flat on a table with the least attractive side up, place the strip on the stem of the marabou, and pin to hold in place. Using stitches approximately 12mm in length, alternating with shorter stitches of 6mm, take two diagonal stitches in each place to attach the feathers to the strip.

Step 2

- To attach the marabou to the garment, turn the feather strip to the right side and lay in place on the right side of the garment. Lift the feathers away from the tape and stitch the tape to the garment with running stitches along its edge; the stitches will be hidden beneath the feathers when you lay them back in place. Repeat on the other side.

Ribbon work

Ribbon comes in a variety of widths, textures, and colors, from pure silk to velvets and sheer organza. Ribbon can be worked the same as any other thread – you can make French knots, bullion stitch roses, and detached chain stitches. Ribbon work embroidery was much used on the couture lingerie of the 1920s.

You will need a needle with a large eye to be able to thread the ribbon. Work with short lengths of ribbon so that you can keep an even, gentle tension. Ribbon needs to be handled gently, with the stitches kept loose and unfolded.

Some of the basic ribbon embroidery stitches are shown in the next few pages.

Ribbon stitch

Ribbon stitch forms pretty little flowers, buds, and leaves.

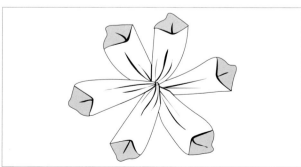

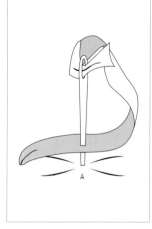

Step 1
- Anchor the ribbon at the back of your work and bring it through to the front. With the point of the needle, hold the ribbon at the desired stitch length, at A. Push the ribbon back a little away from A so that it is not stretched flat against the fabric, then pull the needle through the center of the ribbon to the back, being careful not to pull too hard.

Step 2
- You can work these stitches around in a circle to create a flower. To add a twist to the stitches, instead of pulling the needle through the center of the ribbon, push it through the left- or right-hand side and pull through to the back. You can finish the flower with a bead or French knot in the center.

Spider web ribbon roses

Ribbon can also be used to create an Art Nouveau rose, not unlike the rose motif designed by Charles Rennie Mackintosh.

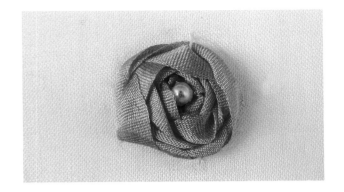

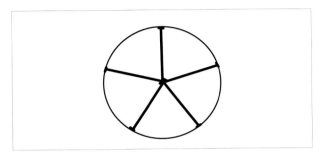

Step 1

- Make a mark to position the center of the rose on your fabric and draw a circle around this the size you want the finished rose to be. Divide the circle into five even sections and mark. Using either embroidery floss or ribbon, bring your needle up at the center point and make a straight stitch into the first mark on the circle. Repeat this straight stitch from the center to the circle edge until you have five even stitches. Secure the floss or ribbon.

Step 2

- Thread your needle with ribbon again and pull through the center point between two straight stitches, anchoring the ribbon at the back of your work. Lightly twist the ribbon and weave it under and over the five straight threads until you have a rose the size you want. Take the ribbon to the back and secure.

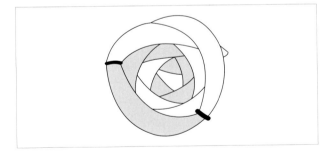

Three-dimensional ribbon flowers

Ribbons can also to be used to make three-dimensional flowers and leaves, employed on their own or mixed with other embellishments. By simply rolling the edges of different lengths and widths of ribbon, and gathering across the bottom before stitching them together, you can create many different varieties of flower. You can then use a group of French knots, beads, or a ribbon knot to create the center of the flower.

When working with ribbon you will often measure the length of ribbon required by working in multiples of the width of the ribbon. Some flowers, for example, may require a length of ribbon four or more times its width.

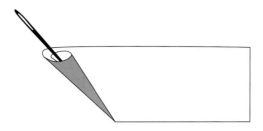

To roll the edges of the ribbon, apply a drop of adhesive to the corner to be rolled. Lay a darning needle or other large needle diagonally across the corner of the ribbon and roll both edges until you have the petal shape you want. Slip the needle out and leave to dry.

Pansies

Work the back two petals in a contrasting color and wider ribbon than the front petals for a realistic-looking flower.

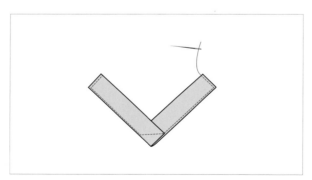

Step 1

- For the back petals, cut two pieces of ribbon four times the ribbon width. Overlap the ends at a right angle and sew gathering stitch across the end of one piece, down the side, diagonally across the overlap, and up the other piece, leaving a thread tail. Stitches should be about 6mm in length.

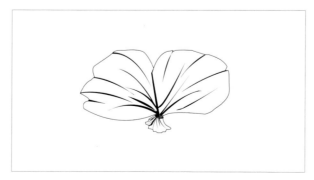

Step 2

- Loosely gather the ribbon so that it forms two petals. You can then either attach the petals to a backing piece of crinoline or directly to the garment.

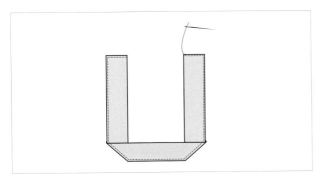

Step 3

- For the three front petals, or face, cut a piece of ribbon twelve times the ribbon width. Divide into three, fold the two ends up on the diagonal, and pin to hold. Stitch across the top of one end, down the side, along the diagonal fold, across the bottom, and up the other side, leaving a thread tail.

Step 4

- Gather and finish with a back stitch into the beginning knot, to form a small circle. Form a small knot of ribbon and place it in the center of the circle, pulling the tails to the back. Place the face of the pansy on top of the two back petals and stitch in place.

Leaves

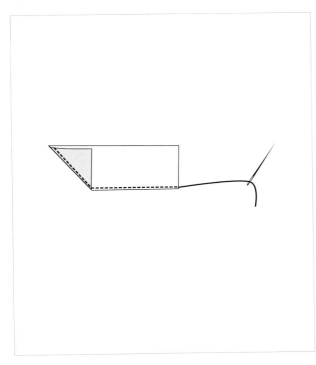

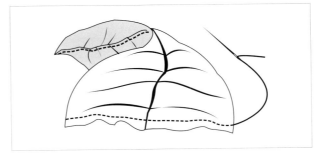

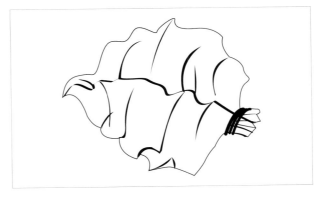

Step 1

- Cut a 2in (5cm) length of 1in (2.5cm)-wide ribbon; fold in half lengthwise and fold back one corner. Run a gathering stitch along the folded edge to the cut edge. Gently gather up the stitches.

Step 2

- Stitch across the cut end, and tightly gather up. Open out the leaf and stitch in place.

Ribbon bows

Small bows are often used on lingerie – just as an embellishment, or to hide the join of the strap to the body of the garment.

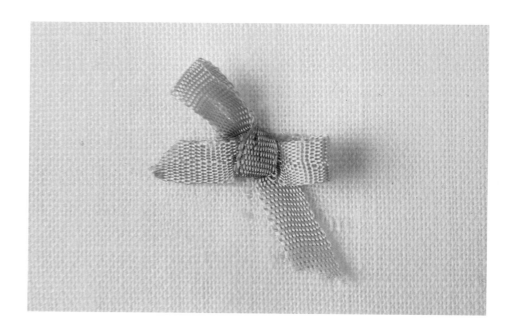

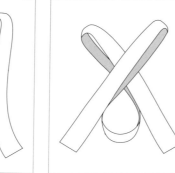

Step 1

- Take a small length of narrow ribbon and loop both ends back on themselves. Hold a loop in each hand.

Step 2

- Cross one loop over the other, forming a lower loop in the center.

Step 3

- Take the upper loop to the back, thread through the lower loop, and pull to form a bow.

Scalloped hems and edges

Scalloped hems can be finished with a self facing, perhaps in a contrasting color, or finished with edging lace or binding. You can use the decorative satin stitch found on some sewing machines, or a wing needle and the decorative shell stitch, to give you a pinstitched seam to hold the facing in place – or when attaching a contrasting colored hem to the scalloped edge. Scallops can also be used as a decorative insert.

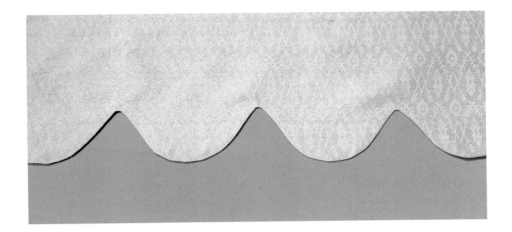

Bound scalloped hem

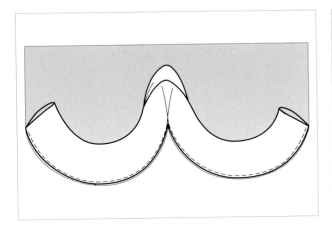

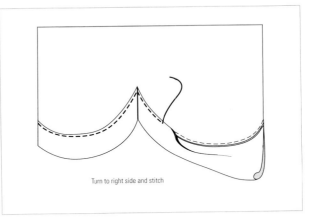

Turn to right side and stitch

Step 1

- Decide on the size of the scallop and draw it on the hemline of your pattern pieces, working from the center to the side seam. Add a seam allowance. Cut the binding on the bias or cross grain four times the finished width, plus seam allowance. Fold the binding in half and attach to the back of the scalloped hemline. Clip the seam allowance at the inside curve.

Step 2

- Fold the binding over the seam allowance, bringing it to the front of the scalloped hemline. Stitch along close to the upper folded edge.

A hemline attached to a scalloped edge

Attaching a hem flounce or frill to a scalloped edge gives you the option of having a contrast color, print, sheer, or shiny hem that shows up the scallop detail.

Shaping the scalloped edge

Use a shorter stitch length of 1½–2mm, so that you get a better rounded shape to the scalloped edge.

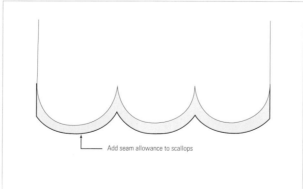

Add seam allowance to scallops

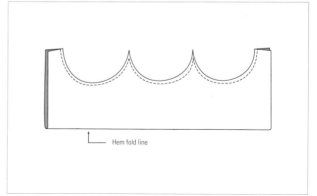

Hem fold line

Step 1

- Mark the scallop pattern on the body of the garment (see Step 1, page 283) along the hem placement line, and add a seam allowance.

Step 2

- Cut the fabric that will form the hemline double, so that the fold becomes the edge of the hemline, and mark the scallop placement; add a seam allowance. Baste together along the scallops so that they don't move when attaching to the garment scallops.

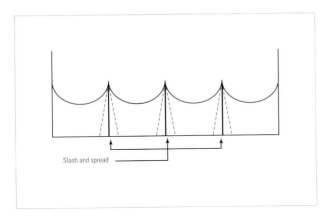

Slash and spread

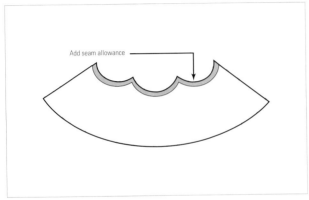

Add seam allowance

Step 3

- If attaching a flounce or frill, mark the scallop placement on pattern paper. Slash and spread the paper to add the correct amount of fullness under the scallops. Add a seam allowance.

Step 4

- Sew the hem fabric to the scalloped edge. You can finish this seam with a decorative satin or pin stitch, to help control any fabric fraying. You can use a wing needle on your sewing machine to create a decorative finish – this needle has two small flanges on its sides that separate the fabric fibers to make small holes or eyelets held open by the stitching. Because the eyelets give an heirloom effect to hems and borders, the needle is also referred to as a hem-stitching needle.

Variations on a scalloped edge

Add a scalloped edge to a collar or sleeve cuff for a pretty finish. Add the flounce to the scalloped edge to give a collar a caped effect. Scallop a slip dress around the hipline before adding the skirt. Take it one step further and work two rows of scallops one to two inches apart to create a hip yoke. Scallop a neckline and front or back opening.

Machine-made scalloped hems

The stitch on your sewing machine will look like this.

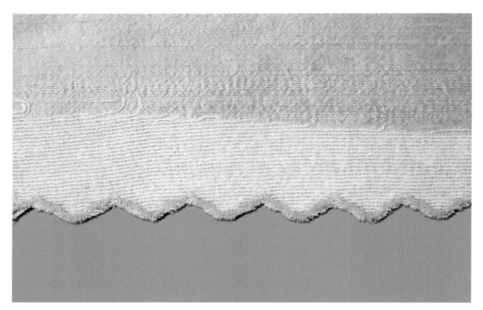

- Place stabilizer both under and on top of the hem to be scallop stitched. Mark the scallop pattern on the top piece of stabilizer and secure in place.

- Begin stitching, following your machine manual for the correct stitch settings. Make a few practice runs beforehand to get all the settings correct, before stitching the final hem.

Shell hem

A shell hem can be created on most sewing machines, or by hand by stitching over a small rolled hem or bound edge.

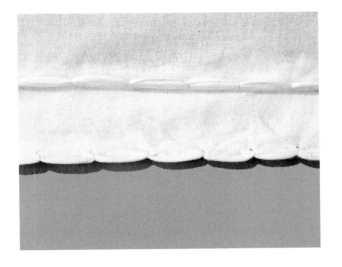

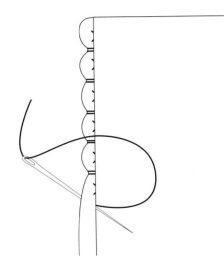

Hand-worked shell hem

Make the rolled hem by double folding the fabric and finger pinching it in place. Secure the knotted thread in the fabric fold and make two or three running stitches along the top fold, through all the fabric thicknesses, finishing at the point of the first shell indentation.

- Wrap the needle and thread over the hem and reinsert in the same place, then pull up the thread to complete the stitch. Wrap the needle and thread over the hem a second time in exactly the same place, and pull up the thread. Run the needle through the hem by approximately ⅜in (1cm) and then repeat the wrapping technique.

Machine shell hem

This hem works well on a soft or sheer material, making it ideal for lingerie.

- Use the 4mm roll hemmer foot, which is available for most sewing machines – make sure that yours has a wide needle opening for decorative stitching. You can use a zigzag stitch or the shell edging stitch. Place the fabric under the foot and set the zigzag or shell edging stitch so that it is wide enough to pass over the edge. The stronger the thread tension, the more the fabric edge will be pulled up or indented.

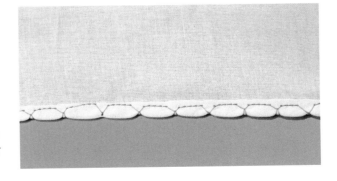

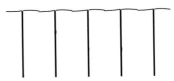

Pin tucks

These are narrow tucks, seamed at ⅛in (3mm) from their folded edge, which are sewn in rows on lightweight fabric. Pin tucks can be purely decorative, or they can be used to create and control shape in a garment. Pin tucks are an essential part of heirloom garments, where they are combined with laces and trims. They add texture and interest to the fabric, whether sewn in straight lines or curved.

A thin cord can be added to the pin tuck, and the easiest and quickest way of doing this is with a pin-tucking foot, available for most sewing machines. The underside of the foot has grooves and the tuck is formed in these indentations. The foot can also be used as a spacing guide, with the previously made tucks sitting up in the grooves as you make the next tuck so you do not have to mark position lines. You can also use a twin needle with or without a pin-tucking foot. Twin needles are available in various spacings, the smallest giving you a tiny tuck. When using a twin needle you will use two spools of thread, so consider a contrasting color or a metallic thread. Adjust the machine's tension to create the raised section of fabric between the needles; if the tension is too loose you will get two rows of stitching and no tuck.

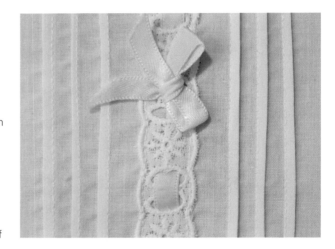

The first step is to estimate the amount of fabric required for the tucking. Establish the measurement between the tucks – the visible space between one tuck and the next from the stitching line. The amount of fabric for each pin tuck is three times its width. The width of the tuck plus the visible space, multiplied by the number of tucks required, gives you the amount of fabric needed.

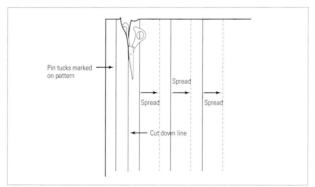

Step 1
- Before cutting out your pattern in the fashion fabric, mark the placement of the pin tucks on your pattern piece. Cut down this line and expand or spread the pattern to allow for the width of each tuck.

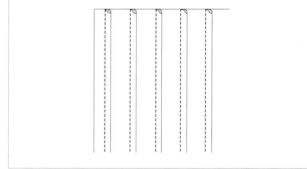

Step 2
- To make the tucks, mark the tuck placement on the fabric using either an invisible pen or chalk. Fold the fabric down each placement line and machine stitch ⅛in (3mm) from the fold line.

Twisted tucks

Twisted tucks can be purely decorative when worked horizontally around a garment or worked vertically down a bodice, the tucks then releasing to add fullness in the skirt. Decorative or contrast coloured stitching can add extra interest. The width of the pleat and the space between the pleats can change to give interesting effects.

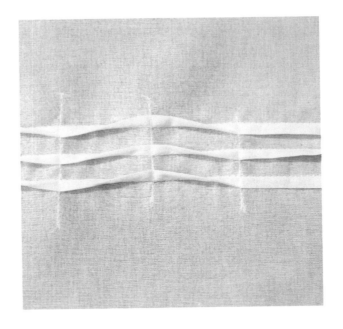

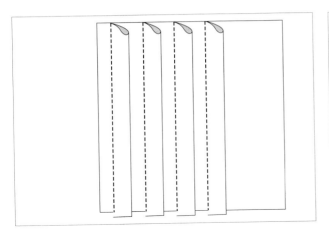

Step 1

- Follow the instructions opposite to estimate the fabric amount and spread the pattern as for regular pin tucks. These tucks can be spread farther apart, though; the visible space and the tuck width can be wider than a pin tuck. Make the tucks as for pin tucks.

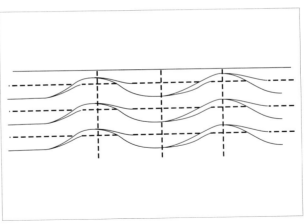

Step 2

- Now topstitch across the tucks, stitching parallel rows that alternate the direction of the tucks.

Inset lace

Before you start to attach any lace placement, stabilize it with spray starch and allow it to dry. Inset lace should have a drawing thread along each edge that you can use to gather or shape the lace. Alternatively, you can use a sewing machine and a strong thread to run a gathering stitch along the edge.

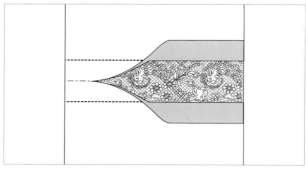

Step 1
- Draw the lace placement on the fabric. Place the lace in position on the right side of the fabric and pin or baste in place.
- Sew along the very edge of the lace, using a small, straight stitch.

Step 2
- On the wrong side cut the fabric away under the lace down the center, and press to the sides.

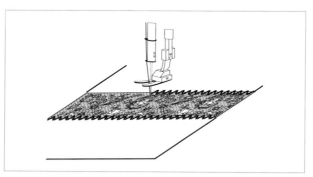

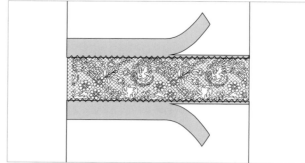

Step 3
- Using a zigzag stitch with a stitch length of 1½–2mm, and a stitch width of 3mm, sew down the edge so that the zig is on the fabric and the zag is on the lace. This will secure the hem on each side of the lace insert and finish the edges.
- Alternatively, working by hand, whip stitch the lace to the fabric.

Step 4
- Cut off any seam allowance on the wrong side.
- Inset lace can also be used to attach a frilled hem of lace or fabric by joining the two together with zigzag stitch or by whip stitching by hand.

Appliqué

Appliqués are small, shaped fabric pieces used to add pattern or embellishment to a base fabric. They can be attached by hand or machine. Appliqués can be attached to the right side of your work, or to the wrong side so that the appliqué acts as a shadow.

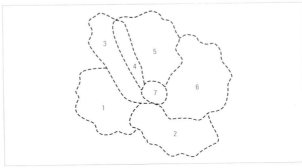

Step 1

- Stabilize the back of the base fabric with a commercial stabilizer. Using the straight stitch on your sewing machine, outline the design to be appliquéd. This makes it easier to place the pieces to be appliquéd in their correct positions.

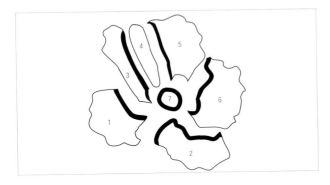

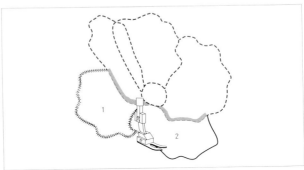

Step 2

- Work out how to cut the pieces, adding a ¼in (6mm) seam allowance on edges that underlap so that there will be no gaps in the finished design.

Step 3

- Lay the pieces in position. Beginning with the under pieces – which here would be 2 followed by 1 – baste in place close to the cut edge.
- The last pieces to be placed – 4 and 7 – will be placed after all other pieces have been attached in Step 4.

Step 4

- Using a satin stitch presser foot, or clear embroidery presser foot, work around the shapes, with the center of the presser foot set to straddle the edge of the appliqué. Lift the foot and pivot with the needle down in the base fabric at the corners and any sharp angles.
- If you are using more than one appliqué and edges will overlap, place the background appliqué on the base fabric first and only stitch around edges that will not be covered. This will avoid any hard stitching edges shadowing through the foreground appliqué.

Appliqué stitching

- Hem stitch can be used instead of satin stitch, or a mixture of both.
- Appliqué work can be attached with tiny blind stitches worked by hand.
- Using a contrasting or metallic thread will make the stitching really stand out.
- When cutting out an appliqué shape add a ¼in (6mm) seam allowance. This allowance can be clipped into for curves, and corners can be trimmed back before being turned under as you attach each piece.

Lacing the corset

Correctly lacing a corset will give a stronger closure
with little or no movement or slippage.

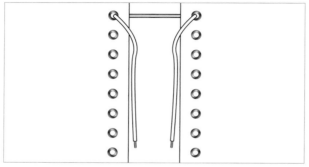

Step 1

- Place lace behind the corset eyelets at the top of the
  closure and bring up one end up through the eyelet on
  the left-hand side of the corset closure and one through
  the eyelet on the right-hand side.

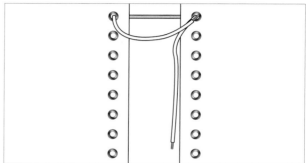

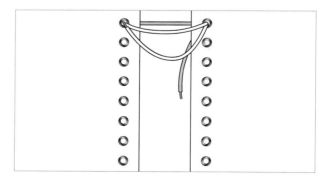

Step 2

- Take both laces directly across to the opposite side so
  that they form a straight line and thread through the
  eyelets toward the back.

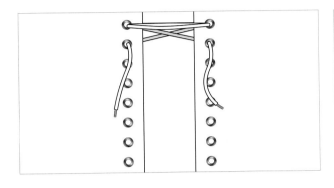

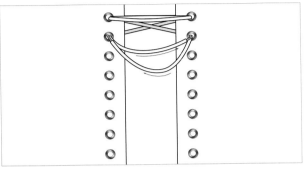

Step 3

- Cross the laces over at the back and thread back toward the front through the next opposite set of eyelets.

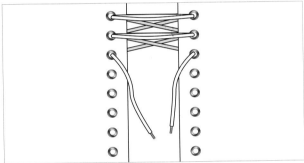

Step 4

- Take both laces straight across to the opposite eyelet again and thread through to the back. Repeat Step 3, and then repeat these two steps, all the way to the bottom.

Rouleau buttonhole loops

Because lingerie and sleepwear is made from soft, lightweight fabrics it is easy to make rouleau buttonhole loops from matching fabric.

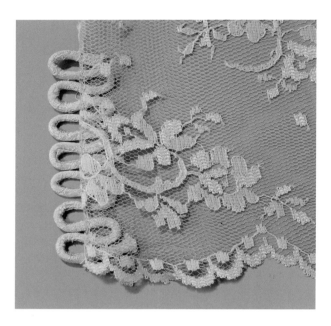

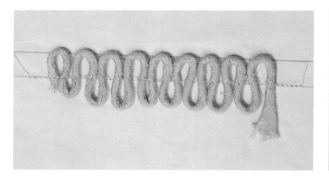

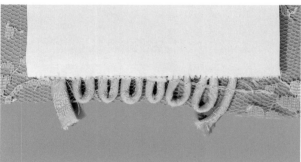

Step 1
- For the rouleau buttonhole loops begin by making a length(s) of rouleau (see Chapter 8, Steps 8 and 9, page 233).
- To keep the loops even, make a paper template by drawing three parallel lines on paper the length of the area to be closed by the loops.
- Mark one line as the seam line.
- Mark equal divisions between the three lines for each loop placement, taking into account the width of the rouleau and the width of the button that will go through each loop – which in lingerie is usually kept small and flat for comfort.

- Stitch down the seam line of the paper template, twisting and folding the rouleau back and forward to create the rouleau buttonhole loops as you work.

Step 2
- Place the paper template with the rouleau loops face down, with the top of the loops facing away from the edge of the fabric and with the seam line sitting on the seam line of the opening.
- Stitch down the seam line drawn on the paper template before tearing the paper from the loops.

Supplier List

USA and Canada

Bra-makers Supply
308 Ottawa Street North
Hamilton, ON L8H 3Z9
Canada
1-905-538-1396
www.bramakerssupply.com

Corset Making Supplies
Delicious, LLC
212 E. Girard Avenue
Philadelphia, PA 19125
USA
1-215-413-8259
www.corsetmaking.com

Farthingales Corset Making Supplies
sales@farthingalescorsetmakingsupplies.com
1-519-275-2374
www.farthingalescorsetmakingsupplies.com

Richard The Thread
1960 S. La Cienega Boulevard
Los Angeles, CA 90034
USA
1-800-473-4997
1-310-837-4997
www.richardthethread.com

UK

Sewing Chest
Kellie Riccardo
The Old School
Walkerith Road
East Stockwith DN21 3DG
www.sewingchest.co.uk

MacCulloch & Wallis
25–26 Poland Street
London W1F 8QN
Tel: 020 7629 0311
www.macculloch-wallis.co.uk

Australia

Aussie Corset Supplies
www.aussiecorsetsupplies.com.au

General information about thread:
www.ylicorp.com/cpanel/document/a_thread_of_truth.pdf

Further Reading

Fischer, Anette, *Sewing for Fashion Designers*.
Laurence King Publishing, 2015.

Haggar, Ann, *Pattern Cutting for Lingerie, Beachwear and Leisurewear*.
Blackwell Publishing, 2004.

Lynn, Eleri, *Underwear: Fashion Detail*.
V&A Publishing, 2014.

Matthews-Fairbanks, Jennifer Lynne, *Underwear: Construction & Pattern Drafting for Lingerie Design* (Bare Essentials).
Los Angeles Fashion Resource, 2011.

Salen, Jill, *Vintage Lingerie: 30 Patterns Based on Period Garments Plus Finishing Techniques*. St Martin's Griffin, 2011.

Shin, Kristina, *Patternmaking for Underwear Design*.
Amazon Publishing, 2010.

Specification Sheet

A specification sheet is filled in for the manufacturer after the pattern is made and includes all relevant information and measurements about the garment. Here is a sample.

Date: 01-Jul-16

Name: underwired long line bra

Fabric: 100% polyester, nylon, elastane

Trimmings: 6x lace motifs

Accessories: strap rings and adjusters

Season: Spring/Summer

Style: 2011

Description: long line push-up cup bra

Label: Pamela Powell

		Part	Part	Pattern piece	Total length	Sketch	
Lower cup to bust point				2 ¾"			
Upper cup to bust point				2 ½"			
Bust point to cup underarm				4 ½"			
Bust point to center front				3 ¼"			
Top bridge width				1"			
Center front band length				6 ½"			
Under cup band length				3"			
Side front band length				2"			
Lower back band width				6 ¾"			
Top back band width				6 ¾"			
Center back band length				5 ¼"			
Strap length to adjusters		7" strap length		length with adjuster 10 ¼"			
Top underarm band elastic			10 ¾"	14"	24 ¾"		
Neckline elastic trim & strap		4" neckline from center front	strap 11"	total 15"	full length 30"		
Hem elastic							
Hook and eye closure			hook & eyes, total 7		total length 5 ¼"		
Underwire casing				one side 9 ½"	total 19"		
						Remarks/other specs: 34B bra underwires	

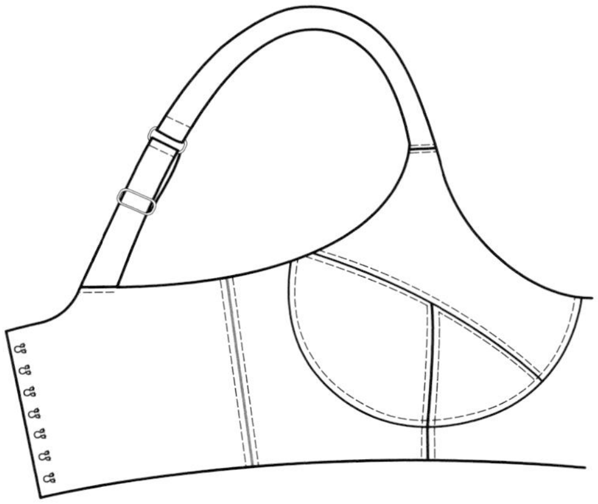

Glossary

Italic words indicate cross-references within this glossary

action stretch Horizontal stretch across the *weft* grain of a fabric.

appliqué A decoration made of fabric pieces sewn onto a base fabric or garment.

armscye Another name for the armhole in a garment or sewing pattern.

bar tack A short row of stitches used to hold part of a garment in place or reinforce a join.

bias The diagonal direction of a piece of fabric, at 45° between the *warp* and the *weft*.

bias binding Binding cut on the *bias* to give it stretch and flexibility.

bias tape Another name for *bias binding*.

binding Strip of fabric used to fold over and cover a fabric edge.

bishop sleeve A very full, gathered sleeve.

block Another name for a *sloper*.

boning Strips of stiffening material, traditionally made of bone but now often plastic, used to strengthen corsets and bras.

buckram A stiff, hardwearing cotton or linen fabric.

bum roll A sausage-shaped pillow worn around the back of the waist to act as a bustle.

busk Another name for a *stay*.

bustier A bra-like garment that reaches down to the waist and can be worn as underwear or outerwear.

bustle A layer of ruffles or padding worn under a skirt to make the skirt stick out at the back below the waist.

button stand Edging attached to a *placket* for buttons to be sewn onto.

cami-knickers All-in-one garment combining a corset and knickers. Also called a "teddy".

camisole A vest-style, waist-length undergarment, also worn as outerwear.

channeling Tube-like pieces of fabric attached to bras for underwires to fit into.

channel stitch Close, evenly spaced, parallel rows of stitching.

charmeuse A type of lightweight fabric with a satin texture on one side.

chemise A loose shirt-style undergarment.

combination Another name for *cami-knickers*.

cording Adding tubes or channels of fabric to a garment, which are then filled with lengths of cord.

coutil A firm, tightly woven cloth, used for making corsets.

crinoline A stiff underskirt or cage-like framework worn under a skirt to give it shape.

cross grain The direction of the *weft* threads in a fabric.

déshabillé A lingerie-style outerwear dress.

facing A piece of fabric used as a lining or as an inner layer to add thickness.

fagoting Attaching two pieces of fabric by leaving a gap in between and filling it with decorative stitches.

findings The non-fabric parts of bras, such as clips and hooks.

flat fell seam A seam that folds over and lies flat against the outside of a garment.

flossing Decorative stitching over a piece of *boning* or cord.

flutter sleeve A very loose and open short sleeve, made in a lightweight fabric.

frame Another name for a *power bar*.

French knickers Another name for *tap pants*.

French seam A seam that folds in on itself, keeping the raw edges hidden inside.

fusible interfacing Interfacing that bonds to fabric when pressed with an iron.

galloon lace A decorative, patterned lace trim with both edges scalloped.

gate A bra fastening made of triangles of strip elastic.

gathering stitch A simple stitch used to gather fabric together when pulled tight.

godets Triangular inserts that add fullness to a garment or hem.

grosgrain A type of heavy, stiff woven ribbon with a ribbed texture.

grain The direction of the *warp* threads in a fabric.

interfacing A layer of stiff fabric used inside collars and *plackets* to add stiffness.

knickerbockers Loose, longish, shorts-style undergarment.

lapped zipper A zipper inserted into fabric with one side of the fabric overlapping the other on top of the zipper.

mandarin collar A simple collar that stands up from the fabric around the neck.

mousseline A fine, sheer, crisp woven fabric, usually made of cotton or silk.

muslin A basic, often lightweight cotton cloth. Also another name for a *toile*.

negligee A short or knee-length sheer or lace nightdress or dressing gown.

oak tag A type of stiff paper used for making sewing pattern templates.

pannier A layer of ruffles or padding worn under a skirt to make it stick out sideways at the hips.

peignoir A type of long, often sheer or lightweight dressing gown.

Peter Pan collar A flat, folded-down collar with rounded corners.

pick stitching Light stitching that only picks up a few threads from the wrong side of a fabric, so the stitching does not show on the right side.

picot A trim made of tiny loops along the edge of fabric or elastic.

placket An opening in a shirt, skirt or other garment to make it easier to put on and take off.

power bar A curved piece of fabric fitted inside a bra to add support and strength. Also called a "frame" or "sling".

raglan sleeve A type of sleeve that extends up to the collar of a garment and curves over the shoulder.

rigilene A type of flexible, plastic boning material.

right side The patterned, printed, embroidered, or finished "outer" side of a fabric.

rouleau A strip of rolled or folded fabric used to make straps, loops, or ties.

rouleau loops Button loops made from strips of rouleau.

rouleau turner A tool used to turn a strip of fabric inside out.

serger A machine that trims, sews, and encloses a seam or fabric edge in a loose, zigzag stitch.

sling Another name for a *power bar*.

sloper A basic pattern design that has not yet had seam allowances added, and that can be altered to make a variety of patterns. Also called a "block".

smocking Gathering fabric together so that it can move and stretch.

stay The central piece of *boning*, or boned clasp, fitted into the front of a corset.

stitch in the ditch Sewing along a seam line on the right side of the fabric.

tap pants Loose, shorts-style undergarment often made from satin or lace. Also called "French knickers".

teddy Another name for *cami-knickers*.

toile A trial-run garment made in a cheap fabric, such as *muslin* (the fabric also known as toile).

trapunto Delicate quilting with raised or stuffed patterns and shapes.

tulle Stiff netting fabric used to make petticoats and veils.

warp The long threads that run along the length of a fabric.

warp stretch Vertical stretch along the *warp* grain of a fabric.

weft The threads that run across the width of a fabric.

wrong side The back or unfinished side of a fabric.

yoke A piece or strip of fabric, usually at the top of a shirt or skirt, from which looser fabric can hang.

Index

Index

Picture Credits

p.6 Roger Viollet/Topfoto; **p.8** Roger Viollet/Topfoto; **p.9** Lucile; **p.10** (top) courtesy of Sally Edelstein Collection; (bottom) Bordelle **p.11** Richard Reissig of Silver Screen Loungerie; **p.12** courtesy of Sally Edelstein Collection; **p.13** (top) © 2015 copyright The Metropolitan Museum of Art/ Art Resource/Scala, Florence © Photo Scala; **p.13** (bottom) © Photos 12/ Alamy; **p.14** iStock; **p.16** (fig 1.1) www.bramakerssupply.com; **p.16** (figs 1.2, 1.3, 1.4, 1.5, 1.6) www.macculloch-wallis.co.uk; **p.18** (fig 1.7) www. macculloch-wallis.co.uk; (fig 1.8) www.bramakerssupply.com; **p.19** (figs 1.9, 1.10) www.macculloch-wallis.co.uk; **p.22** (fig 1.11) www.macculloch-wallis.co.uk; **p.24** Kerry Taylor Auctions; **p.37** (fig 2.2) Myla London www. myla.com; **p.38** (fig 2.3) MGM Studios/Getty Images; **p.42** (fig 2.4) Rigby & Peller; **p.43** (fig 2.5) Rigby & Peller; **p.44** (fig 2.6) Rigby & Peller; **p.45** (fig 2.7) Rigby & Peller; **p.46** (fig 2.8) Rigby & Peller; **p.51** (fig 2.10) Richard Reissig of Silver Screen Loungerie; **p.53** (fig 2.11) Rigby & Peller; **p.56** (fig 2.12) Pascal le Segretain/Getty Images; **p.59** (fig 2.13) Rigby & Peller; **p.60** © Victoria and Albert Museum, London; **p.68** (fig 3.1) Richard Reissig of Silver Screen Loungerie; **p.75** (fig 3.2) Richard Reissig of Silver Screen Loungerie; **p.80** (fig 3.3) © Victoria and Albert Museum, London; **p.89** (fig 3.4) Richard Reissig of Silver Screen Loungerie; **p.97** (fig 3.5) Richard Reissig of Silver Screen Loungerie; **p.99** (fig 3.6) Myla London www.myla.com; **p.102** Reza Estakhrian/Getty Images; **p.124** Pierre Verdy/Getty Images; **p.126** (fig 5.1) Victor Virgile/Getty Images; (fig 5.2) Myla London www.myla.com; **p.127** (top right) Pascal le Segretain/Getty Images; (fig 5.7) Los Angeles County Museum of art/www.lacma.org; **p.128** (fig 5.8) Created by Joanne Argririadis/photo by David Reiss; **p.141** (fig 5.9) Charly Hel/Prestige/Getty Images; **p.144** (fig 5.10) catwalking. com; **p.145** (fig 5.11) Michel Dufour/Getty Images; **p.147** (fig 5.13) catwalking.com; **p.148** (fig 5.14) Photo by Chicago History Museum/Getty Images; **p.160** © Atlantide Phototravel/Corbis; **p.171** (fig 6.1) Antonio de Moraes Barros Filho/Getty Images; **p.173** (fig 6.2) Pierre Verdy/Getty Images; **p.178** Wendell Teodoro/Getty Images; **p.184** (top left, top middle, top right) Rigby & Peller; (bottom left) Myla London www.myla.com; (bottom middle) Rigby & Peller; (bottom right) lingerie by What Katie Did/ photography by Steve Hart/model Slinky Sparkles; **p.185** (top left, top middle) Rigby & Peller; (top right) Panache Sport; (bottom left) Photo courtesy of FocusInOn.Me at TylerPaper.com; (bottom middle) Cristian Baitg/Getty Images; **p.203** (fig 7.1) catwalking.com; **p.204** (fig 7.2) Eugene Adebari/Rex; **p.211** (fig 7.4) Panache Lingerie; **p.213** (fig 7.5) © Scott McDermott/Corbis; **p.220** (fig 7.7) © Victoria and Albert Museum, London; (fig 7.8) Rigby & Peller; **p.221** (fig 7.9) Ritratti Milano; (fig 7.10) Panache Lingerie; **p.222** © Patricia Canino; **p.260** © Victoria and Albert Museum, London; **p.268** (fig 9.1) catwalking.com; **p.273** (fig 9.2) © Leicestershire County Council; **p.274** (fig 9.3) © Victoria and Albert Museum, London. All other photography by Simon Pask, with garments sewn by the author. All illustrations by Thom Olson.

Acknowledgments

Thanks to Thom Olson for his hard work on the illustrations. Special thanks also to Richard Reissig, of Silver Screen Loungerie, for all his assistance providing photographs.